Religion and Law in Greece

Religion and Law in Greece

Second Edition

Constantine Papageorgiou

This book was originally published as a monograph in the International Encyclopaedia of Laws/Religion Law

Founding Editor: Roger Blanpain
General Editor: Frank Hendrickx
Volume Editor: Wouter Druwé

Wolters Kluwer

Published by:
Kluwer Law International B.V.
PO Box 316
2400 AH Alphen aan den Rijn
The Netherlands
E-mail: international-sales@wolterskluwer.com
Website: lrus.wolterskluwer.com

Sold and distributed by:
Wolters Kluwer Legal & Regulatory U.S.
7201 McKinney Circle
Frederick, MD 21704
United States of America
Email: customer.service@wolterskluwer.com

ISBN 978-94-035-3943-0

e-Book: ISBN 978-94-035-3992-8
web-PDF: ISBN 978-94-035-3993-5

The Author

Constantine Papageorgiou is an Associate Professor of Ecclesiastical Law at the Aristotle University of Thessaloniki (Law Faculty). He is a member of the Bar Association of Thessaloniki and has worked as a lawyer since 1994. For the last ten years, he has also sat on the scientific committee of the journals *Theory and Practice of Administrative Law* and *Theory and Practice of Civil Law & Civil Procedure Law*.

Born in Thessaloniki (Greece) in 1963, he gained his Doctorate in Law in 1999 (Thessaloniki).

Asst. Prof. C. Papageorgiou has participated in numerous conferences at European universities.

His research interests lie mainly in the area of the domestic and international legal protection of the right to religious freedom and relations between State and Church, especially in the areas of property and the tax status of religions. A selection of the author's publications (in Greek) includes:

- *Ecclesiastical Law*, Athens ^{3}2019.
- *Ecclesiastical Property,* Thessaloniki 2017.
- *The Limits of Ecclesiastical Authorities*, Thessaloniki 2012.
- *Religious Law. Special Legislation – Bibliography – Jurisprudence*, Athens 2009 (in collaboration with Emeritus Professor Sp. Troianos).
- *An Introduction to Hellenic Ecclesiastical Law. Religious Freedom – State and Church Relations – Administration of the Church*, Thessaloniki 2012.
- *The Tax Status of Religions. Tax Equality and Religious Freedom*, Athens-Thessaloniki 2005.

The Author

Table of Contents

List of Abbreviations

§1. General Abbreviations

AIP	Agricultural Insurance Organization
AP	Areios Pagos (Greek Supreme Court in Civil and Criminal Matters)
Art(s)	Article(s)
CC	Civil Code
CCProc	Code of Civil Procedure
CCrimProc	Code of Criminal Procedure
cf.	*confer* (compare)
Ch.	Chapter
Const.	Constitution
CoS	Council of State (Symvoulio tis Epikrateias: Greek Supreme Court in Administrative Matters)
CUN	Charter of United Nations (1945)
e.g.	*exempli gratia* (for example)
ECFS	Ecclesiastical Central Financial Service
ECHR	European Convention for the Protection of Human Rights and Fundamental Rights (1950)
ECtHR	European Court on Human Rights
ed.(s)	edited, edition, editor
EEC	European Economic Community
esp.	especially
etc.	*et cetera* (and so forth)
ff.	following
GOC	Genuine Orthodox Christians
HSH	Holy Synod of Hierarchy
i.e.	*id est* (that is)
ICCPR	International Covenant on Civil and Political Rights (1966)

List of Abbreviations

ICESCR	International Covenant on Economic, Social and Cultural Rights (1966)
IntrLCC	Introductory Law of the Civil Code
L	Law
LCS	Legal Council of State
LD	Legislative Decree
LD/1926	Legislative Decree of 10/16-9-1926, 'Ratification of the Statutory Charter of Mount Athos'
lit.	*littera* (letter)
n.	note
no(s)	number(s)
OAEP	Organization for the Administration of Ecclesiastical Property (Church of Greece)
ODMP	Organization for the Administration of Ecclesiastical Property (Church of Crete)
OGG	Official Government Gazette
OL	Obligatory Law
p.(s)	page(s)
para(s).	paragraph(s)
PC	Penal Code
PD	Presidential Decree
PHS	Permanent Holy Synod of Church of Greece
RD	Royal Decree
Reg.	Regulation
SCCG	Statutory Charter of Church of Greece (L 590/1977)
SCMA	Statutory Charter of Mount Athos (1924)
UDHR	Universal Declaration of Human Rights (1948)
UNCHR	United Nations Commission on Human Rights
UNO	United Nations Organization
VAT	Value Added Tax
vol(s)	volume(s)

§2. Abbreviations of Periodical Titles

AchNom	Achaiki Nomologia (Court Rulings of Achaia)
AEKD	Archeion Ekklisiastikou kai Kanonikou Dikaiou (Archive of Ecclesiastical and Canonical Law)
AID	Archeio(n) Idiotikou Dikaiou (Archive of Private Law)

ArcN	Archeio(n) Nomologias (Archive of Court Rulings)
Arm	Armenopoulos
BS	Balkan Studies
Chr	Christianos (Christian)
ChrIdD	Chronika Idiotikou Dikaiou (Chronicles of Private Law)
D	Diki (Trial)
D&P	Dikaio kai Politiki (Law and Politics)
DA	Dikaiomata tou Anthropou (Human Rights Review)
DFN	Deltio Forologikis Nomothesias (Taxation Law Bulletin)
DiDiki	Dioikitiki Diki (Administrative Trial)
DiDni	Dioikitiki Dikaiosyni (Administrative Justice)
Dig	Digesta
E	Ekklisia (Church)
EAD	Epharmoges Astikou Dikaiou (Theory and Practice of Civil Law)
EDD	Epharmoges Dioikitikou Dikaiou (Theory and Practice of Administrative Law)
EDDD	Epitheorisi Dimosiou kai Dioikitikou Dikaiou (Review of Public and Administration Law)
EEN	Ephimeris Ellinon Nomikon (Journal of Greeks Jurists)
HEED	Helliniki Epitheorisi Evropaikou Dikaiou (Hellenic Review of European Law)
HellDni	Helliniki Dikaiosyni (Greek Justice)
NC	Nomocanonica (Nomocanonical Magazine)
ND	Neon Dikaion (New Law)
NoV	Nomiko(n) Vima (Law Tribune)
ÖARR	Österreichisches Archiv für Recht & Religion
PChr	Poinika Chronika (Criminal Chronicles)
PDni	Poiniki Dikaiosyni (Penal Justice)
RHDI	Revue Hennénique de Droit International
Them	Themis
ToS	To Syntagma (The Constitution)
TPDD	Theoria kai Praxi Dioikitikou Dikaiou (Theory and Practice of Administrative Law)
Y	Yperaspisi (Defence)

List of Abbreviations

Preface of 2nd Edition

Nearly seven years after the publication of the first edition, this monograph is being republished in order to present a significant series of remarkable legal changes that have occurred in recent years concerning the legal status of religions in Greece.

Although the recent constitutional reform (2019) did not succeed in effecting any changes in the relations between the so-called prevailing religion (the Orthodox Church, Article 3 paragraph 1 of the Constitution) and the State (*see* General Introduction), nevertheless the relevant system (which exists for almost two centuries!) is no longer characterized by the same stifled relations. Numerous State legal provisions, coupled with the release of recent ecclesiastical regulations, permit us to speak of a different and quite interesting new institutional framework which embraces the whole field of religions, on many levels and from different perspectives.

Mention should be made of the following innovations as being the most representative of the new legal framework concerning the churches and religions in Greece:

(1) The provisions of L. 4301/2014, which has established the new institution of the 'religious/ecclesiastical legal entities in private law' in the sphere of Greek legal order; an analytical approach to the provisions of L. 4301/2014 in conjunction with the relevant jurisprudence, *see* in Part I.
(2) The abolition of numerous anachronistic provisions of the Penal Code regarding the protection of religions, for ex., the removal of the crimes of 'malicious blasphemy' (198 § 1 PC) and of 'blasphemy concerning religions' (199 PC), *see* Parts III, VII.
(3) The issuance of important ecclesiastical by-laws/regulations which deepened the self-administration of the Church of Greece and of Crete [Part III], as ex.: Regulations 267/2015 and 317/2020 (Ecclesiastical Central Service of Finances), 281/2015 and L. 4582/2018 (Pilgrimage Tours), 305/2018 (Priests and Deacons), 307/2018 (Communication and Education Service), 317/2020 (Organization of the Ecclesiastical Service of Finance), 318/2020 (Leases, Sales and Management of the Property). About the Church of Crete should be mentioned Regulations 2/2014 (Metropolitan Councils), 3/2015 (Church Architecture Council and the Building Service), 4/2015 (Code of Ecclesiastical Employees), 5/2015, 6/2015 (Synodical Office of the Holy Provincial Synod), 7/2015 (Holy Temples and Parishes).

(4) The publication by the European Court on Human Rights of a series of landmark decisions on Greek religious issues, as, for example, in the cases: *Kosmas* (29.6.2017: ecclesiastical property), *Molla Sali* (19.12.2018: Islamic law of sharia), *Pantelidou* (10.10.2019: the right to use places of worship), *Papageorgiou* (31.10.2019: on the religious education in schools), *Stavropoulos* (25.6.2020: birth certificate including information about the religious beliefs of the child), etc.

(5) A long series of judgments published by courts of all ranks (Council of State, Supreme Civil and Penal Court, Appellate Courts, Multi- and Single-Member Courts) and updated until April 2021.

(6) A qualitative bibliography updated with the most recent noteworthy books and studies on the religious and ecclesiastical legal matters in Greece and furthermore on the recent developments about the human right to religious freedom (*see* the updated catalogue in 'Selected Bibliography').

Many thanks are addressed to all those colleagues who helped in many ways to the present 2nd revised edition.

Thessaloniki, 1 May 2021
Assoc. Professor Constantine Papageorgiou

Preface of 1st Edition

In each member country of the European Union, the legal relations between the State and the Churches/Religions are formed in a distinct way, following the local historical and cultural tradition that exists between these two institutional entities – as this tradition has become crystallized in the constitutional and legal order of the country concerned.

For the same reasons, in few branches of the law are the historical experience, emotional bonds and basic ideological convictions of a people more clearly and influentially expressed than in Ecclesiastical Law (or 'Law of Religions').

Greece is one of the few countries in Europe in which the above observations are borne out so clearly, as is evident in Articles 3, 13, 72 §§ 1 and 105 of the current Constitution.

More specifically, Article 3 Const. recognizes the Eastern Orthodox Church as the 'prevailing' religion of the Greek State – that is to say, the one to which the vast majority of the Greek people belong.

Furthermore, Article 13 Const. – in conformity with Article 9 of the European Convention on Human Rights (Rome, 1950) – protects the religious freedom of all 'known' religions in Greece.

Finally, with regard to the relations between the Greek State and the Churches/Religions in Greece, both the above and other constitutional provisions (including Article 72 § 1 of the Constitution) establish the peculiar system of 'State-law rule'.

For many decades now, the web of provisions mentioned above has generated a diverse range of theoretical views and produced a very rich body of case law consisting of decisions not only by Greek courts but also by the European Court of Human Rights (Strasbourg).

The present volume aims to provide a brief though, wherever necessary, critical presentation of all this theory and case law interpreting the legal relations between the State and Churches/Religions in Greece.

I would like to thank all those who supported me in the execution of this study.

Finally, I wish to express my sincere gratitude to Prof. Rik Torfs, editor of the internationally recognized series with the general title *International Encyclopedia of Laws: Religion*, for our excellent collaboration.

Thessaloniki, 5 August 2014
Asst. Prof. Constantine Papageorgiou

General Introduction

§1. General Background of the Country

1. Greece is a country located on the south-eastern tip of Europe, and more particularly, in the southern extremity of the Balkan Peninsula. It was officially recognized as an independent state on 3 February 1830 ('London Protocol'), whereas since 1945 it is one of the founding members of the United Nations Organization (UNO).

2. It acceded as Greek Republic to the European Economic Community (currently, 'European Union') as a full member in 1981[1] and to the eurozone in 2001, adopting the euro as its common currency. The city of Athens is the capital of Greece and its official language is Greek.

3. The total population of Greece comes to about 10.800.000 inhabitants. During the last few decades, the country absorbed a large wave of immigrants, whose total number reached nearly 10% of the total population, according to recent estimates. However, from all these immigrants only an estimated half live in the country legally. This fact may be attributed to the lack of a rational immigration policy, to the geographical position of Greece, and to the political or economic instability of those foreign countries, where many of the immigrants are coming from.

4. Under the current Constitution (enacted on 11 June 1975 and revised in 1986, 2001, 2008, 2019), the Greek Republic is a presidential parliamentary democracy. The Greek Constitution contains extended guarantees of the freedoms and rights of the citizens, which were further reinforced with the 2001 constitutional revision.[2] The particular revision established – for the first time on a constitutional level – five independent authorities, three of which (the 'Ombudsman', the 'Authority for the Protection of Communication Privacy', and the 'Authority for the Protection of Personal Data') are consecrated to the protection and entrenchment of individual rights. Greece is also a signatory state of the European Convention on Human Rights (enacted in Rome, on 4 November 1950).

---

1. The treaty of accession was ratified on 29.6.1979 (L. 945/1979).
2. In general, *see*: Chrysogonos/Vlahopoulos, *Individual and social rights*, passim.

5. On a state and organizational level, the Constitution distinguishes three powers: the legislative, the executive and the judicial (Article 26). The Greek Parliament and the President of the Greek Republic represent the legislative power; the President of the Greek Republic and the government share the executive power, whereas the judicial power is exercised by the courts in the name of the Greek people.[3]

§2. Social Facts about Religion

6. The 'International Religious Freedom Report',[4] which the State Department of the United States drafts every year, mentions the following about Greece (2019):

> The U.S. government estimates the total population at 10.8 million (midyear 2019 estimate), with 81 to 90 percent identifying as Greek Orthodox, 4 to 15 percent atheist, and 2 percent Muslim. In Thrace, there are approximately 140,000 Muslims, according to government sources using 2011 data; they are largely descendants of the Muslim minority officially recognized in the 1923 Treaty of Lausanne. According to a Pew Research Center study released in November 2017, an additional 520,000 Muslims – mostly immigrants and asylum seekers from Southeastern Europe, South Asia, Southeast Asia, the Middle East, and North Africa – reside throughout the country, clustered in communities by their countries of origin or in reception facilities. Government sources estimate half reside in Athens.
>
> According to data provided by other religious communities, their members combined constitute 3 to 5 percent of the population. These include Old Calendarist Orthodox, Catholics, Protestants, Jehovah's Witnesses, Jews, members of polytheistic Hellenic religions, Scientologists, Baha'is, members of The Church of Jesus Christ of Latter-day Saints, Sikhs, Seventh-day Adventists, Buddhists, and members of the International Society of Krishna Consciousness (ISKCON). Independent and media sources estimate Ethiopian Orthodox number 2500, and Assyrians less than 1,000. The Armenian Orthodox Archbishop, interviewed in 2018, estimated there are 100,000 Armenian Orthodox.

7. As it arises from the statistical data, the Greeks are a very religious people[5] – although this does not necessarily mean that they faithfully observe the relevant dictates of the Orthodox Church). The very high degree of formal integration of Greeks into this Church has, among others, two crucial constitutional consequences.

3. In detail: Chrysogonos, *Constitutional law*, 353 ff; Venizelos, *Lessons of constitutional law*, 62f, 82f, 131f, 160, 381ff; Mavrias, *Constitutional law*, Athens [5]2016, 102f, 319f, 333, 369, 392, 449.
4. United States of America, Department of State, *2019 Report on international religious freedom*, Office of International Religious Freedom.
5. Indicatively, *see* the comparative data cited by the European Social Research (ESR) dated 2003, in the article by Drettakis, 'The religiousness of Greeks', in newspaper 'The Kathimerini' (Sunday edition), issue dated 11.04.2004, p. 15, where, on a scale 0-10, the averages of religiousness are the

8. (i) In Greece, when we refer to church and state relations, we primarily mean not only the constitutional and legislative regulation but also the sociopolitical collaboration of the Greek Republic with the Orthodox Greek Church, since the near-total number of Greeks belongs to it (Article 3 Const.).

9. (ii) This reality had in previous decades led to the granting of economic and administrative privileges for the benefit of the said Church.[6] But because today similar beneficial statutory provisions exist under law for nearly all creeds, the privileged treatment of the Orthodox Church focuses rather on a form of ideological support on the part of the State, since for historical and tradition-based reasons, the Orthodox creed is considered an integral part of the modern Greek identity.

§3. Historical Background

I. The Impact of History

10. The relations between the State and the church develop in a specific manner in every Member State of the European Union, following the local historical and cultural tradition between the two institutional entities – as this has hitherto crystallized and has been embedded in their respective constitutional and overall legal civilization.

11. In Greece, the State maintains – for reasons which are customarily ascribed to a common historical trajectory and traditional social and cultural ties – a closer constitutional and administrative relationship with the Eastern Orthodox Church in particular. Consequently, the reference to history is deemed necessary in order to interpret and deeply comprehend the contemporary existing constitutional relationship between the State and the church in this country.[7]

II. The Byzantine Period

12. The form and the institutional content of the relations that developed between the Byzantine state and the church have historically constituted a point of interpretative conflict and friction for the scholars who specialize in the study of this period. Several historians have argued that the two institutions had been in constant

following: Greece (7.68), Italy (6.14), Ireland (5.78), Portugal (5.71), Finland (5.57), the Netherlands (5.06), Belgium (4.96), Spain (4.40), Denmark (4.36), United Kingdom (4.30), Germany (4.24), Luxembourg (3.96), Sweden (3.70).

6. For example, *see* Papageorgiou, *The tax regime of religions: Tax equality and religious freedom*, especially 5ff, 43ff, 331ff; *ibid.*, 'The special tax treatment of religions', Arm 74 (2020) 953–969.
7. On all these points, *see* Papageorgiou, *Ecclesiastical law*, 82 ff; Close, *Greece (1945-2004): Policy-society-economy*, 159–162; Makridis, 'The orthodox church in the 20th century: A historico-sociological survey', 860ff; Frazee, *Orthodox church and Greek independence (1821-1852)*, 245–247 and passim; Prinzipas/Karagiannis, *Church and hellenism from 1821 till today. An historical overview*, 13ff and passim.

competition – milder or harsher at different times and depending on the interests at stake – during the entire century-long history of the Byzantine period, contesting the allocation of power and the dominance of one over the other.

13. Nevertheless, according to other researchers, state and church collaborated in the context of the political theology of the Byzantines, with the common goal of achieving or preserving a coherent and undivided Christianity, in a state which was vulnerable due to its ethnic diversity and non-homogeneity.[8]

14. It is an undisputed fact that the emperors or other state agents and political emissaries of the Byzantine state acted as systematic supporters in the entrenchment and promotion of ecclesiastical political ideology. Nevertheless, they identified the organizational coherence or territorial integrity of the Byzantine 'imperium' with the administrative stability and doctrinal purity of the Church, thus pursuing their interference, either systematically or occasionally, even in manifestly internal ecclesiastical affairs.[9]

15. Assessing the full range of viewpoints which have been put forth, we should not overlook the fact that any uncertainty as to the validity of our conclusions may be attributed to the discontinuity or non-credibility of the relevant sources, on which the historical-legal research studies are grounded. However, in addition to this problem, since neither constitutional law nor canon law stipulates theoretical principles for a more systematic regulation of church and state relations, we contend that approaching the issue ultimately relates directly to the personal world view, the pursuits and even the strategies of particular individuals, who in each historic occasion embodied the two institutions. Put differently, in addition to any systematic or typological approaches, we believe that a decisive criterion for the realistic treatment of the whole issue has after all proven to be the individual world view of the personalities which in every instance represented the relevant institutions, with their choices of personal accountability substantiating and infusing meaning to the policy of the State or the church.[10]

---

8. From the especially extensive bibliography, *see* mainly: Runciman, *Byzantine theocracy*, 15–56 and passim; Glykatzi-Arhweiller, *Why byzantium* (especially Part III: 'State and Church', 141–170), and, *The political ideology of the Byzantine empire*, 118ff; Kiousopoulou, *King or seneschal? political power and ideology before the fall*, esp. 217ff; Beck, *A History of the orthodox church in the Byzantine empire*, passim.
9. The intervention of the Emperor in ecclesiastical affairs aimed at deterring the disruptive tendencies among his subjects, which may have originated from the absolute insistence on different doctrinal opinions. Thus, the imposition of the imperial volition sometimes in an outright, unconditional manner ('*sic volo, sic jubeo*') reduced any existing centrifugal propensities, homogenizing the imperial with the ecclesiastical ideology.
10. This is, in any case, corroborated by the contemporary reality in Greece: for example, the personality of the occasional ecclesiastical leaders, decisively tainted church-state relations, on a scale that ranged from the complete submission of the official ecclesiastical policy to the mandates of the State to open conflict (like the one which broke out with the enactment of L. 1700/1987 or, more recently, with the issue of the mention of religious affiliation on identity cards. *See* in general Manitakis, *The relations of the church with the nation-state under the shadow of the identity* (Athens 2000). *See* further below for both issues.

16. However, it was true that, from the aspect of its both morphological structure and internal function, the ecclesiastical organization constituted, throughout the entire Byzantine period, an institution with prominent state characteristics. For this reason, organizational or administrative issues of ecclesiastical interest were also regulated by provisions of the imperial state legislation.[11]

17. These legislative interventions in ecclesiastical administration either were direct and explicit or followed more indirect methods of influence; however, it was not allowed for them to distort the Orthodox doctrinal teaching, as this had crystallized in decisions of the ecclesiastical synods or writings of the fathers; in any cases when this occurred, their action of the church was, as a rule, straightforward and strong, towards the direction of the preservation of its spiritual freedom and doctrinal integrity – certainly as long as its various internal tendencies consented.

III. The Rule of the Ottomans

18. According to the Islamic Ottoman tradition, the so-called People of the Bible (Christians and Hebrews), as long as they had not shown resistance and regularly fulfilled their tax obligations, maintained their religious self-governance, observing their respective religious or community traditions. For this reason, Sultan Mehmed II, the Conqueror, evaluating the religious and political conditions that had already been shaped after the Fall of Constantinople (1453), granted the Patriarch Gennadius Scholarius an array of general and special privileges for the self-administration of the Orthodox Church. Their implementation set the institutional bases for the coexistence of the ecclesiastical organization in the context of the gigantic Ottoman administrative machine, aiming at the most harmonious integration and operation of the former in alignment with the Ottoman legal order.[12]

19. These privileges regarded either the Patriarch himself, as the religious leader of the Orthodox (*special privileges*), or the Orthodox Church in its entirety (*general privileges*). The privileges provided freedom of worship, internal self-administration of the Christian communities or its foundations, the unhindered administration and management of the ecclesiastical property assets, tax exemptions, the exercise of spiritual or judicial jurisdiction on the part of the competent ecclesiastical organs in cases of family or inheritance law, and so on.

20. Nevertheless, these same privileges often did not become respected, especially in regions where the Christian populations were more vulnerable to the oppression of the local Ottoman authorities, without more direct monitoring on the part of the central state administration.

---

11. *See* indicatively: Runciman, *Byzantine theocracy*, 15ff; Glykatzi-Arhweiller, *Why byzantium*, 1412ff.
12. On this issue, *see* Kambourides, *Modern Greece through Ottoman archival sources: Economy, institutions and society in the 17th century Thessaly*, 15ff.

IV. The Modern Greek Period

21. The onset of the national liberation struggle of the Greeks in 1821 brought about the disruption of communication between the ecclesiastical eparchies of the Greek territories which were in revolt and the Ecumenical Patriarchate.[13]

22. All the constitutional Greek texts contained provisions which recognized, by official wording, the Eastern Orthodox Church as 'prevailing' in the country. However, these same texts, permeated by a liberal spirit, provided in an equally festive fashion the establishment and protection of religious freedom, with the free exercise of worship of any other doctrines or creeds under the guarantee of state authorities.[14]

23. For reasons which were attributable to foreign policy, the Decree of 23-7/4-8-1833 proclaimed the Greek Orthodox Church as autocephalous and administratively independent from the Ecumenical Patriarchate, maintaining since that time only a doctrinal unity with Constantinople. In parallel, this Decree launched a new period in which the State closely supervised the Church, whose bishops were appointed by the government. The Holy Synod of the Church of Greece was under the complete control of King Otto (who was a Roman Catholic!). No synodal decision took any effect, unless it was ratified by the government itself.[15]

24. However, the Ecumenical Patriarchate issued the Patriarchal and Synodal Decision of 29 June 1850, officially proclaiming the Church of Greece as 'autocephalous', laying down certain terms concerning its administration.[16]

25. With the promulgation of the Patriarchal and Synodal Acts of 1866 and 1882, the ecclesiastical eparchies of the Heptanese and of Thessaly were permanently joined with the Autocephalous Church of Greece, as was the case with the region of Arta in Epirus.[17]

---

13. About this period, *see* instead of others: Frazee, *Orthodox church and Greek independence (1821-1852)*, 119ff; Diamantouros, *The origins of the formation of the contemporary state in Greece (1821-1828)*, 73–79; Petropoulos, *Politics and state formation in the kingdom of Greece (1833-1843)*, passim; Sherard, *Essays on the new hellenism*, 294 ff.
14. Mavrias/Pantelis, *Constitutional texts*, passim; Alivizatos, *The constitution and its enemies in modern Greek history (1800-2010)*, especially 33–72 ('The modern Greek Enlightenment and the Constitutions of the Revolution'); Kitromilidis, *Modern Greek enlightenment. The political and social ideas*, 372–380 and passim.
15. More analytically, *see* Frazee, *Orthodox church and Greek independence (1821-1852)*, 161–213.
16. Papageorgiou, *Ecclesiastical law*, 57–60; Troianos/Dimakopoulou, *Church and state. Relations between them during the period 1833-1852*, 51–58; Matalas, *Nation and orthodoxy: The adventures of a relationship*, 90ff; Prinzipas/Karagiannis, *Church and hellenism from 1821 till today. An historical overview*, 35–51.
17. Papageorgiou, *Ecclesiastical law*, 85ff; Matalas, *Nation and orthodoxy. The adventures of a relationship*, passim; Prinzipas/Karagiannis, *Church and hellenism from 1821 till today: An historical overview*, 65ff.

26. The public presence of the Church during the first few decades of the 20th century was marked by its active participation in political affairs, which later spiralled into the national dichotomy between royalists and liberals (1917). The events of this period led, among others, to the dethronement and replacement of the archbishop, as well as numerous other bishops, demonstrating the extent to which ecclesiastical decisions or acts could supersede their spiritual role and deviate to become regular interferences in political passions or party politics.[18]

27. The 'Statutory Charter', which was enacted in 1923, established the Holy Synod as the highest administrative body of the Autocephalous Church of Greece, entrenching the synodical system of governance and stipulating, in this same context, the direct election of bishops by the Synod. By virtue of provisions of the same Statutory Charter, the metropolitan of Athens was renamed as Archbishop, whereas the local archbishops as metropolitans.[19]

28. Two years later, a second synodal organ was established, the Permanent Holy Synod, whereas in 1928, the Patriarchal and Synodal Act of 4 September 1928 was issued, and ratified by L. 3615/1928,[20] bringing under the jurisdiction of the Church of Greece 'temporarily'[21] the administration of the ecclesiastical eparchies of the New Lands (namely of Epirus, of course without the eparchies of Arta, Macedonia, Western Thrace and certain islands of the Northern Aegean Sea).[22]

29. Statutory charters of the Church of Greece, L. 5187/1931 and L. 5438/1932, were enacted, followed by L. 671/1943,[23] as well as by L.D. 126/1969, which was in force during the period of the dictatorship.[24] Soon after the beginning of the post-Junta era, L. 590/1977 was enacted, which is currently in effect and which we will explore more closely below.

---

18. In general *see* Tsironis, *Church in politics (1913-1941)*, 41–175 and passim; Prinzipas/Karagiannis, *Church and hellenism from 1821 till today: An historical overview*, 67–104.
19. Tsironis, *Church in politics (1913-1941)*, 171ff; Papageorgiou, *Ecclesiastical law*, 86ff; Prinzipas/Karagiannis, *Church and hellenism from 1821 till today: An historical overview*, 91f; Konidaris, *Lessons of ecclesiastical law*, 125ff.
20. Prinzipas/Karagiannis, *Church and hellenism from 1821 till today. An historical overview*, 93f.
21. In 2003, on the occasion of the alignment with the content of the said Act, the relations of the Ecumenical Patriarchate with the Autocephalous Church of Greece were marred by a profound crisis, which reached the limits of a schism between the two Churches; on this matter, *see* Feidas, 'The constitutional entrenchment of the Patriarchal Act of 1928', D 35 (2004) 903ff; Beis, 'The revocation/termination of the Patriarchal Synodal Act of September 4th 1928', D 35 (2004) 581ff. Cf. Prinzipas, *The great crises in the Church: Five landmarks in the relations between the church of Greece and the ecumenical patriarchate*, passim.
22. CoS 4068/1981, NoV 32 (1984) 181; CoS 534/1999, EDDD 43 (1999) 558–563, and CoS 603/1999, ArchN 50 (1999) 581–585.
23. This statutory charter secured ecclesiastical self-administration to a greater degree than all previous ones. More extensively, *see* the doctoral thesis of Theodoridis, *Conflict between legality and canonicity: The case of archbishop of Athens and all Greece damaskinos*, especially 463ff; Tsironis, *Church in politics (1913-1941)*, 237ff; Papageorgiou, *Ecclesiastical law*, 87 f; Konidaris, *Lessons of ecclesiastical law*, 128ff.
24. For an analysis of the historical events which institutionally traumatized the Church of Greece during the period of the dictatorship (1967–1973), *see* in Marinos, 'Thoughts on the crisis in the church

30. The post-war period was characterized by a plethora of arbitrary interventions of the State in the internal affairs of the church. Some of them were so violent and flagrant that they moved far beyond any statist logic. Nevertheless, one should not ignore the fact, which has been confirmed by multiple sources, that some of these interventions became favourably accepted – if they were not directly encouraged – by groups of members of the governing church, with the ultimate goal of promoting their own personal interests and ambitions.

31. From the chronicle of the numerous (obvious and less obvious) interventions, it is worth noting here that the Greek military junta (1967–1973) appointed a great many archbishops as members of the Permanent Holy Synod (PHS), who in many instances provided the necessary ideological 'legitimation' which was required by the dictatorship of the colonels on the part of the Church in order 'to bear good testimony'.[25] Archbishop Serapheim (1973–1998) was also appointed by the military regime which succeeded the dictatorship for a brief period of time. A primary characteristic of his term was the generalized indifference towards the image and the presence of the Church in public affairs.[26]

32. The most recent sharp public clash between the church and the State occurred in 2001. The occasion was the intention of the Greek government, following a recommendation of the Authority for the Protection of Personal Data,[27] to remove the indication of religious affiliation on the identity cards of Greek citizens. However, this attempt met with the fierce resistance of the dynamic Archbishop Christodoulos, who organized, among others, two huge public demonstrations ('Gatherings of the People', as he himself called them) in Athens and Thessaloniki.[28]

33. Ultimately, the inscription of the creed on identification cards was held to be unconstitutional by the Greek Council of State[29] and the whole matter was forgotten, proving once more how fragile church and state relations are and how susceptible to the unfathomable ambitions of their occasional representatives.

---

of Greece', *Church and law: Theory and case law*, 604–637, *ibid.*, *Relations between church and state (under the constitution of 1975 and the new statutory charter of the church of Greece),* 100–116 (in which *see* esp. Chapter III: 'Interventions in the administration of the Church attempted during the period spanning from 21-4-1967 until 23-7-1974'); Mavrias, *Constitutional law*, 791ff.

25. Close, *Greece (1945-2004): Politics-society-economy*, 334f; Prinzipas/Karagiannis, *Church and hellenism from 1821 till today. An historical overview*, 151–172.
26. It is no coincidence that enlightened theologians identified this period as one of a sad 'ecclesiastical apathy' which characterized it: the Church 'was there', but in practice it was inert and essentially absent from any serious public action, a fact which dramatically aggravated the climate of disgrace felt by the citizens, directed especially against its higher administrators.
27. *Authority for the Protection of Personal Data 510/17/2000*, ToS 26 (2000) 948.
28. For the wide range of opinions (mainly) within the Church on this issue, *see* the collective volume *The church and identities: A theological and legal consideration of the identity card issue*, Athens, 2d ed. 2000, a publication of the Holy Synod of the Church of Greece.
29. *See* CoS 2279-2282/2001, Arm. 55 (2001) 1111–1135: the elements which are cited in police identity documents comprise personal data and their indication constitutes processing; the obligatory mention of religious affiliation on citizens' identity cards is unconstitutional. *See also* the decision of the European Court of Human Rights of 12-12-2002 in the case *Sophianopoulos v. Greece*, NoV 51

34. One of the most controversial issues in the recent revision of the Greek Constitution (2018–2019) was the relations between the State and the Orthodox Church, as governed principally by Article 3 of the Constitution. More specifically, in February 2019, the parliamentary group of the SYRIZA party[30] proposed that: (a) a clause should be added to Article 3 paragraph 1 Const. establishing the so-called religious neutrality of the State; and (b) a political oath should be established through the revision of Article 13 paragraph 5 (freedom of religion), Article 33 paragraph 2 (oath of the President of the Republic) and Article 59 paragraphs 1 and 2: oath to be taken by Members of Parliament; oath to be taken by Members of Parliament of a different religion or creed; also Members of Parliament who do not wish to give any kind of religious oath may give an oral promise that they will execute their duties according to their moral conscience (*secular oath*).

35. The final vote on the revision of the Constitution was held on 25 November 2019. However, the majority of the Greek Parliament did not accept the above-proposed changes and so Church-State relations have remained unchanged in constitutional terms. The new Constitution was published in the Government Gazette on 24 December 2019 (Issue A no. 211).[31]

V. Conclusions

36. Attempting a final evaluation of the relations between State and Church, as they developed from the period of the National Revolution (1821) until the end of the 20th century, we may deduce their dynamically dialectic nature: the relations between the two institutions went through, naturally not in a linear direction, all possible degrees on a scale which ranged from a smooth and reciprocal collaboration, in the context of the classic viewpoint about 'distinct roles',[32] all the way to a direct and open confrontation, for reasons usually appertaining to political choices.

(2003) 801–805: the identity card issued by the police constitutes a public document, whose content cannot be determined by the wishes of the interested party; the non-indication of the citizens' religion in the information contained on their identity cards does not violate their right to religious freedom (Art. 9 ECHR).

30. It should be mentioned that the Coalition of the Radical Left – Progressive Alliance (SY.RIZ.A – Progressive Alliance) is a Greek political party. It was founded in 2004 as an alliance of left-wing parties and organizations. The President of SY.RIZ.A is Alexis Tsipras. Since 2012, SY.RIZ.A. is one of the two dominant political parties in the political scene of Greece along with New Democracy. Ο ΣΥ.ΡΙΖ.Α. served as the government of Greece from January 2015 to July 2019, with Prime Minister Alexis Tsipras. Today the party is represented in the Greek Parliament by 86 deputies and is in the position of the official opposition.
31. Analytically: Sotirelis/Xiros, *The fourth revision of the constitution of 1975 (2014-2019): Introduction, history, proposals, amendments, reports, ballots, resolution, sources, scientific articles, press publications*, passim.
32. For illustrative historical examples, *see* in Close, *Greece (1945-2004): Politics-society-economy*, 159ff; Feidas, 'The function of the distinct roles of church and state and the responsibility of the polity', E. 78 (2001) 232–247.

37. A point of continuous contestation was the way in which the Church functioned in the framework of constitutional institutions, as well as its social or political role, in a country which could easily, at least in the past, invest clergymen with competencies belonging to ethnarchs.

Part I. Legal Framework and Sources

Chapter 1. The Constitutional Status of Religion

38. The institutional relations between the State and the creeds within the Greek territory are regulated by the following provisions of the Constitution that are currently in force:

- Article 3: recognition of the Eastern Orthodox Church of Christ as the 'prevailing religion' of the Greek state; the character of this Church as 'autocephalous' (self-governing); the Holy Synod of Hierarchy, as the highest ecclesiastical authority of the above Church; constitutional entrenchment of the holy canons.[33]
- Article 4 § 6: alternative military service of conscientious objectors.[34]
- Article 5 §§ 1–2: free development of the personality, without distinction based on, among others, religious beliefs.
- Article 13: right to religious freedom – freedom of religious conscience and freedom of worship – concept of 'known' religion – constitutional limitations of religious freedom.[35]
- Article 14 § 3: requirements for the seizure of newspapers and other publications because of an offence against the Christian or any other known religion.[36]
- Article 16 §§ 1–2: religious education – teaching of the lesson of religion in schools.[37]
- Article 18 § 8: protection of a part of ecclesiastical property.[38]
- Article 33 § 2: the oath of the President of the Republic, before assuming the exercise of his duties.
- Article 55 §§ 1–2: the oath taken by Members of Parliament, before they assume the exercise of their duties.

---

33. The relevant bibliography is quite rich; *see* indicatively: Papastathis, *The Hellenic republic and the prevailing religion*, 815ff; *ibid.*, *Nomocanonical studies*, 65–84; Marinos, *Religious freedom*, 92–100; Christophilopoulos, *Greek ecclesiastical law*, 70ff; Papageorgiou, *Ecclesiastical law*, 98ff; Venizelos, *The relations between state and church*, 107ff, passim.
34. Chrysogonos/Vlahopoulos, *Individual and social rights*, 194ff.
35. *See* the relevant Part II.
36. Chrysogonos/Vlahopoulos, *Individual and social rights*, 345ff.
37. Chrysogonos, *Religious education and prevailing religion*, ToS 25 (1999) 993–1024; Troianos, *Religious education in the context of the individual right of religious freedom*, 285–301; Venizelos, *The relations between state and church*, 119–129.
38. Papageorgiou, *Ecclesiastical property*, passim; Papastathis, *Nomocanonical studies*, 41–54.

- Article 72 § 1: the competence of the Parliament in full session to vote on bills pertaining to issues arising from the relations between the State and the creeds.
- Article 105: the content and the protection of the ancient and local privileged regime of the Monastic State of Mount Athos.[39]
- Article 110 § 1: the provisions of the Constitution relating to religious freedom are not subject to revision.

39. As it becomes obvious from the aforementioned constitutional arrangements, in Greece there is *a form of unity of the State with the Orthodox Church.* We will discuss at greater length in the pages that immediately follow the specifics of the concept, the content and the consequences of this 'statocratic' regime. Here we will limit ourselves to underlining that a direct consequence of the said system of unity is that the State is legitimized to intervene and to regulate – even the internal ecclesiastical affairs – by law which is enacted by the Parliament in Plenary Session (Article 72 § 1 Const.).

40. The 'Preamble' to the Constitution of Greece ('In the Name of the Holy and Consubstantial and Indivisible Trinity') constitutes a matter of different institutional significance because, as it is widely believed, this reference is of a symbolic and not a normative nature.[40]

41. As for the broader legal consequences that the aforementioned constitutional arrangements will have on all the creeds of the country, these will be systematically and analytically explored in the individual chapters of the monograph. Because of the system of unity between the Greek State and the Orthodox Church – and we should remind the readers that over 90% of the Greek people belong to it – this chapter will be devoted to a more particular discussion of the constitutional status of this Church and of its institutional impact.

42. It is clarified that, with the general term 'Church', the present work refers to the totality of Christians of the same denomination, whose religious communities have an indivisible legal organization. The concept consequently is used to include the Orthodox Church, the Roman Catholic Church, the different Protestant or Evangelical Denominations, the Anglican and the Lutheran Church, and so on. Furthermore, by the term 'religions', we denote mainly the Judaic and the Muslim religion. Lastly, it is worth reminding the readers that the term 'Ekklesia' in classic antiquity meant the 'Assembly of the People' (*Ekklesia tou Dimou*).[41]

39. Skandamis, *Mount Athos and the European Communities*, HEED 3 (1983) 271–285; Pavlopoulos, *The legal nature of the administrative bodies of Mount Athos and the collection of the fines that it imposes according to the code for the collection of public revenues*, D 28 (1997) 547–558.
40. Tsatsos, *Constitutional law*, vol. II, Athens 1993, 592ff; Papageorgiou, *Ecclesiastical law*, 93f.
41. Christophilopoulos, *Greek ecclesiastical law*, 8; Troianos, *Lectures in ecclesiastical law*, 32f.

Chapter 2. Other Legislation with Regard to Religion

§1. Generally

43. A decisive breach in the system of statocracy characterizing the relations between the State and the Orthodox Church was that the latter was empowered by law to issue administrative acts of a regulatory (legislative) content.

44. More particularly, initially with the provisions of LD 126/1969 and subsequently of L. 590/1977 (Statutory Charter of the Church of Greece), the Holy Synod, acting as the highest authority of the Autocephalous Church of Greece, was authorized to issue regulatory acts concerning the organization, administration and operation of ecclesiastical legal entities and ecclesiastical administrative authorities.[42]

45. The issuance of these regulations – whose effect expands and deepens the self-administration of the Church – is grounded on the provision of Article 43 § 2 Const.[43] and aims to regulate matters of a particular, technical or local nature. These ecclesiastical regulations are subject to the powers of annulment and recourse of the Council of State for a possible *lack or transgression of legislative authorization,* but not for abuse of power.[44]

46. The large number of ecclesiastical regulations that were enacted in this manner led to the multifaceted normative self-regulation of the ecclesiastical organization and to the impressive enrichment of its self-administration, through a very broad law-giving function.

47. The institutional fields of the internal administrative organization of the Church, which were regulated with approximately sixty-seven such regulations to date, during the period spanning from 1977 to 2020, include the following:

(1) the operation of the synodal bodies and committees;[45]
(2) the status of priests and deacons;[46]

42. On this issue, *see* particularly Papageorgiou, *The limits of ecclesiastical self-administration*. I: *Regulatory jurisdiction*, Thessaloniki 2012.
43. According to this provision: 'The issuance of general regulatory decrees, by virtue of special delegation granted by statute and within the limits of such delegation, shall be permitted on the proposal of the competent Minister. Delegation for the purpose of issuing regulatory acts by other administrative organs shall be permitted in cases concerning the regulation of more specific matters or matters of local interest or of a technical and detailed nature.'
44. According to decision CoS 960-961/1978 (Plenary Session), there is a clear transgression of legislative mandate when the ecclesiastical administrative body issues a regulation whose content directly contradicts the statutes of the Charter.
45. Reg. 1/1977, 'Proceedings of the Holy Synod of the Church of Greece' (OGG A' 275); Reg. 160/2004, 'Operation of the Synodal Committees' (OGG A' 100); Reg. 214/2010 (OGG A' 185); Reg. 279/2015.
46. Reg. 305/2018 (OGG A' 153).

(3) the employment status of ecclesiastical employees;[47]
(4) the organization and administration of churches and parishes;[48]
(5) the fiscal review of church finances;[49]
(6) the organization of the financial agency of the Church of Greece;[50] and
(7) the protection and management of ecclesiastical real estate property.[51]

48. L. 2456/1920, 'On Israelite Communities', provides for similar legislative authorizations for the internal self-administration of the Israelite communities within the Greek territory.[52]

§2. Law 4301/2014 on Religious Communities and Associations

49. The right to associate for religious purposes is the most direct consequence of the constitutionally safeguarded right of religious communities to govern themselves, as part of the broader right to religious freedom (Article 13 Const., Article 9 ECHR).[53] In accordance with their right to self-government, religious communities may, in order to realize their aims, find, organize and operate legal persons,[54] within the framework of the terms of their approved charter or statute.

50. The right of association for religious purposes has frequently preoccupied Greek theory and jurisprudence. It achieved particular prominence in legal circles through the ECtHR ruling in the *Canea Catholic Church v. Greece* case (16.12.1997), which accepted that: (a) regardless of their legal personality, religious communities are entitled to enjoy the rights guaranteed in the ECHR and may exercise these rights in the name of their members; and (b) in the case of the Canea Catholic Church, the Greek court's refusal to recognize its legal personality restricted its procedural right to a fair trial (Article 6 paragraph 1 ECHR).

47. Reg. 5/1978, 'Code for Ecclesiastical Employees' (OGG A' 48).
48. Reg. 8/1979–1980, 'Holy Churches and Parishes' (OGG A' 1/1980).
49. Reg. 210/2010, 'Division for the Fiscal Review of the Church of Greece' (OGG A' 135).
50. Reg. 267/2015, 'Operation of the Ecclesiastical Central Financial Agency' (OGG A' 120); Reg. 317/2020, 'Organisation of the Ecclesiastical Central Financial Agency' (OGG A' 97).
51. Reg. 229/2011, 'Protection of the ruined monasteries and ecclesiastical monuments' (OGG A' 253); Reg. 318/2020, 'On hiring, sale and management of church property' (OGG A' 121).
52. Troianos/Papageorgiou, *Religious legislation*, 1737f.
53. Analytically: Kastanas, in Sicilianos, *European Convention on Human Rights: Interpretation to articles*, 363–393. Robbers (ed.), *Church autonomy: A comparative survey*, Frankfurt, Berlin, Bruxelles, Oxford, Wien 2001; Doe/Sandberg (ed.), *Law and religion: New horizons*, European Consortium for Church and State Research: Law and Religion Studies 7, Peeters, Leuven-Paris-Walpole, MA 2010.
54. As a rule, legal entities in private law – such as unions, foundations, civil non-profit companies or fundraising committees – according to the provisions of Arts 61 et seq.

51. Article 1 of Law 4301/2014[55] introduces for the first time into Greek law the term 'religious community' to denote 'a sufficient number of individuals with a specific Confession of Faith in a known religion who are permanent residents of a specified geographical region and whose aim is to carry out collectively the duties of worship and observance required by the common Confession of Faith of their members'.

52. Article 2 establishes the new term 'religious legal person', denoting a union of individuals belonging to the same religious community whose purpose is to exercise their religious duties in an organized manner. A religious legal person acquires its personality when it is registered in the 'Special Public Register of Religious Legal Persons', which is kept in the First Instance Court of the area in which the religious legal person is based. According to the same article, in order for a religious legal person to be established, a minimum number of three hundred individuals is required – a requirement that clearly constitutes a restriction on the freedom of worship.

53. According to Article 3, in order for a religious community to be registered as a religious legal person in the above-mentioned register, its administrative board must submit a relevant application to the competent First Instance Court. The application should be accompanied by: (a) the instrument of incorporation of the religious legal person, signed by all its founder-members, with full details of their identity and residence; (b) the community's 'Confession of Faith'; (c) the names of the members of the administrative board, including the name of the community's religious minister; (d) the full curriculum vitae of the latter, showing any religious studies pursued by him/her and the manner and date of his/her selection or appointment to his/her position; (e) a list of the places of worship used by the community applying for the status of religious legal person; and (f) the applicants' statute. No member of a religious legal entity may participate in another religious legal entity.

54. The statute of a religious legal person (Article 4) should not offend public order or good usages (good morals) as such offences constitute restrictions of religious freedom (Article 13 [2] ii Const.). The statute must state: (a) the name of the religious legal person, which must include the basic Greek word defining the religion or a faithful transcription of it in Greek, together with the indication 'Religious Legal Person'; (b) the seat of the religious legal person; (c) its internal organizational structure; (d) its governing bodies, the procedures for their selection, appointment or dismissal and their rules of operation; (e) the selection or appointment procedures for its religious ministers; (f) its means of representation in and out of

55. Modified by Art. 39 of L. 4589/2019; *AP 678/2019*: the name of the religious legal entity must be immediately indicative of the religion that follows it, so as not to confuse its identity; *First Instant Court of Xanthi 75/2020*; *First Instant Court of Thiva 195/2018*; *First Instant Court of Athens 1279/ 2016*.

court; (g) the procedures for the admission, departure and expulsion of its members, as well as the rights and obligations of the latter; (h) the procedures under which its supreme body meets and decides; (i) its funds and sources of funding; (j) any relations of interdependence or spiritual or administrative ties it has with an 'ecclesiastical person' in Greece or religious communities or organizations abroad; (k) the procedures for amending the statute; (l) the procedures for the dissolution of the legal entity. The statute must clearly state the religion, doctrine and Confession of Faith to which the legal person adheres. It must also describe the legal person's teachings and worship events and mention all the sacred texts and rules by which it is bound and which form the basis of its organization.

55. If the First Instance Court decides that the legal conditions have been met, the application is accepted and the Court (Article 5) orders that the Confession of Faith and a summary of the statute with its most important elements be published in the press, and that the legal person be registered in the above-mentioned Register of Religious Legal Persons. The statute is ratified by the President of the Court, notified to the Public Prosecutor of the First Instance Court and deposited in the archives of the First Instance Court. The religious legal person acquires legal personality the moment it is registered in the Register. The registration takes place immediately after the Court has issued its decision.

56. The property of the religious legal person may not be distributed or transferred to its members. In the event of its dissolution, however, it may be received by another religious legal person of the same Confession of Faith, or a church of the same religion or confession, provided that this is expressly provided for in the statute. Otherwise, it becomes the property of the State.

57. According to Article 8, the religious legal person must be governed in accordance with its statute by its religious minister or a multi-member body. The statute of the religious legal person may designate its general assembly of members as its governing body with the competence to decide on any matter that does not lie within the competence of another body.

58. Religious legal persons are entitled to establish, organize and operate, anywhere in Greece, places of worship, camps, private schools, educational institutions, charitable institutions, non-governmental organizations and other legal persons of a non-profit character for the purpose of promoting their activities and developing the services they offer.

59. Of particular importance is Article 12 of L. 4301/2014 (on 'Ecclesiastical' Legal Persons), which, in our opinion, is the most problematic. According to this article, a 'Church' is an association of at least three religious legal persons of the same religion with an episcopal, synodical or other type of central structure, operates in accordance with its statute and is governed by individual or collective bodies that are either elected or appointed. As can be seen, the creation of such an association requires the existence of at least nine hundred church members, although it is not clear what the reasoning behind this number is.

60. An exception to these strict requirements for the recognition of a legal personality, which applies to all other religions, is introduced by the very lengthy Article 13 entitled 'Recognition of legal personality of the Catholic Church in Greece', which, among other things, provides for the following:

(a) The Catholic Church in Greece, which is based in Athens and governed by the Holy Synod of the Catholic Hierarchy of Greece, is recognized as an ecclesiastical legal person of private law 'with no further formalities and with no need to follow the procedures laid down in Articles 3 and 12, even if the minimum number of members or religious legal persons stipulated in the previous articles is not met'. The approximately 240 dioceses, parishes and monasteries of the Catholic Church that are clearly specified later in Article 13 are recognized as religious legal persons.
(b) Similar recognition is given (paragraph 5) – also without the need to follow the procedures laid down in Articles 3 and 12, even if the minimum number of members is not met – to the following religious communities: (i) the Anglican Church in Greece (based in Athens); (ii) the Ethiopian Orthodox Church (based in Athens); (iii) the Egyptian Coptic Orthodox Church of Greece; (iv) the German-speaking Evangelical Church (based in Athens); (vi) the Greek Evangelical Church (based in Athens), including its parishes in Athens, Katerini, Thessaloniki, Volos, Ioannina, Corfu and Alexandroupoli, which are also recognized as religious legal persons; (vii) the Assyrian Orthodox Church (based in Aigaleo, Attica); and (viii) the Armenian Evangelical Church (based in Piraeus).
(c) Similar privileges are to be found in Article 16 (on the 'Maintenance of Specific Legal Regimes'), which exempts the following groups from the obligation to comply with the provisions of Law 4301/2014: (i) the religious ministers and the organization of religious communities under the jurisdiction of the Orthodox Church of Greece, as specified in Article 3 of the Constitution, or the other Churches, Patriarchates, Bishoprics or Monasteries of the same religious denomination, within or outside Greece, that are united in doctrine with the Ecumenical Patriarchate and, like the latter, observe the holy canons and traditions; ii) the religious ministers and the organization of religious communities that adhere to the Jewish faith, which are subject to the legal provisions on the Jewish Communities; and iii) the religious ministers and the organization of religious communities of Muslims in the areas under the jurisdiction of the Muftiates.

61. Article 14 stipulates that the Ministry of Education and Religious Affairs must keep an electronic register of religious legal persons and religious ministers who perform religious ceremonies with civil law effects, including both ministers who belong to a religious community organized in some legal form and those who belong to a community without legal personality.

62. Finally, the question of the transfer of property is regulated by Article 18, which stipulates that associations, foundations or non-profit civil law partnerships that have been established by religious communities and are operating at the time L. 4301/2014 is published may, by means of donation, transfer their property to the religious legal persons established by the same religious communities.

Chapter 3. Typology of the System

§1. The Community of the Orthodox Churches

63. The Orthodox Church does not possess *in globo* a pyramid-shaped hierarchical structure in its organization; it is not characterized by absolute organizational homogeneity and is not structured into a uniform administrative corpus. It is more appropriate to see the Orthodox Church as a broad community of 'autocephalous' and 'autonomous' churches: these local churches are connected by a common doctrinal faith and canonical order, but without being structured into a unified and solid legal organization, because they fall under the legal system of the State, in which they are located. In other words, each autocephalous or autonomous Orthodox Church functions in the context of the legal order of a particular nation state. The legislative power of this State may many times intervene in internal ecclesiastic affairs, regulating the form or even the legal content of ecclesiastical institutions.

64. Even if it is not possible to give a comprehensive and generally accepted definition, nevertheless:

- an *autocephalous* church is the church that is fully self-administered, by means of organs that it selects itself; whereas;
- an *autonomous* church is a church in which the Ecumenical Patriarchate either elects its 'First Bishop' or simply ratifies his election. For all other matters, autonomous churches also enjoy very broad self-administration.[56]

65. Every autocephalous church is equal to all others. The Ecumenical Patriarchate of Constantinople holds an honorary primacy among other patriarchates: it is considered par excellence to be the first among equals *(primus inter pares),* but it is not entitled to intervene in the internal administration of autocephalous churches.[57]

66. The highest legislative, administrative and judicial authority in the Orthodox Church is the Ecumenical Synod:[58] it is comprised of all the bishops of the local autocephalous churches, under the presidency of the Ecumenical Patriarch of Constantinople.

---

56. On all these matters, *see*: Christophilopoulos, *Greek ecclesiastical law*, 104ff; Troianos, *Lectures in ecclesiastical law*, 128ff; Vlasios Feidas, 'L'Église locale: autocephale ou autonome – en communion avec les autres Églises. Autocephalie et communion', in (collectif) *Église locale et Église universelle,* ed. du Centre orthodoxe du Patriarcat oecuméique, Chambesy-Geneve 1981, 148ff.
57. In general, *see*: Maxime de Sardes, *Le Patriarcat oecumenique dans l'Église orthodoxe*, Paris 1975.
58. For example, *see* the collection of Joannou, *Discipline generale antique,* vol. I/1: *Les canons des conciles oecumeniques* vol. I/2: *Les canons des Synodes Particuliers* vol. II: *Les canons des Peres Grecs,* Grottaferrata (Roma): Tipografia Italo-orientale 'S. Nilo', 1962–1964.

§2. The Principle of Ethnicities

67. Although it is a fact that autocephalous or autonomous churches have been functioning for many centuries, the modern-day reality of the local Orthodox Churches has been to a large extent shaped during the nineteenth and twentieth centuries, as a result of the 'principle of ethnicities'. This ideological and political current, which prevailed in Europe during the aforementioned historical period, led to the creation of nation states in the wider region of the Balkan Peninsula, by peoples who claimed political independence from the Ottoman Empire.

68. The gradual formation of a new geopolitical map in the region had a significant impact on the field of ecclesiastical jurisdictions, which was admittedly always sensitive to political rearrangements. The nationalities of the wider Balkan Peninsula consolidated new state entities, at the same time pursuing their ecclesiastical independence.

69. This trend by necessity restricted the jurisdiction of the Ecumenical Patriarchate, which until then operated as a hyper-national ecclesiastical authority for all the Orthodox peoples of the Balkan area. The new order of political affairs incited the establishment of 'national' churches (autocephalous or autonomous), corresponding to the newly formed nation states.[59] The jurisdiction of these national churches was exercised within the limits of the respective independent state.

§3. The Canonical Foundations of Ecclesiastical Autocephaly: Autonomy

70. The demands for ecclesiastical independence invoked mainly Holy Canon 14 of the Fourth Ecumenical Synod (year 451) and Holy Canon 38 of the Synod in Trullo (year 691). According to these canons – which are protected by the Article 3 Const. – it is expedient that ecclesiastical administration follows the development of the respective policy. As it derives from the content of the holy canons previously mentioned, practical reasons – and more particularly, the possibility of exercising more effective or unhindered ecclesiastical administration – constituted the criterion for granting autocephaly or autonomy to a local church.

71. However, to a far greater extent than the pressure exerted by the practical needs for better administration, the main incentive to pursue ecclesiastical independence from the Ecumenical Patriarchate was the establishment of churches having a national or racial character, something which was completely unknown to the Orthodox Church until the nineteenth century. This historical juncture brought the Patriarchate before a number of difficult and challenging problems. The extensive bibliography on issues of autocephaly and autonomy provides a detailed picture of these problems.

---

59. In general *see* Matalas, *Nation and orthodoxy: The adventures of a relationship*, Iraklio, Crete 2003.

§4. Doctrinal and Canonical Unity

72. As it was already noted, the local Orthodox Churches are bound by a relationship of doctrinal and canonical unity, which is understood mainly as a spiritual concept – and not merely an administrative one.

73. Doctrinal unity has as its content the precise observation of the teachings of the Bible/Holy Scriptures, the respect for tradition and doctrines, as these were set down by the synods or the holy fathers.

74. Canonical unity is expressed in the implementation of the basic, at the very least, institutions of Church administration and in the lively communication between the local Orthodox Churches.

75. Finally, we should consider that the main consequences of doctrinal and canonical unity are the 'communion' among the Orthodox Churches, that is, their participation in a common Holy Communion, and the universality of ecclesiastical penalties, that is their common effect and implementation on any one of its members. Exiting the aforementioned spiritual-doctrinal and canonical framework is considered to constitute a sect or a schism.[60]

§5. The Internal Organization of Autocephalous Churches: The Synodical System of Administration

I. Generally

76. The parish is the administrative and spiritual cell of every autocephalous church. A greater number of parishes comprise a self-administered diocese (or metropolis). The bishops (the metropolitans), as the administrative and spiritual leaders of their ecclesiastical eparchies, comprise the *Synod of the Hierarchy,* which constitutes the highest administrative organ of every autocephalous church.[61]

77. The synodical system of administration is the cornerstone of the ecclesiastical regime in the Eastern Orthodox Church: this means that the Church is administered collectively by a Synod of Bishops (Metropolites), whose decisions are made on the basis of the rule of majority. In this Synod, the first in rank is the one who always presides, that is, the Patriarch if it is a Synod of the Patriarchate, and the Archbishop if it is a Synod of an autocephalous or autonomous church.

60. Panagiotakos, *System of ecclesiastical law during its enforcement in Greece*, vol. C: *The penal law of the church*, 341ff, 404ff; Papageorgiou, *Ecclesiastical law*, 327.

61. Troianos, 'Die Synode der Hierarchie als höchstes Verwaltungsorgan der einzelnen Autokephalen Orthodoxen Kirchen', Kanon 2 (1974) 192–216; Jean Zizioulas, 'L'institution synodale: Problèmes historiques, ecclésiologiques et canoniques', Istina 47 (2002) 14–44; Jean de Saint-Denis, 'L'organisation de l'Église [le 34e canon apostolique], Présence Orthodoxe nos 9–10 (1970) 79–85; Konstantinidis, 'Authority in the orthodox church', Sobornost 3 (1981) 197ff.

78. A fundamental principle of the synodical system of administration of the ecclesiastical organization is the rule of majority:[62] the person who presides in the collective bodies of the Church has only one vote *(primus inter pares).* However, this does not apply as to the internal organization of the bishops, where the respective bishop is recognized nearly always (and wrongly so, in our opinion) as the most prevalent decisive organ in what concerns all issues of an ecclesiastical nature.

79. The synodical system of administration has been in effect in the Church already since the second century, in the form of the local (episcopal or metropolitan) Synod. This was an assembly of the neighbouring bishops of an eparchy, with the common objective of discussing and resolving the serious administrative or judicial ecclesiastical issues arising in this region. These synods were convened twice annually in the capital of the eparchy (the metropolis) under the presidency of its bishop, that is, of the 'metropolitan', implementing primarily the 34th Holy Canon of the Apostles.[63]

80. But in addition to the local synods, the ecumenical synods are considered to be the highest collective organ of the Church: these were convened in irregular time periods, with an invitation to participate extended to all bishops and similarly a right to vote for all bishops. The main focus of the synods' proceedings was the resolution of doctrinal and of administrative issues of fundamental significance. However, today it is no longer possible to convene an Ecumenical Synod because we can no longer speak of the Church's doctrinal unity. It is nevertheless possible to convene a Pan-Orthodox Synod, with the participation of all or most Orthodox autocephalous churches.

81. A Pan-Orthodox Synod with the participation of many Orthodox Churches has been met in Crete from 19 to 27 June 2016. A series of decisions of this Synod concerned the obstacles of marriage and the proclamation – recognition of a church as autonomous.

82. In certain autocephalous churches, because the Synod of the Hierarchy is a multi-member organ which meets periodically, a 'Permanent' Synod of only a few members also operates in parallel. This Synod is composed of a limited number of bishops, it handles the current affairs of the Church and it represents the Synod of the Hierarchy.

---

62. Canon 6 of the First Ecumenical Synod: ' … let the choice of the majority prevail'.
63. According to which: 'The bishops of every nation must acknowledge him who is first among them and account him as their head, and do nothing of consequence without his consent; but each may do those things only which concern his own parish, and the country places which belong to it. But neither let him (who is the first) do anything without the consent of all; for so there will be unanimity … .'

II. Presbygenous Patriarchates

83. In the hierarchical order of the Orthodox Church, the following patriarchates hold honorary prevalence today:[64]

- the *Ecumenical Patriarchate of Constantinople:* it was recognized by the Second Ecumenical Synod. It exercises jurisdiction, in addition to the Orthodox faithful of Turkey, and to those who live in other countries ('diaspora');
- the *Patriarchate of Alexandria:* it was recognized by the First Ecumenical Synod and its jurisdiction encompasses all of Africa;
- the *Patriarchate of Antioch:* it too was recognized by the First Ecumenical Synod; it holds jurisdiction over the greatest part of the Middle East;
- the *Patriarchate of Jerusalem:* it was recognized by the Fourth Ecumenical Synod; its jurisdiction encompasses Israel, Jordan and the Palestinian lands.

III. More Recent Patriarchates

84. These are more specifically:

- the *Patriarchate of Russia:* this church was proclaimed autocephalous in 1459, while it was recognized as a Patriarchate in 1589 and 1593;
- the *Patriarchate of Serbia:* the Church of the Serbs was proclaimed autocephalous in 1879 and as a Patriarchate in 1919;
- the *Patriarchate of Romania*: this Church was proclaimed autocephalous in 1885 and as a Patriarchate in 1925;
- the *Patriarchate of Bulgaria:* the Church of the Bulgarians was proclaimed autocephalous in 1870 and it was recognized as a Patriarchate in 1961;
- the *Patriarchate of Georgia:* it was proclaimed as a Patriarchate in 1990.

IV. Autocephalous Churches

85. According to the chronological order of their establishment, these are the autocephalous Churches (which until today have not been recognized as patriarchates):

- the *Church of Cyprus:* it was recognized by the 8th canon of the Third Ecumenical Synod (431);
- the *Church of Greece:* it was self-proclaimed as independent in 1833, and it was officially recognized as autocephalous by the Ecumenical Patriarchate in 1850;
- the *Church of Poland:* it was proclaimed in 1924;
- the *Church of Albania:* autocephalous since 1937, but it was re-established in 1992 with the election of a new Archbishop of Tirana by the Synod of the Ecumenical Patriarchate;

64. Troianos, *Lectures in ecclesiastical law*, 138; Papageorgiou, *Ecclesiastical law*, 170ff.

– the *Church of the Czech Republic and Slovakia:* initially and since 1923 it was an autonomous church, but it was elevated to an autocephalous church in 1998.

V. Autonomous Churches

86. The *Archdiocese of Finland* and *the Church of Estonia* have since 1923 been subject to the jurisdiction of the Ecumenical Patriarchate.[65] Finally, the *Archdiocese of the Sinai (Holy Monastery of Saint Catherine)* is in a loose state of dependence on the Patriarchate of Jerusalem.

§6. The Different Orthodox Ecclesiastical Regimes in the Greek Territory

I. Generally

87. The regime of the Orthodox Church is not unified even within the geographical confines of Greece. National and historical reasons have shaped today's reality, whereby the entire Greek territory is subdivided into five regions, each one of which implements a particular ecclesiastical regime.

88. These are the ecclesiastical orders of:

– the Autocephalous Church of Greece;
– the Metropolises of the New Lands;
– the Monastic Polity of Mount Athos;
– the Semi-Autonomous Church of the Island of Crete; *and*
– the Ecclesiastical Provinces of the Dodecanese.

89. These regions are subject to the same Greek legal order, but they do not apply the same ecclesiastical institutions. The criterion of their differentiation is the degree of administrative dependence of every region on the jurisdiction of the Ecumenical Patriarchate. The difference ranges from the full administrative independence enjoyed by the Autocephalous Church of Greece to the complete dependence on the Patriarchate which holds true for the island complex of the Dodecanese. On different points along this scale whose two extremes are the aforementioned ecclesiastical regimes (and based on the criterion of the intensity and the content of canonical dependence on the Patriarchate), we can place the local regimes of the Metropolises of the New Lands, of the Monastic Polity of Mount Athos and of the Semi-Autonomous Church of the Island of Crete.

65. Troianos, *supra*, 141; Papageorgiou, *supra*, 186ff.

II. The Autocephalous Church of Greece

90. The Revolution of 1821, which led to the independence from the Turkish yoke, had as its inevitable result the breach of relations of the Church in Greece with the Ecumenical Patriarchate. By way of the Declaration of 23 July 1833, which was drafted by the Regency of Otto, the Bavarian King of Greece, the national Orthodox Church was arbitrarily proclaimed as autocephalous and independent, headed by a King and maintaining only its doctrinal unity with the other Orthodox Churches.[66]

91. The aforementioned action (which was blatantly anti-canonical) provoked the strong disapproval of the Ecumenical Patriarchate. Finally, on 29 June 1850, the Patriarchate proclaimed the Church of Greece as autocephalous, issuing a relevant Patriarchal and Synodical Tome.[67] The proclamation took place under explicit terms, which secured the canonical unity of the Greek Church with the 'Great Church of Christ' (i.e., Ecumenical Patriarchate) and the other Orthodox Churches. Among the terms, we find the provision that the Church of Greece shall be ruled by a Synod which will be presided over by the Metropolitan of Athens, 'in accordance with the divine and holy canons, freely and in a manner unhindered by any secular intervention'.

92. In 1866, two years after the union of the Ionian Islands with Greece, the ecclesiastical eparchies of the Heptanese were emancipated from the Ecumenical Throne by a special Patriarchal and Synodical Act and were permanently annexed to the Autocephalous Church of Greece.[68]

93. The ecclesiastical eparchies of Thessaly and of a part of Epirus (Arta) were annexed conclusively to the Autocephalous Church of Greece, by way of an analogous Patriarchal and Synodical Act in 1882.[69] A year earlier, these territories had already been liberated from the Turkish occupation and had been politically annexed to the Greek territory.

94. Today, the Autocephalous Church of Greece is administratively composed of the Archdiocese of Athens and the forty-four metropolises belonging to the geographical administrative units of southern Greece (Sterea Ellada, the Peloponnese,

66. Ch. Frazee, *Orthodox church and Greek independency (1821-1852)*, 161ff; Prinzipas/Karagiannis, *Church and hellenism from 1821 till today. An historical overview*, passim; Matalas, *Nation and orthodoxy. The adventures of a relationship*, 35ff; Manitakis, *The relations of the church with the nation-state under the shadow of the identity*, 23ff; Troianos/Dimakopoulou, *Church and state: Relations between them during the period 1833-1852*, 51ff.
67. The text of the Patriarchal Tome, *see* in Troianos/Papageorgiou, *Religious legislation: Special legislation – bibliography – case law,* 183–187.
68. The text of the Synodical Act, *see* in Troianos/Papageorgiou, *ibid.,* 188–190.
69. *Ibid.*, 191–192.

the Cyclades, the Heptanese, Thessaly, the region of Arta in Epirus). Its administrative organization is governed by L. 590/1977, 'Statutory Charter of the Church of Greece'.[70]

III. The Metropolises of the New Lands

95. The aforementioned practice of the final concession of ecclesiastical eparchies to the Autocephalous Church of Greece was not observed in the case of the Metropolises of the New Lands. These are the ecclesiastical regions of Macedonia, Epirus, the islands of the Aegean and of Crete, which were politically annexed to the Greek territory after the Balkan Wars (1912–1913).

96. After negotiations with the Greek State, the Ecumenical Patriarchate, issuing the Patriarchal and Synodical Act of 4 September 1928 (which was ratified by L. 3615/1928),[71] temporarily assigned the administration of these ecclesiastical eparchies to the Autocephalous Church of Greece, under ten Conditions, such as: the egalitarian participation of the prelates of these eparchies in the administrative organs of the Church of Greece, the submission of annual reports to the Patriarchate, the preservation of full rights on the part of the Patriarch over the stavropegial monasteries that lie within these territories, etc.[72] However, these Conditions were not always observed by the Church of Greece, a fact that constituted a source of conflict between it and the Ecumenical Patriarchate.

97. Finally, as was already made obvious, L. 590/1977 is also implemented in the Metropolises of the New Lands.[73]

IV. The Monastic Polity of Mount Athos

98. Mount Athos enjoys a regime of privileged self-administration, in accordance with the provisions of Article 105 Const., of the Statutory Charter of Mount Athos (issued in 1924) and its ratifying LD (*see* in greater detail 'Part III').

---

70. The text of L. 590/1977, *see* in Troianos/Papageorgiou, *ibid.*, 199–267.
71. *See* both the texts in Troianos/Papageorgiou, *ibid.*, 193–198. CoS (Plenary Session) 410/2008, CoS 2576/2017.
72. Generally *see* Markos, *The legal regime of patriarchal and stavropegic monasteries on Greek territory*, Athens-Thessaloniki 2012.
73. Papastathis, *Nomocanonical studies*, 27–34; Beis, *The revocation/termination of the patriarchal synodal act of September 4th 1928*, D 35 (2004) 581–592; Feidas, 'The constitutional entrenchment of the patriarchal act of 1928', D 35 (2004) 903–915; Prinzipas, *The great crises in the church: Five landmarks in the relations between the church of Greece and the ecumenical patriarchate*, 213ff.

V. The Semi-Autonomous Church of Crete

99. It enjoys partial autonomy in relation to the ecclesiastical jurisdiction of the Ecumenical Patriarchate, in accordance with the provisions of its own Statutory Charter (L. 4149/1961, *see* in greater detail 'Part III').

VI. The Ecclesiastical Eparchies of the Dodecanese

100. It includes five metropolises and the patriarchal exarchy of Patmos, which are subject to the full ecclesiastical jurisdiction of the Ecumenical Patriarchate (*see* in greater detail 'Part III').

§7. The 'Statutory Charters'

101. The *technicus terminus* 'Statutory Charter' is used to denote the law that is enacted by the Greek Parliament with the purpose of regulating the relations between the State and the Orthodox Church in a particular region of the Greek territory.

102. Today three Statutory Charters are in effect:

(1) *L. 590/1977,* which applies to the legal relations of the Autocephalous Church of Greece and the Metropolises of the New Lands.
(2) *L. 4149/1961,* governing the regime of the Church of Crete.
(3) the Statutory *Charter of Monastic Polity of Mount Athos,* which was passed by the monks in 1924 and was ratified by L.D. of the State in 1926.

§8. Church-State Relations under the Constitution of 1975

I. Fundamental Characteristics

103. The contemporary relations between the State and the Orthodox Church in Greece constitute the object of an ongoing and open dialogue among the members of the scientific community, expressed in various theoretical approaches.[74] The semantic content of Article 3 § 1 of the current Constitution is not only nearly always the normative point of departure but also the interpretative focal point of the relevant debate. Before we proceed with the overview of the range that these viewpoints cover, it is necessary to clarify that the analysis of the said relations mainly pertains to the limits between the jurisdiction of state organs and the jurisdiction of

74. *Inter alia, see*: Marinos, *Relations between church and state under the constitution of 1975 and the new statutory charter of the church of Greece*, 25ff, 51ff, passim; Papageorgiou, *Ecclesiastical law*, 93ff; Tsatsos, *Constitutional law*, vol. B', 581; Spyropoulos, 'The system of church and state relations in Greece', EDDD 25 (1981) 332–343.

the Church, namely the degree of autonomy and self-administration which the Church enjoys as a legal entity, vis-à-vis the legislative interventions of the State in its sphere of autonomy.

104. The constitutional status of the Orthodox Church in the Greek territory is regulated primarily by Article 3 § 1 Const., which stipulates *ad litteram* that:

Relations of Church and State

Article 3

1. The prevailing religion in Greece is that of the Eastern Orthodox Church of Christ. The Orthodox Church of Greece, acknowledging our Lord Jesus Christ as its head, is inseparably united in doctrine with the Great Church of Christ in Constantinople and with every other Church of Christ of the same doctrine, observing unwaveringly, as they do, the holy apostolic and synodical canons and sacred traditions. It is autocephalous and is administered by the Holy Synod of serving Bishops and the Permanent Holy Synod originating thereof and assembled as specified by the Statutory Charter of the Church in compliance with the provisions of the Patriarchal Tome of June 29, 1850 and the Synodical Act of September 4, 1928.
2. The ecclesiastical regime existing in certain districts of the State shall not be deemed contrary to the provisions of the preceding paragraph.
3. The text of the Holy Scripture shall be maintained unaltered. Official translation of the text into any other form of language, without prior sanction by the Autocephalous Church of Greece and the Great Church of Christ in Constantinople, is prohibited.[75]

105. It is widely accepted that, with the enactment of the Constitution of 1975 by the Fifth Revisionary Parliament of the Greeks (1975), a mature step was taken towards relaxing the regime of suffocating statocracy, which until that day characterized Church and State relations, in the context of the system of 'State-law rule' which was in force.[76] This observation arises from the legal-comparative study of the provisions of the current Constitution in juxtaposition with those contained in the previous Constitution of 1952.[77]

106. As to the conceptual content of the term 'prevailing religion', the dominant view holds that it constitutes a mere proclamation of the fact that Greeks are, in their

75. Troianos/Papageorgiou, *Religious legislation: Special legislation – bibliography – case law*, 17–30; Papastathis, *Nomocanonical studies*, 65–85; Venizelos, *The relations between state and church*, 55ff, 107ff, passim; Spyropoulos, 'The system of relations between church and state in Greece', EDDD 25 (1981) 332–343; *ibid., Die Beziehungen zwischen Staat und Kirche in Griechenland unter besonderer Berucksichtigung der orthodoxen Kirche*, Freiburg 1981.

76. As it is noted, a 'statocratic' system is one in which the primacy of the state's volition is enforced. The system of statocracy often presents the tendency for the exhaustive legislative regulation of Church and State relations: Papastathis, *ibid.*, 66.

77. Which continued, with minor differences, the relevant ecclesiastical policy of the previous Constitutions of 1844, 1864 and 1911: Mavrias/Pantelis, *Constitutional texts*, vol. A', 82, 92, 102.

overwhelming majority, Christian Orthodox.[78] Therefore, according to this opinion, the constitutional term 'prevailing religion' is of a descriptive and not a normative nature.[79] Reverting to the will of the constitutional legislator, as this was embodied in the relevant deliberations for the enactment of the Constitution during the proceedings of the Fifth Revisionary Parliament, lends credence to this dominant interpretative stance.

107. However, the system of unity between State and Church was in essence maintained in the present Constitution – despite the declared intention on the part not only of the government which was then in office but also of the opposition parties, to proceed with a constitutional separation of the two institutions.

108. The 'relaxed phase' of these relations arises from the following new constitutional facts:

- the provisions pertaining to Church-State relations are for the first time located in the third, and not the first, article of the Constitution;
- the President of the Republic, as the Head of State, is no longer required to be a Christian Orthodox (as the King in previous decades had to be: Articles 47, 51–52 Const. 1952). During the oath-taking ceremony of the President of the Republic before the Parliament, the Holy Synod is not present, whereas the President no longer vows to protect the prevailing religion (Articles 31, 33 § 2 Const.), as was the case under the Constitution of 1952;
- proselytism is now generally prohibited, when it is conducted against any 'known' religion (Article 13 § 2 sect. c' Const.) and not only against the Orthodox Church (as the Constitution which was previously in force stipulated);
- the confiscation of newspapers and other publications is allowed exceptionally after their circulation if they contain an offence against the Christian or any other 'known' religion (Article 14 § 3 sect. a' Const.).

109. In parallel, however:

- the convocation of the Holy Trinity was maintained in the Preamble to the Constitution, a reference which undoubtedly holds a symbolic and not a legal significance;

78. *Administrative Court of Appeal of Athens 1700/1983*, EEN 52 (1985) 113–114: the proclamation of the Eastern Orthodox Church of Christ as the prevailing religion in Greece is of an affirmative nature; in this sense, it is recognized as the most populous religion in Greece, under whose rites the official ceremonies are conducted, the feast days are determined, etc.
79. A rather moderate viewpoint is put forth by Venizelos, *Relations between state and church,* 146: 'the term "prevailing religion" bears a content that is on the one hand historical and cultural, which however is not legally crucial, while on the other hand it possesses a factual content, which is legally crucial, since it describes the Orthodox Church as the most populous collective subject for the exercise of religious freedom'; Papastathis, *Nomocanonical studies*, 65ff.

- the current Constitution also characterizes the Orthodox Eastern Church as 'prevailing',[80] with the aforementioned semantic content;
- a religious convocation is contained in the oath taken by not only the President of the Republic but also the Members of Parliament (Article 59 § 1 Const.); it is however stipulated that Members of Parliament who are of a different religion or creed may take the same oath according to the form of their own religion or creed (Article 59 § 2 Const.);
- education aims at the development of religious consciousness on a general level (Article 16 § 2 Const.);
- bills of law which relate to matters pertaining to the known religions (Articles 3 and 13 Const.) shall be voted on by the Parliament in plenum (in full session), and not one of its Sections (Article 72 § 1 Const.).

110. In addition to the aforementioned elements, it should not be overlooked that:

- the feast days, the official ceremonies and the official holidays of the public service sector are mainly determined according to the feast day cycle of the Orthodox Church;
- Article 2 § 1 of L.D. 90/1973, 'On the Religious Body of the Armed Forces'[81] provides for the purely Orthodox character of the religious agency of the armed forces;
- nearly all of the ecclesiastical organizations within the Greek territory (Orthodox metropolises, churches and monasteries) are vested with a legal personality of public law, a fact which renders them agents which exercise public authority (the Church of Greece in particular is considered, by virtue of Article 1 § 4 L. 590/1977, as a legal entity under public law, however as regards its legal relations);
- the decisions of ecclesiastical authorities are executed primarily by state organs (Articles 53, 54, 62, 107 L. 5383/1932 'On Ecclesiastical Courts and the Procedure Before Them');[82]
- the near total of the operating expenses of the Orthodox Church has been covered through public funding (OL 536/1945, 'Wages of the Orthodox parish clergy of Greece, manner of their payment and coverage of the relevant expenditure',[83]

80. All of the previous Constitutions contained a similar recognition, namely that of Epidaurus (§ a', 1822), of Astros (§ a', 1823), of Troizina (1827, Art. 1: 'religion of the Territory'), of the 'Hegemonic' Constitution (1832, chp. B' § 1), of 1844 (Arts 1–2), 1864 (Arts 1–2), 1911 (Arts 1–2), 1927 (Art. 1), 1952 (Arts 1–2). For the aforementioned texts, *see* consecutively in the historical-comparative research of Zoi/ Lasthiotakis/Giannopoulos, *The historical evolution of the provisions of the constitution (1822-2001),* Institute for Constitutional Research, Sources of Greek Public Law 11, Athens-Komotini, 2003; cf. Mavrias/Pantelis, *Constitutional texts,* vol. A', passim.
81. Troianos/Papageorgiou, *Religious legislation: Special legislation – bibliography – case law,* 1340–1344.
82. Troianos/Papageorgiou, *ibid.,* 1677–1727.
83. *Ibid.,* 616f.

OL 469/1968, 'On the salary gradation of the parish clergy of the Church of Greece',[84] Article 8 L. 1041/1980,[85] concerning the state salaries of prelates, etc.).

111. Consequently, the constitutional framework of the relations of the Greek State with the Orthodox Church cannot be considered, as the history of the previous decades has repeatedly demonstrated, to be characterized by stability. And this is because it is influenced to a great degree both by the persons representing the institutions and by the current state or ecclesiastical policy which was implemented on each occasion. Ultimately, the abstract content of the constitutional provisions regulating the above-mentioned relations assumes its meaning depending on the political, historical and ecclesiastical conditions which prevailed in each instance. For this reason, any attempt to integrate these perpetually changing relations into a coherent and absolutely homogeneous system can be considered only minimally persuasive and consistent. In addition, the content of Article 3 Const. does not suffice on its own to paint a complete image of the relations between the State and the Church in Greece today, since these are governed, and perhaps to a more critical degree, by the provisions of parallel normative scope contained in Articles 13, 14 § 3 section a', 16 § 2, 33 § 2, 59 § 1 and 72 § 1 Const.[86]

112. Without a doubt, even today *the regime of statocracy* is in effect (i.e., a regime of 'State-law rule') since the State is legitimized to intervene legislatively in ecclesiastical affairs, with laws (Statutory Charters) enacted by Parliament (Article 72 § 1 Const.). It is however well known that this legislative competence is often accompanied by unconstitutional or extra-institutional interferences, which violate the constitutionally guaranteed right to ecclesiastical self-administration.[87]

II. The Issue of the Constitutional Entrenchment of Holy Canons

113. Both Greek case law and legal theory have repeatedly and already since the beginning of the nineteenth century dealt with the problem of the extent to which the Constitution safeguarded holy canons, that is, the provisions of ecclesiastical

84. *Ibid.*, 618–621.
85. *Ibid.*, 627f.
86. *See* the approach of Tsatsos, *Two advisory notes on church-state relations and on religious freedom*, D&P 15 (1987) 195–203.
87. CoS 1476/1975 (Plenary Session), ToS 1 (1975) 887–890, with a commentary by S. Troianos: the annulment of a regulatory act which contravenes the constitutional provisions relating to the self-administration of the Church; CoS 1136/1983, Arm. 38 (1983) 63: Art. 3 Const. establishes the authority of the Church to decide on its affairs with its own bodies and to be governed by the Holy Synod of the Hierarchy and the Permanent Holy Synod, as well as to exercise exclusive administration over the legal entities which depend on it and which lack a primarily religious nature. This authority must certainly be exercised always within the framework of the general rules enacted by the legislator, who cannot on his own proceed so far as to effectuate radical changes in fundamental administrative institutions which have been firmly established in the organization and operation of the Church. *See also* Marinos, *Relations between church and state under the constitution of 1975 and the new statutory charter of the church of Greece*, 100–116.

origin which organize and regulate the internal life of the church. The whole issue was deemed to be one of critical importance because of the crucially significant impact that any interpretative version would have in the field of the self-administration of the Church.[88]

114. The different interpretative versions sprang from the wording of Article 3 § 1 Const., which stipulated on the one hand that the Church of Greece is inseparably united in doctrine with the Ecumenical Patriarchate of Constantinople and with every other Church of Christ of the same doctrine, and on the other hand that this Church observes 'unwaveringly', as they do, the holy apostolic and synodical canons, as well as the sacred traditions.

115. There are three main opinions that have been put forth as to the resolution of the above-mentioned interpretative matter.

116. According to the chronologically first opinion, supported by those who approach the matter in a rather theological manner, the Constitution safeguards all the holy canons without exception, whether these are of doctrinal content or they simply relate to the administrative organization of the Church. Therefore, not only is the abrogation or amendment of canonical provisions by ordinary law not possible but also any laws which are contrary to the holy canons must – according to this particular interpretative stance – be considered unconstitutional.

117. The second viewpoint, distinguishing holy canons into two categories, doctrinal and administrative,[89] argues that constitutional entrenchment is limited only to the former. Its supporters argue that, in the context of the existing statocracy, the State may decide without any hindrance about the revision and even the abrogation of holy canons, as long as the latter are of administrative content only. Conversely, no intervention is permitted on holy canons of a doctrinal or spiritual nature.

118. The case law of the Council of State initially moved steadily within the framework of the second viewpoint: considering that constitutional entrenchment does not extend to the administrative holy canons, it ruled that the latter may be amended for the common interest of the State and the Church.

---

88. Orfanoudakis, 'The holy canons and the constitution (a counter-comment or "the other" interpretative approach)', Arm 35 (1981) 82–83; *ibid.*, 'The separation of state and church: Necessity or palillogy?', 3ff; Venizelos, *The relations between state and church*, 66–71; Feidas, 'The constitutional entrenchment of the patriarchal act of 1928', D 35 (2004) 903–915; Marinos, *Relations between church and state under the constitution of 1975 and the new statutory charter of the church of Greece*, 137–148; Papageorgiou, 'Findings from the ecclesiastical case law of the council of state of the year 1987', Arm Scientific Yearbook 17 (1996) 35f.
89. The decisive criterion is their regulatory field of reference to the doctrine or the administration of the Church. Although it is accurate to claim that the content of every canon may be considered as primarily doctrinal or primarily administrative, the Church itself never distinguished its voluminous (comprised of 770 canons) *corpus canonum* into doctrinal and administrative canons.

119. Nevertheless, the implementation of the Constitution of 1952 pushed the Council of State to an interesting turning point in its case law, introducing the distinction of administrative holy canons into basic and non-basic. Furthermore, setting a limit, the Council of State decided that the ordinary legislator cannot revise or amend basic canonical institutions pertaining to ecclesiastical administration, which are all those canons that have been established in a stable and long-standing manner within the Church.

120. Moreover, under the scope of the current Constitution (1975), this same Court, without departing from its prior decisions, differentiated their legal substantiation: now drawing arguments mostly from Article 13 §§ 1–2 Const. (and less from Article 3 § 1 Const.), it added that, since the right to religious freedom also protects the adherents of the prevailing religion, it undoubtedly safeguards all the holy canons permeating its 'life'.

121. Finally, from the standpoint of the European Court of Human Rights, we should mention that in its decision dated 3 May 2011, on the case of *Negrepontis-Giannisis v. Greece* (appeal no. 56759/08), the Court expressed noteworthy reservations as to whether holy canons, whose enactment dates back to the seventh and eighth centuries, on the one hand, fulfil the necessary prerequisites of contemporary positive law, and, on the other hand, the criteria of precision, accuracy and predictability, so that they do not ultimately clash with the principle of proportionality.

III. Aspects of State Supervision

122. Under the present system, the State exercises administrative supervision over the Church, mainly through agency units which are competent for ecclesiastical matters in the Ministry of Education and Religious Affairs, as well as in the Ministry of Foreign Affairs.

123. In general overview, state supervision includes:

- the assistance of the State for the completion of an act issued by an ecclesiastical authority, under the well-known procedure of complex administrative actions;[90]
- or the participation of civil servants in collective administrative bodies, as is the case in the councils of metropolitans;
- or finally, the granting of the State's authorization so that the acts of ecclesiastical administrative authorities or organs can become enforceable.

90. For example, the assumption of duties on behalf of a metropolitan presupposes, in addition to his election by the Holy Synod of the Hierarchy and his ordination to the episcopal rank (if he is not already a title holder), the issuance of a presidential decree under the competence of the Ministry of Education, relating to the recognition and 'enthronement' of the said metropolitan (Art. 15 § 6, 26 § 1 L. 590/1977). Consequently, only after the issuance and publication in the Official Government Gazette of the relevant presidential decree is it possible for the aforementioned ecclesiastical administrative organ to assume his duties.

124. The Orthodox Church, although it is a spiritual (religious) foundation, exercises secondary administrative power, by issuing, either as a legal entity under public law or more generally as an administrative authority, enforceable administrative acts. The latter are subject to the judicial review (annulment) of the Council of State, a fact that had until today incited the production of an especially rich case law, formative to a decisive degree of the content of ecclesiastical administrative institutions.

125. The enforceable administrative acts of the Church indicatively pertain to:

- the composition, formation and operation of the central and peripheral administrative organs of the Church;
- the civil service regime of the staff comprised of clergy or laity, serving in the various ecclesiastical legal entities;
- the administrative structure of the Church and the regulation of matters arising from ecclesiastical administrative regions;
- the granting or non-granting of a marriage licence, as well as the certification of its spiritual dissolution, following a judicial decision declaring the divorce.

126. Ecclesiastical acts of an individual or regulatory nature (CoS 866/1974, 960/1978) are subject to the review of the Council of State, while their interlocutory review is also possible.

127. The following acts escape the annulling review of the Council of State:

- any ecclesiastical acts pertaining to internal, evidently spiritual, matters of the Church (such as the ordination or the monastic rite of *'koura'* or tonsure, the penance of solitude, the election of a metropolitan); and
- the decisions of ecclesiastical courts, when they impose penalties of a spiritual nature. Nonetheless, when ecclesiastical penalties have an impact on the employment status of clergy, then they are subject to the review of the Council of State, because in this case, the ecclesiastical courts function rather as disciplinary councils (CoS 825/1988).[91]

---

91. CoS 825/1988 (Plenary Session), NoV 36 (1988) 615–624: the disciplinary organs of the Church, when they operate collectively, have the character of disciplinary councils, which must follow, at least with regard to their case and the disciplinary procedure, the fundamental principles of disciplinary law, in order to ensure the principles of rule of law and good administration; the decisions that are issued by them may be appealed before the Council of State with an application for annulment; CoS 2928/1996 (Plenary Session), NoV 46 (1998) 1345–1351, with comments by Katselas; CoS 2739/1997, DiDiki 10 (1998) 367–369: ecclesiastical courts have the character of collective disciplinary councils; their decisions, when they impose penalties of a merely spiritual nature, are not subject to judicial review, but when they impose penalties which directly influence the employment relationship of clergymen with the Church and the rights derived therefrom, they are subject to an appeal for annulment before the Council of State.

§9. Sources of Greek Ecclesiastical Law

I. Categories

128. A fundamental distinction in the literature is the distinction of the sources of Greek Ecclesiastical Law, on the basis of their origin from a state or an ecclesiastical legislative body.

129. In the first category, we can subsume the *constitutional provisions* regulating the relations between state and church or creeds (Constitution of 1975, amended three times, in 1986, 2001 and 2008, not in 2019 as it has been above written); the *international conventions or treaties* that were integrated in the Greek legal order after their ratification by law of the Greek legislature (Article 28 § 1 Const.); the *common state legislation* (laws, decrees or ministerial decisions); and *custom,* as a long spanning and uniform observation of a particular social behaviour, as long as it is characterized by conscience of law *(opinio juris).*

130. The sources of ecclesiastical derivation include the Holy Testament, the Holy Tradition, and the holy canons, namely all the statutes enacted by ecumenical or local synods as well as by the Church Fathers. In the same category, we classify the various decisions or circulars of regulatory character or content which are issued by the existing synodical bodies and establish secondary rules of law.

131. From the immediately aforementioned decisions, we must exclude those 'Regulations' or 'Regulatory Statutes' that are issued by the Holy Synod of the Church of Greece or by the Provincial Synod of the Church of Crete, following the legislative authorization provided for in the respective Statutory Charter (L. 590/1977 and L. 4149/1961, as it was amended by Article 43 § 6 L. 3848/2010).

II. Matters of Interpretation: The Institution of 'Ecclesiastical Economy' ('Oikonomia')

132. The well-known methods of interpretation of all legal texts in general (grammatical, historical, teleological, systematic interpretation, etc.) are also implemented to discover the 'right' meaning of the rules of Ecclesiastical Law.[92] But in addition to them, the principle of implementation by proportionality (Article 25 § 1

92. The prevailing opinion holds that, especially in what regards the interpretation of the rules of Ecclesiastical Law, priority should be given to the historical-subjective interpretation. This opinion invokes as its main argument the special weight that the will of the historical, ecclesiastical or other, legislator holds for this branch of law in particular. It is my view that this may be true for those advocating the particularly historical nature of Ecclesiastical Law. However, a central position of the present monograph is that our discipline constitutes a branch of the existing internal and international law. For this reason, I consider that here also the teleological interpretation of the law should prevail, in alignment with contemporary legal theory.

Const.)[93] has proven to be a valuable interpretive tool which finds an increasing application in case law, especially on issues relating to restrictions of religious freedom (Article 13 § 2 Const.).

133. The sui generis institution of 'ecclesiastical economy' is found only in the field of Ecclesiastical Law and is today a part of everyday ecclesiastical reality: it consists of the non-precise implementation of a particular holy canon on the part of a body of ecclesiastical (executive or judicial) power, in a particular case and for reasons of equity towards the interested parties.

134. However, in the same line of thinking, one cannot rule out even the stricter implementation of a holy canon. The only limitation to the implementation of economy is the Orthodox dogma, which should not be permissibly violated by its exercise.[94]

135. It is argued that economy is not yet another interpretive method, but an (empirical?) way to settle the conflict between a particular canonical mandate and a historical fact. For this reason, according to the same opinion, the observed repetitive or constant application of economy on similar cases does not allow the creation of custom.[95]

136. Pursuant to Article 4 Cases (d) and 6 § 3 SCCG, economy is exercised by the Holy Synod of the Hierarchy, with an increased majority of the two-thirds of the totality of its members (in the Church of Crete, Mount Athos and the Dodecanese, there is no such restriction).

137. Nevertheless, it should be acceptable that in matters of lesser significance, economy is also exercised by the local bishop, as is in any case provided for by canon law.

---

93. In general *see*: Orfanoudakis, *The principle of proportionality in the Greek legal order: From its implementation in case law to its constitutional entrenchment*, Athens-Thessaloniki 2003; Voutsakis, 'The principle of proportionality: from interpretation to rule-making', in: Manitakis/Paschos/Stamatis (dir.), *Aspects of rule of law. A historical retrospective to Greek theory and contemporary insights*, Critical Studies 5, Thessaloniki 1990, 207–254; Kontogiorga-Theoharopoulou, *The principle of proportionality in domestic public law*, Thessaloniki 1989.

94. Papageorgiou, *Ecclesiastical law*, 75ff; Irene Tsagri, 'The legal nature of the ecclesiastical economy', EEN 39 (1972) 876–879.

95. This view, however, cannot be considered as absolutely correct: as it is reasonable and evident, every time the ecclesiastical body exercises economy, it is actually interpreting (basically in teleological manner) a particular legal rule. In any case, precision, as the flip side of economy, does not cease to fall within the context of the grammatical interpretive implementation of holy canons.

Part II. Religious Freedom in General

Chapter 1. Individual Religious Freedom

§1. Constitutional Protection

138. Religious freedom in Greece is conceptually distinguished from 'religious tolerance', which is the tolerance or indifference of the State for the religious beliefs of its citizens. Religious freedom is a concept that is considerably broader than religious tolerance and has a constitutionally specified guaranteeing function: it secures the right of citizens to shape or manifest freely their religious conscience, demanding that the State not merely remains neutral but also undertakes every necessary institutional initiative or measure (legislative, administrative or judicial) to safeguard and satisfy the particular right.[96]

139. Constitutional references to religious tolerance and consequently to religious freedom were included – with a definite influence from the liberal ideas of the French and the American revolutions – in the provisions of all modern Greek Constitutions (Article 1 Const. of 1844, 1864, 1911 and 1927; Article 2 Const. 1952).[97]

140. Presently the legal protection of religious freedom in our country is predicated mainly in the constitutional provisions of Article 13 (freedom of religious conscience and freedom of worship), Article 2 § 1 (respect for privacy and human dignity),[98] Article 5 § 1 (free development of personality),[99] as well as the relevant statutes of international treaties,[100] especially of the ECHR.[101]

141. More particularly, Article 13 of the Constitution stipulates:

---

96. About all these matters, *see*: Papageorgiou, *Ecclesiastical law*, 120; Chrysogonos/Vlahopoulos, *Individual and social rights*, 309–330; Papastathis, *Nomocanonical studies*, 93–117; Troianos, *Lectures in ecclesiastical law*, 74f; Mavrias, *Constitutional law*, 791ff; Konidaris, *Lessons*, 77ff.
97. Marinos, *Religious freedom,* 82ff; Mavrias/Pantelis, *Constitutional texts,* vol. A', 7f, 25f, 34f, 43f, 54f, 82f, passim; Alivizatos, *The constitution and its enemies in modern Greek history (1800-2010),* 33ff, 74ff, 107ff, passim.
98. Article 2 § 1 Const.: 'Respect and protection of the value of the human being constitute the primary obligations of the State.'
99. Article 5 § 1 Const.: 'All persons shall have the right to develop freely their personality and to participate in the social, economic and political life of the country, insofar as they do not infringe the rights of others or violate the Constitution and the good usages.'
100. Papageorgiou/Papastathis, 'Formes de collaboration conventionelle ou non-conventionelle entre l'État et les communautés religieuses en Grèce', 65–77.

Article 13[102]

§ 1.Freedom of religious conscience is inviolable. The enjoyment of civil rights and liberties does not depend on the individual's religious beliefs.
§ 2.All known religions shall be free and their rites of worship shall be performed unhindered and under the protection of the law. The practice of rites of worship is not allowed to offend public order or the good usages. Proselytism is prohibited.
§ 3.The ministers of all known religions shall be subject to the same supervision by the State and to the same obligations toward it as those of the prevailing religion.
§ 4.No person shall be exempt from discharging his obligations to the State or may refuse to comply with the laws by reason of his religious convictions.
§ 5.No oath shall be imposed or administered except as specified by law and in the form determined by law.

142. As it is construed from the aforementioned constitutional provisions, the general right of religious freedom is made up of two manifestations of equal significance: the freedom of religious conscience (Article 13 § 1 Const.) and freedom of worship (Article 13 §§ 2–3 c' Const.).[103]

143. We will elaborate on these two freedoms and analyse them in greater detail below. At this point, we will make clear that, since the constitutional provisions previously cited do not make such a distinction, the subjects of the right to religious freedom are not only Greek citizens but also foreign citizens.[104]

101. It constitutes a part of internal Greek law, since it has been ratified by the State for a second time with LD 53/1974 (Art. 28 § 1 Const.). *See also* Venizelos, 'The European Constitution and the religious phenomenon' in *ibid., The challenge of the European Constitution,* 119ff; on the same issue, *see* more in Part IV: International, Transnational, Regional Effects on Religious Communities.

102. Mavrias/Pantelis, *Constitutional texts*, vol. A', 300. *See also* Karakostas, 'The constitutional foundations of religious freedom and the possibility of revision of the relevant statutes (interpretative issues of emphasis and tension on religious freedom)', D 26 (1995) 817–841f; Papastathis, *Nomocanonical studies*, 95ff.

103. Papageorgiou, *Ecclesiastical law*, 121ff; Marinos, *Religious freedom*, 102ff, 154ff; Troianos, *Lectures in ecclesiastical law*, 76ff; Venizelos, *The relations between state and church*, 107f, 133ff, 157ff, passim; Papastathis, *Nomocanonical studies*, 98; Konidaris, *Lessons*, 80ff.

104. As it has been already mentioned, the protection of the right of religious freedom in Greece is limited, mainly because Art. 3 Const. stipulates the existence of a 'prevailing' (dominant) religion (i.e., the Eastern Orthodox Church). According to science and case law (CoS 3533/1986, 3356/1995, 2176/1998), 'prevailing' is the religion of the majority of the Greek people; *See*, for example, Venizelos, *The relations between state and church,* 55ff; Papastathis, *Nomocanonical studies,* 98. However, this characteristic has been linked by the common legislator with certain privileged equitable effects which, in some cases, lead to an unequal treatment of other religions. *See also*: Papageorgiou, *Ecclesiastical law*, 120; Troianos, *Lectures in ecclesiastical law,* 91ff; Papastathis, *Nomocanonical studies*, 65ff.

§2. Freedom of Religious Conscience

I. General Aspects

144. Article 13 § 1 Const. stipulates that freedom of religious conscience *(forum internum)*[105] is inviolable. More particular manifestations of this right are the following:

(a) A person's right to *follow any or no religion* (irreligion/irreligious) or *not to believe in God* (atheism/atheist/godless). In this context, the right of *unhindered change of religious beliefs* is also protected, as well as the acceptance of religious beliefs that other religions consider as 'heretic', without the advent of any negative effects.[106] This is because the term 'sect',[107] having no legal but a purely religious content, concerns only the religious community in question and does not affect the exercise of constitutional rights and freedoms.

It is clarified that the aforementioned constitutional protection also extends to anyone who accedes to a religion which is not considered 'known' (i.e., whose worship clashes with public order or good morals),[108] given that this particular limitation concerns the freedom of worship (Article 13 § 2 Const.) and not that of religious conscience.

(b) The right to *manifest* (or even *not reveal*) *religious convictions,* provided that this does not happen in a manner that constitutes proselytism.[109] The protection encompasses the possibility of proclaiming religious opinions in any way or means, such as in writing or orally, individually or in community, through printed documents or electronic press. In the latter case, special legislation concerning the press applies.

However, it is recognized that the State has the right to restrict the exercise of this right on grounds of public order, as long as this does not occur in a disproportionately onerous manner, that would violate the principle of proportionality (Article 25 § 1 section d Const.).[110]

---

105. About this substantial meaning of the term *'forum internum'*, *see* Ktistakis, *Religious freedom and the European Convention on Human Rights*, 51–84.

106. Papageorgiou, *Ecclesiastical law*, 121; Marinos, *Religious freedom*, 102–105; Troianos, *Lectures in ecclesiastical law*, 76ff.

107. On this issue, *see* Kyriazopoulos, 'Les nouveaux mouvements religieuses en Grèce: la reconnaissance des organisations religieuses en Grèce', *Les Cultes et l'État en Grèce. Les identités religieuses dans la République hellénique, Quatrième colloque sur la notion d' 'Églises nationales'*, L'Année Canonique 2003, 249–259.

108. On the term of 'known' religion, *see* Papageorgiou, *Ecclesiastical law*, 125f; Troianos, *Lectures in ecclesiastical law*, 89f.

109. *See* Argyropoulos, 'Freedom of religious conscience and the obligation to declare one's religious affiliation in public documents', 21ff; about the peculiar penalization of proselytism in Greece, *see* Part VII: Religious Communities and Protection of the Individual.

110. On this matter, *see* in general Orfanoudakis, *The principle of proportionality in the Greek legal order. From its implementation in case law to its constitutional entrenchment*, Athens-Thessaloniki 2003; Voutsakis, 'The principle of proportionality: From interpretation to rule-making', in: Manitakis/Paschos/Stamatis (dir.), *Aspects of rule of law: A historical retrospective to Greek theory and contemporary insights*, 'Critical studies 5', Thessaloniki 1990, 207–254; Emiliou, *The principle of proportionality in European law: A comparative study*, London-The Hague-Boston 1996;

The refusal to reveal religious convictions is not protected when the relevant declaration is required for the advent of legal consequences (e.g., for the formation of religious marriage). However, as it is observed, in this case, the declaration must be made in the context of confidentiality.

(c) The right to found associations for religious purposes.[111]
(d) The right of religious equality.[112]
(e) The right of religious education.[113]
(f) The right of a person *not to be coerced into actions which are contrary to his or her religious beliefs.* Thus, non-Orthodox students are not obliged to attend the school subject of religion of the prevailing religion,[114] prisoners are not obliged to participate in the joint congregation, etc.

145. The *refusal to give a 'procedural oath' in a court of law or a 'confirmatory oath'* when a person swears into public service can be considered as an implementation of the same right, when this action clashes with the religious convictions of the involved parties. Under Article 385, 408 και 423 of the CCProc and Articles 194, 218, 220 and 236 of the CCrimProc, the non-Orthodox take an oath according to the conventions of their religion, if it recognizes oath-taking. If the person taking an oath is irreligious or an atheist or if his religion prohibits (or does not recognize) oath-taking, then in place of an oath, a person can give a confirmatory statement, invoking his honour and conscience.[115]

Drooghenbroeck, *La proportionnalite dans le droit de la convention europeenne des droits de lhomme. Prendre l'idee simple au serieux*, especially 433ff; Muzny, *La technique de proportionnalite et le juge de la Convention Europeenne des Droits de VHomme. Essai sur un instrument necessaire dans une societe democratique*, tom. I, 259ff.

111. *See* more below in: 'Chapter 3. Organizational Religious Freedom'.
112. *See* more below (paragraphs 146–160).
113. *See* more below in paragraph 161 and 'Part IX. Education'.
114. According to CoS 3356/1995: the right of religious freedom that is enshrined in Art. 13 Const. and the relevant provisions of the ECHR allow that one or more students, or their parents, state in any manner before the School Principal that on grounds of religious conscience, namely because they are followers of another creed, religion or atheists, that they do not wish to attend the course of religion or to participate in other religious events that are provided for in the school programme. In this case, the principal has the duty to proceed with all the necessary actions under law to ensure that these students do not participate in the said religious events and do not attend the teaching of the school subject of religion, without this absence entailing any form of scholastic sanction for these students (absences, conduct unbecoming, disciplinary penalties, etc.).
115. CoS 2601/1998: the mandatory taking of a religious oath in the context of the graduation ceremony of a graduate of the Department of Theology contravenes the constitutionally enshrined religious freedom when the graduate believes that the taking of such an oath offends his Orthodox faith. *AP 489/1972*: the confirmatory statement of a minister on his prelacy has the legal force of a common oath. *See also* the cases of Alexandridis and Dimitras before the ECtHR, in the list of Greek cases concerning religious freedom (below: 'Part IV: International, Transnational, Regional Effects on Religious Communities'). On the same issue see the following studies: Papageorgiou, 'Die Verpflichtung, anlässlich der Eidesleistung seine religiöse Überzeugung vor Gericht zu erklären, verletzt die Gewissens- und Religionsfreiheit. EGMR 21. 2. 2008, 19.516/06 (Alexandridis/Griechenland)', ÖARR 58 (2011) 372–379; Philippou, 'The freedom of religious conscience and the obligation to give an oath. Comments on decision 2601/1998 of the Council of State', DA 2 (1999) 409–423.

II. Right of Religious Equality

146. According to the teachings of the Greek constitutional law, this right provides that the different religious convictions of citizens shall not constitute grounds for their unequal treatment on the part of the State, in relation to other subjects. Religious equality exists when the members of a given society enjoy the various individual, political, civil, taxation or other rights that the respective legal order provides for, regardless of their religious beliefs or their involvement with a particular religious community. Put differently, the essential and complete protection of religious equality does not allow that the enjoyment of the full spectrum of individual rights will depend on or be influenced by (either evidently or latently) criteria of citizens' religious integration.[116]

147. The right to religious equality is enshrined in the Greek Constitution:

(a) explicitly and specifically by § 1, section B, Article 13 Const., stipulating that: 'The enjoyment of civil rights and liberties does not depend on the individual's religious beliefs';[117] and
(b) within the framework of the general principle of equality (4 § 1 Const. 'All Greeks are equal before the law'), whose particular manifestations include religious equality. The general principle of equality constitutes one of the cornerstones of every contemporary democratic state of law, and it demands that equality before the law filters into every specific aspect and form of public life.[118]

148. Exceptions to the application of the principle of equality apply when positions in the public sector are closely connected to a particular creed. For this reason, Article 16 of L. 1771/1988 provides for the appointment of grade school teachers and kindergarten teachers of a different creed or religion only to grade schools employing many teachers or kindergartens employing over two kindergarten teachers, so that the teacher who will teach the subject of religion in one-teacher schools shall be Orthodox.[119]

---

116. Sicilianos, *European Convention on Human Rights: Interpretation to articles*, 437ff; Marinos, *Religious freedom*, 118–124; Troianos, *Lectures in ecclesiastical law*, 79–81.
117. In particular, *see* Philippou, 'Religious equality and the principle of the interpretation of laws in accordance with the constitution: A comment on decision 1064/1998 of the Single-Member Administrative First-Instance Court of Thessaloniki', DA 7 (2000) 689–696.
118. In general, *see*: Chrysogonos/Vlahopoulos, *Individual and social rights*, 157ff; Vlahopoulos, *Fundamental rights: Individual, social and political rights*, 47ff.
119. CoS 3533/1986: the refusal to appoint a classics high school teacher on grounds that he is a Jehovah's Witness is unlawful. More particularly, it is based neither on the statutes concerning the qualifications of educators nor on the statutes of the Greek Civil Servant Code regarding their qualifications, nor on any general statutes about the mission of education. Furthermore, it is unconstitutional, since it violates the provisions of Arts 4 and 13 § 1 Const. (1975) safeguarding equality and religious tolerance. This is so because the main mission of high school teachers who teach literature and the classics is not the development of the students' religious conscience, for which the

149. The principle of equality obliges the legislator, the administration and the judiciary to an equal, impersonal and object treatment of similar cases or situations, with a simultaneous prohibition of any arbitrary discrimination. In parallel, a clear logical outcome of this same principle, with an equally binding force, is the obligation to treat essentially dissimilar cases or situations unequally because the inverse would lead to a not less arbitrary violation of the constitutional principle of equality.[120]

150. Legal treatment is unequal when it lacks an objective, rational and convincing justification. This happens mainly when similar situations are treated dissimilarly (by the legislator, the administration or the judiciary) or the inverse: when the law treats as similar situations and cases that are substantially different from the average case. Finally, as it is evident, legal distinctions can never be presented as justified when it contravenes fundamental rights because equality is conceived, above all else, as equality in the enjoyment of rights.

151. More particular applications of the general principle of equality enshrined in Article 4 Const. – that are safeguarded by provisions of that same article and are connected indirectly with religious equality – are:

- the equality of the two sexes ('Greek men and women have equal rights and equal obligations', Article 4 § 2 Const.);
- the equality of access to public service ('Only Greek citizens shall be eligible for public service, except as otherwise provided by special laws', Article 4 § 4 Const.);[121]
- the equality before the military draft ('Every Greek capable of bearing arms is obliged to contribute to the defence of the Fatherland as provided by law', Article 4 § 6 Const.);[122]
- the social equality ('Titles of nobility or distinction are neither conferred upon nor recognized in Greek citizens', Article 4 § 7 Const.), whereas more specifically equality in the field of tax burdens is grounded on Article 4 § 5 Const., expressly stating that 'Greek citizens contribute without distinction to public charges in proportion to their means'.[123]

152. The constitutional protection of the right to religious equality cannot be considered as absolute in our country because of the parallel force of the provision

---

follower of another religion would be unsuitable, particularly in what concerns the students of Greek junior high schools and high schools, who in their overwhelming majority are Christian Orthodox.

120. CoS 1422/1986; *AP 690/1983 (Plenary Session)*.

121. Koukiadis/Papastathis, 'Droit du travail et religion en Grèce', *Churches and labour law in the EC countries,* 115f, passim.

122. Chrysogonos/Vlahopoulos, *Individual and social rights*, 194ff; Vlahopoulos, *Fundamental rights: Individual, social and political rights*, 65f. But *see* CoS 2837/1015: the exemption of the monks of Mount Athos from the military obligations is justified by the special constitutional regime (Art. 105 Constitution).

123. Manitakis, 'The constitutional principle of equality and the concept of general interest', ToS 3 (1978) 433–465.

of Article 3 § 1 section a' Const., which sets apart the Eastern Orthodox Church from all other religions, recognizing it as the 'prevailing' religion in Greece.[124] The exact conceptual content of this term, but in reality the issue of the normative or non-normative effects that its mention in the Constitution itself entails, comprises the topic of an especially interesting and still ongoing scientific debate currently unfolding in our country. The prevailing opinion advocates that the nature and the meaning of this provision are limited to the simple proclamation that Greeks are, in their overwhelming majority, Christian Orthodox. According to this interpretative position, the term 'prevailing religion' in the present Constitution has a merely descriptive and not a normative character.

153. I believe that a strong argument for the prevailing interpretative position is turning to the will of the constitutional legislator – a fact that the relevant theoretical argumentation that was developed was not sufficiently emphasized. More specifically, during the deliberations leading to the voting of the Constitution and despite the final outcome of the discussions, all the political wings of the then Parliament, without any exception, asserted that the best system of church and state relations is the one of separation between church and state.

154. At this point, we will make some observations of a more general nature. The fact that even today democratic states often encounter insurmountable difficulties in every one of their efforts to implement the principle of religious equality, observing equal distances before all creeds, justifies absolutely the conclusion that religious equality constitutes the most elusive, as to its actual implementation, manifestation of religious freedom. These difficulties in implementation are exacerbated by the very nature of religious equality as a polyprismatic right which is connected, directly or indirectly, to all the other previously mentioned manifestations of religious freedom. For all these reasons, the de facto (and not merely nominal, as is usually the case) protection of religious equality in a country enhances the full and substantial enjoyment of all other manifestations and aspects of religious freedom, ultimately becoming a genuine barometer for the latter.[125]

155. A realistic outlook on the situation forces us to acknowledge that the absolute pursuit of the goal of religious equality of the citizens is not feasible. And this is mainly because legislation is by its very nature not able to observe and regulate not only the very rapid dynamics and developments that all contemporary societies are undergoing but, even more so, the numerous cases of individualized inequality among the members of society. As a result, it is inevitable to neglect at least the less important cases, whose limitation must be left to the devices of justice and to the initiative of administrative organs.

---

124. *See* relatively: Papastathis, *The Hellenic republic and the prevailing religion*, 815–852; Marinos, *Religious freedom*, 92–101; Troianos, *Lectures in ecclesiastical law*, 84ff; Papageorgiou, *Ecclesiastical law*, 93ff.
125. Sicilianos, *European Convention on Human Rights: Interpretation to articles*, 44ff.

156. Nevertheless, it is absolutely feasible to seek a continuous adjustment, amelioration and particularization of the legislative measures and administrative institutions relating to the essential implementation of religious equality. Here the responsibility lies with the legislation, the administration and the justice system, which is obliged, through case law, to implement the relevant statutes in a spirit of rule of law, so that the eradication of any religious inequalities constitutes a goal that should be steadily pursued.

157. One such noteworthy case was Decision 1064/1998 issued by the First Instance Court of Thessaloniki. Proceeding to an implementation of the constitutional principles of religious equality and equality before taxation law, it ruled that the exemption from the Real Estate Tax that was provided for under Article 24 § 7 of L. 2130/1993 in favour of the prevailing religion had to be extended to every piece of real estate of every other known religion, even if this was used not only for worship but also for educational purposes, given that a similar restriction does not apply for the prevailing religion. The same decision aptly emphasized that:

> possible tax exemptions cannot refer exclusively to the Orthodox Church, with a general invocation of the system of regulating church and state relations, according to which the Orthodox Church constitutes the 'prevailing religion' … Since there is no sufficient reason for this privileged treatment, the exemption provisions should be interpreted as encompassing all known religions and creeds in the state. This must be accepted even more so, when in the context of the particular regulation the economic element predominates, in the sense that the privileged treatment is not related to the spiritual role of the Orthodox Church, but it concerns primarily its status as an economic agent, a holder of rights and obligations within the jurisdiction of the Greek State.[126]

III. Law 3304/2005 and the Greek Ombudsman

158. The enactment of L. 3304/2005 'On the implementation of the principle of equal treatment irrespective of racial or ethnic origin, religion or belief' constituted a critical point for the promotion of the principle of equality and the protection of human rights in Greece. This Law incorporated Directives 2000/43/EC and 2000/78/EC of European Union into Greek law.

159. The provisions of L. 3304/2005 seek to combat the effects of both direct and indirect discrimination (Articles 3 and 7) while organizing a complex network of mechanisms for the protection of the individuals, which far exceeds the traditional model of sanctions. New administrative and penal sanctions are provided for (Articles 16 and 17), the emphasis being on the actions to be taken by specific public bodies so as to promote equal treatment and take positive measures.

126. DA 7 (2000) 705–708. *See also* Philippou, 'Religious equality and the principle of the interpretation of laws in accordance with the constitution: A comment on decision 1064/1998 of the Single-Member Administrative First-Instance Court of Thessaloniki', DA 7 (2000) 689–696.

160. This act is primarily implemented by the Greek Ombudsman whose role is strengthened and enhanced by the addition of new functions and competences, which contribute to the effective fulfilment of its mission. The Greek Ombudsman, as shown by the annual reports as of this day, has already spent part of his activity in investigating citizens' complaints regarding unequal treatment on the part of state bodies. As of entry into force of L. 3304/2005 (27 January 2005), the Greek Ombudsman has been receiving complaints of citizens in protest of unfair discrimination, which, according to the Greek Ombudsman, had taken place against those citizens by the administration, also by reason of their religious beliefs.

IV. Right of Religious Education

161. The right of *religious education* includes two fundamental manifestations:

(i) The right of parents to provide their children with the religious upbringing that they deem appropriate.[127] The parents jointly, as bearers of the child's custody, are the ones competent to decide about the child's induction (or not) in a particular religious community. If they disagree, the court decides, taking into consideration the best interests of the child (Articles 1510–1512 CC).[128]

A case demonstrating the abusive exercise of this right is the refusal of parents who are Jehovah's Witnesses to allow the vaccination of their child. Aiming to resolve this serious issue, Article 1534 CC stipulates that:

> In case there is an urgent need for medical intervention, in order to prevent the risk of life or health of the child, the Public Prosecutor at the Court of First Instance may, if the parents refuse, immediately grant the required permission, following the application of the attending physician or the head of

127. Zervogianni L., 'The religion of the child and the parental responsibility', ToS 2020, 537–558.

128. CoS (Plenary Session) 942/2020: church attendance and prayer for kindergarten and elementary school students are legal. The possibility of exemption is in accordance with the Constitution; *Appellate Court of Thessaloniki 1433/2003*: for the judicial regulation of the exercise of child custody, the court takes into consideration the bonds of the child with his parents and siblings, as well as any private agreements that the parents have signed. The court decision should be aimed at safeguarding the child's best interests, but should also be based on the constitutionally enshrined principles of equality, gender equality, the free development of personality and the freedom of religious conscience. The judge should not discriminate on the basis of the parents' religion, but it should take into account the impact of a parent's religious convictions on the exercise of parental custody and care. Depending on the child's maturity, the court should seek and take into consideration the child's opinion concerning parental custody or care in cases of emergency medical procedures, in order to avert a danger to the child's life or health. On this issue *see* in general: Chrysogonos, 'Religious education and prevailing religion', ToS 25 (1999) 993–1024; Michailidis-Nouaros, 'The right to education under the European Convention of Human Rights (Article 2 of the 1rst Protocol of the European Convention', *Anthology in Honor of Phaedon Vegleris*, vol. I: *The crisis of state institutions*, Athens 1988, 1–34; Sotirelis, *Religion and education under the constitution and the European Convention: From catechism to polyphony*, Athens 1993.

the clinic where the child is hospitalized or of any other competent health-care providing organ/health-care provider.[129]

(ii) The right of every creed to found educational institutions with religious purposes, under the condition that no proselytism is exercised in the context of the educational process.[130]

129. Zervogianni, 'The religion of the child and the parental responsibility', *supra* 540; *Public Prosecutor of the Supreme Court 6/1992*: the refusal of parents to consent to medical surgery that is necessary for the life of their minor child may be construed as an abusive exercise of a right and not be taken into consideration. The physician has a special legal obligation to proceed with the surgery *lege artis* even if the parents refuse to give their consent or are absent.

130. CoS 2349/1974: in Greece every private citizen who has not been deprived of his political rights can establish, having been granted a licence by state authorities, academic institutions which shall operate in accordance with the Constitution and general laws. Nobody can be denied of this right solely on grounds of adhering to another creed or religion. It was duly permitted, by act of the Minister of Education, to the Archbishop of Catholics in Athens to accept students not belonging to the Christian Orthodox dogma to the private school of elementary education of his ownership bearing the title of 'Saint Joseph'. About the same issue, *see* 'Part IX. Education'.

Chapter 2. Collective Religious Freedom

§1. Freedom of Worship

I. General Presuppositions

162. The most important expression of the right to collective religious freedom is the freedom of worship (*forum externum:* 13 § 2 Const.). The same right may of course occur individually or in community with others, in private or in public, in specially designated houses of worship or outdoors.

163. The practice of worship is free under the following three main requirements, set by the Constitution:

(1) worship is exercised by people representing a 'known' religion;
(2) the worship of the known religion must not violate public order or morals;
(3) the followers of every religion must not be involved in proselytism.

II. Constitutional Presupposition of 'Known' Religion

164. A significant constitutional limitation of the right of worship is set by the precondition that the religion be 'known', in the sense of not having secret doctrines and an occult worship.[131] Consequently, the various secret organizations that block free entry of the interested parties to their 'dogmatic' positions or to the knowledge concerning the content of their worship are not considered to be known religions and are not protected by the Constitution.

165. It must be clarified that the religion must be 'known' and not 'recognized': the latter case would comprise an extreme limitation of the freedom of worship because it would impose the granting of a state licence-approval concerning the recognition of a religion, a fact that at least in Greece is not required.[132]

131. CoS 1842/1992: Art. 13 Const. safeguards the individual right of the followers of known religions to perform their rites of worship freely and without any hindrance, under the requirements set therein and which consist in the nature of a religious faith/doctrine as known and not occult, the non-violation of public order or morals and the prohibition of proselytism.
132. CoS 310/1997, CoS 493/1997: the concept of 'known religion' does not presuppose an approval or in any manner recognition by means of a state or ecclesiastical act.

166. In its decisions, the Greek Council of State has ruled as 'known religions' the Methodists,[133] the Seventh-Day Adventists,[134] the Mormons, the Evangelical Churches,[135] the Jehovah's Witnesses, and so on.

167. The characterization of a creed or doctrine as 'known' does not depend on its stage of development or on the number of its followers, or even the degree to which its doctrinal teachings diverge from others, already 'known' religions or from the 'prevailing' (Article 3 § 1 Const.) religion. It also does not have any impact whether or not the particular creed maintains ecclesiastical principles or whether its ministers lack priesthood similar to the Orthodox clergy because the acquisition of the property of minister will in each instance be judged on the basis of the statutes of the respective religious law.

168. The ministers of known religions (including the prevailing religion) are subject to the same supervision by the State and to the same obligations (Article 13 § 3 Const.).

III. Right to Establish Places of Worship

169. The followers of every known religion have the constitutional right to found and maintain special places devoted to the exercise of their worshipping duties, such as temples, mosques, and synagogues. The State is required, applying the criterion of the equality of religions before the law, to ensure that all creeds have the requirements and possibilities for the egalitarian enjoyment of their right to establish places of worship.[136]

170. More particularly, the foundation of a church of the prevailing religion presupposes the permission of the local metropolitan and a building licence, which is

133. CoS 2274/1962: the denomination of Methodists constitutes a known religion; however, its members are prohibited from using the term 'Eastern Apostolic Church', which is doctrinally suitable only for the Orthodox Church.
134. CoS 1952/1992, CoS 2004/1991: the denomination of Seventh-Day Adventists fulfils the requirements of a known religion.
135. CoS 2058/1957 (Plenary Session): the Free Evangelical Church constitutes a known religion, adopting beliefs that are widely known and popular among a sufficient number of followers in Greece. The same holds for the Greek Evangelical Church [CoS (Plenary Session) 2358/1952, 2058/1957, 851/1961, 2275/1962].
136. *See* in general: Dervitsiotis, *The establishment of a church as a component of religious freedom*, Athens 2010; Papageorgiou, 'The application of the freedom of religion principles of the European Convention on Human Rights in Greece', in: Emilianides, *Religious Freedom in the European Union*, 187–198; Marinos/Troianos, 'The construction of churches and places of worship', AEKD 21 (1966) 49–84.

granted by the Division of Church Construction at the Ecclesiastical Central Service of Economics. The State, on the other hand, merely supervises the enforcement of the terms of construction, through the competent Ministry of Environment and Energy (Article 32 §§ 2, 8 and 14 L. 4495/2017, Article 14 L. 4585/2018, Article 14 L. 4674/2020).[137]

171. The establishment of places of worship of the other known religions is subject to a different legislative regime, which using as a criterion the size of the construction distinguishes between 'temples' and 'houses of worship' (Article 1 L. 1363/1938, Article 1 L. 1672/1939, Article 41 L. 1369/1938 and the RD of 20.5/2.6.1939). The difference between these two types ('temples' – 'houses of worship') lies in the size and the capacity of the establishments.

172. For the establishment of temples, the requirements are:

(a) the petition of at least fifty neighbouring families. The petition, after it is signed by the heads of the families and the authenticity of their signatures is authorized by the local police authorities, is then submitted to the Ministry of Education and Cults (Article 27 L. 3467/2006);[138]
(b) the district in which the applicants reside must be at a great distance from another temple of their own denomination;
(c) approval from the aforementioned Minister.

173. For the establishment of a 'house of worship', the requirements are:

137. *See* the landmark cases CoS 4202/2012, 1920/2014, 625/2016, 560/2019.
138. The very interesting Art. 27 of L. 3467/2006, 'Selection of primary and secondary education officers, regulation of administrative and educational issues and other provisions' (OGG A' 128) stipulates the following: '(1). The permit or opinion of the local ecclesiastical authorities of the Greek Orthodox Church is not required for the establishment, construction or operation of a temple or church of any religion or doctrine, with the exception of the Greek Orthodox Church. Any other provision stating otherwise shall be repealed [Article 1 of Obligatory Law 1363/1938 (OGG A' 305), as amended by Article 1 of Obligatory Law 1672/1939 (OGG A' 123), Article 41 of Obligatory Law 1369/1938 (OGG A' 317)]. (2). The application for granting permit for the establishment, construction or operation of a temple or church of any religion or doctrine, with exception of the Greek Orthodox Church, shall be directly submitted to the Ministry of National Education and Religious Affairs and not to the local ecclesiastical authorities. Any other provision stating otherwise shall be repealed [Article 1 of the Royal Decree 20.5/2.6.1939 (OGG A' 220)]'. Upon application of the above article, was repealed Art. 1 of the OL 1363/1938, which stipulated the issue of a necessary 'permit' by the local ecclesiastical authorities of the Greek Orthodox Church (i.e., by the competent local metropolitan), so that non-Orthodox citizens (heterodox or of different religion) would be able to establish, construct or put into operation a temple or church of their own religion or doctrine. Based on the new regulation, the application for granting permit for the establishment, construction or operation of a temple or church of any religion or doctrine (with the exception of Orthodox churches) shall be directly submitted to the Ministry of National Education and Religious Affairs (since then, no 'permit' of any kind shall be required by the Orthodox metropolitan). This repealed regulation was repeatedly criticized by the scientific community as violating directly the constitutional provisions safeguarding the right of freedom of worship.

(a) the signed application of the followers, which is submitted by their minister or pastor to the Ministry;
(b) validation of the authenticity of their signatures by the mayor; and
(c) permission (licence) by the Minister.

174. If the aforementioned requirements are satisfied, the administration is obliged to grant the licence. But if it refuses, it must justify its refusal specifically, so that the review of this denial before the Council of State is consequently possible.[139]

IV. The Relevant Case Law of the European Court of Human Rights

175. The anachronistic framework of the above-mentioned provisions (L 1363/1938 – L. 1672/1939 – R.D. on 20.5/2-6-1939) was three times the subject of proceedings in the ECtHR. These were the cases of *Manousakis and others v. Greece, Pentidis and others v. Greece* and *Tsavachidis v. Greece.*

176. In the case of *Manousakis and others v. Greece* (26 September 1996),[140] which can be considered the most important of the three, the ECtHR convicted Greece for the violation of Articles 11 and 13 Const. as well as of Article 9 ECHR. According to the grounds of such decision by the ECtHR, Article 9 ECHR does not exclude the granting of an administrative permit for the operation of temples or other places of worship, provided certain standard requirements are met that do not involve a control of the 'lawfulness' of such religious beliefs. According to the wording of the decision on *Manousakis* case, it seems that the only preventive controls that can be performed by the Minister are whether certain strictly standard requirements are met, such as if there is a certain number of signatures, if the place of residence of the applicants is known and if the signatures have been verified by police authorities.

139. CoS 625/2016; CoS 1411/2003: the establishment and operation of a house of worship take place under a regime of administrative licence, which, as long as the religion is known, is granted following the review of fulfilment of certain legal requirements. This regime is not contrary to the Constitution and the ECHR, as long as it is corroborated that the religion is 'known' and there is a genuine need of the religious community, deduced from the number of the applicants and their place of residence. CoS 1121/1987: Art. 13 Const. safeguards the right of the followers of various religions and creeds to practise their rites of worship freely and without any hindrance, under the requirements set therein, namely the nature of the religion or creed as known and not occult, the non-offence of public order or good morals and the non-practice of proselytism. The investigation of whether these requirements apply has been handed over to the administration by RD of 20.5/2.6.39 (L. 1672/39). When there is an application for the granting of a licence for a house of worship, the administration is required, having enquired into the legitimacy of its submission, to proceed with the relevant enquiry and, if it affirms that all the legal requirements are met, to grant the licence, whereas in the contrary case, it must justify its relevant act of rejection legally and sufficiently. In this sense, the aforementioned provisions are aligned with Art. 13 Const., and for this reason they continue to be in effect after the entry into force of the latter.

140. Lindholm/Durham/Tahzib-Lie, *Facilitating freedom of religion or belief: A deskbook,* 108, 154, 222f, 427–429, passim.

177. On the contrary, the ECtHR did not leave much room for the compliance of the applicable Greek legislative framework with the ECHR, stating that L. 1363/1938 and the R.D. on 20-5/2-6-1939 on 'temples' and 'houses of worship' that do not belong to the Greek Orthodox Church allow far-reaching interference by the political, administrative and ecclesiastical authorities with the exercise of religious freedom.

178. Finally, in the other two cases, Greece granted the permit before the hearing of the case *(Pentidis,* 19 March 1997)[141] and agreed on an amicable settlement *(Tsavachidis,* 21 January 1999)[142] under the threat of being convicted for violation of the ECHR article.

179. The conviction of Greece in the aforementioned *Manousakis* case and the amicable closure of the other two cases requested by the Greek State *(Pentidis, Tsavachidis*) were followed by important court decisions such as the following.

180. The decision of the Plenary Session of the Supreme Court (Areios Pagos) in its decision 20/2001, based on the majority of which the applicable framework for granting permit for the establishment of a 'house of worship', as provided for by the above-mentioned provisions, is not contrary to the Constitution and the ECHR which stipulate that:

(a) The practice of worship is subject to the limitations imposed by public order and morals as well as by the prohibition of proselytism.
(b) A permit issued by the Ministry of National Education and Religious Affairs is required for the construction or operation of a temple of any religion or church. Such permit is granted at the discretion of the Minister and may be refused if the Minister believes that the construction or operation of the temple or house of worship does not serve a real need of the religious community comprising the applicants.
(c) The applicable framework in the Greek legal order regarding the granting of permits for the establishment of a house of worship aims to protect public order and conforms, in principle, with Article 13 §§ 1–2 Const. and Article 9 §§ 1–2 ECHR to the extent that such framework is limited to the control of the requirements laid down in Article 13 § 2 Const. and Article 9 § 2 ECHR ('known' religion, respect of public order or morals, unfair practices of proselytism) as well as of standard requirements laid down by the provisions of OL 1363/1938 and the executive decree for granting permits pursuant to the decision dated 29 September 1996 of the ECtHR on *Manousakis v. Greece* case.

181. According to the same decision (AP 20/2001), the legal requirement of prior administrative permit is not unconstitutional as long as its aim is to check whether certain criteria are met and such permit is granted at all times, unless the exceptions set forth in this provision apply. That is, when contrary to the law: the

141. Lindholm/Durham/Tahzib-Lie, *supra*, 154–155, 222–223.
142. *Ibid.*, 154, 219.

religious belief is secret and not known, or the worship poses a threat to public order or morals, or the aim of this religion is proselytism.

182. These requirements, according to the majority opinion in the Supreme Court decision 20/2001, are not contrary to Article 9 ECHR, provided that the granting of the permit is prescribed by the law; those requirements are necessary in a democratic society in order to protect public order and do not constitute a measure similar to the intended lawful purpose.

183. The minority opinion in this decision was held by the President of the Supreme Court and another judge who believed that Article 13 § 2, section (a) Const. (stating that any known religion is free and that its related worship is practised unhindered under the protection of the law) and that Article 9 § 1 ECHR stipulate the free and unhindered worship of a known religion and do not allow the prior issue of an administrative permit (apart from a simple urban planning or building permit) for the establishment or operation of places of worship, since in this way the worship of a religion is dependent on a prior permit and is hindered in a preventive way.

184. Based on the minority opinion, the above-mentioned constitutional provision and the ECHR allow all limitations imposed for reasons of public order and morals – as well as for reasons of 'public health' and 'the protection of rights and freedoms of others' according to the ECHR – however both the Constitution, using the expression 'it must not pose a threat', and the ECHR, stating that a limitation is acceptable 'as long as it is necessary in a democratic society', exclude any other preventive control that 'would not be necessary in a democratic society' (Article 9 § 2 ECHR), as already accepted by the ECtHR in *Manousakis* case. And this is because the preventive control usually results in unreasonable prohibition or improper refusal of permits on vague grounds. In addition, the annulment of the refusal by the court is not the solution to the problem since it involves long and costly procedures, which discourage the interested parties and may entail the prohibition of freedom of worship for a long period of time. According to the minority opinion, the above-mentioned provisions of OL 1363/1938, etc., are, on the one hand, unconstitutional and, on the other hand, contrary to Article 9 ECHR and thus null and void (Article 111 § 1, 93 § 4 and 28 § 1 Const.).

185. The Report of the Public Prosecutor of the Misdemeanour Court of Kavala no. 212/2001, based on which the offence for the operation of a house of worship without permit, as laid down in the provisions of Article 1, section (b), of OL 1363/1938, is contrary to Article 9 of the ECHR, something that was pointed out in the hearing of *Manousakis v. Greece* case in the ECtHR.

186. The decision of the Court of Appeals of Crete 297/2002, which annulled the judgment of conviction for the operation of a house of worship without prior permit issued by the local ecclesiastical authorities and the Ministry of National

Education and Religious Affairs on the grounds that the conviction constitutes violation of the right of religious freedom pursuant to the decision of the ECtHR in the case of *Manousakis v. Greece* and Article 9 of the ECHR.

187. The decision of the CoS 1411/2003, due to the importance of the issues raised and the various opinions expressed, referred the issue to the seven-member committee of the Court.

188. In the case *Pantelidou v. Greece* (10-10-2019), the ECtHR judged that the use of a public building by Old Calendarists as a place of worship is not contrary to the ECHR, even if it is in violation of urban planning legislation.

§2. Limitations to Freedom of Worship and Religious Freedom

I. Public Order and Good Morals

189. According to Article 13 § 2 section B Const., the exercise of worship is not allowed to offend public order or morals ('good usages'). These are largely indistinguishable concepts, expressing the social, moral, political and economic beliefs that prevail in Greece, within a particular time period. The precise content of these concepts will be judged by the administration or by the judicial system for each particular case, but in a manner that is objective and free from any personal opinions of the competent state agent.

II. Lawful Obligations: Duties Towards the State

190. The invocation of religious beliefs cannot justify the exemption from obligations that the citizens incur towards the law and the State (13 § 4 Const.),[143] such as indicatively the payment of taxes and military service.

191. The issue of 'conscientious objectors'[144] has in the past caused grave legal and practical problems in Greece, as regards their military obligations (Article 4 §

143. CoS 4079/1976: the religious beliefs of individuals do not grant them the right to refuse the fulfilment of their obligations towards the State or their compliance with general laws, such as those concerning education, public defence, public health, the functioning of the civil services, etc. The Seventh-Day Adventists, who are adherents of a religion that is known under the Greek Constitution (CoS 123/1964, 4054/1973 and 2139/1975), maintain that on the day of Saturday they must abstain from their employment and their other activities, so that on that very day they remain free and unhindered to worship God in their churches. The implementation in practice of this belief of theirs, which stems from their religious conscience, on the one hand may not be self-righteously subjected to any limitation, but on the other hand does not provide them with the right to refuse their compliance with the general laws of the State, and more particularly, to demand their exemption from the general rules regulating the consequences of non-attendance for the students of secondary education.

144. *See* generally: Chrysogonos/Vlahopoulos, *Individual and social rights*, 196ff; Alivisatos, 'Conscientius objectors and military service', NoV 36 (1988) 519–528; Anthopoulos, 'The problem of the

6 Const.: 'Every Greek capable of bearing arms is obliged to contribute to the defence of the Fatherland as provided by law').[145] These are individuals who, invoking their religious or ideological conscience, refuse the military draft in general or the armed service in the army.

192. An interpretive statement that was added to Article 4 Const. during the constitutional revision of 2001 stipulates that, in what concerns the mandate of Article 4 § 6 Const., it is possible to prescribe by law the mandatory offer of other services, within or outside the armed forces (alternative service) on the part of those who have a substantiated objection of conscience for the provision of armed or generally military service.[146]

193. Today all those who are recognized as conscientious objectors are obliged to provide 'alternative service' that is double in duration compared to the one they would have provided if they served bearing arms (Article 60 § 1 L. 3421/2005, as this was replaced by Article 78 section f L. 3883/2010 and L. 4609/2019). The alternative service consists in the provision of public utility services in various agencies of the public sector.[147]

194. For corroborating the integrity of the conscientious objectors, the law requires a prior advisory opinion of a five-member committee, comprised of two professors in the highest educational institutions (public universities) specializing in philosophy or in the social and political sciences or in psychology, a consultant or an associate judge of the Legal Council and two higher officers, one serving in the recruiting office and the other in the medical services of the armed forces.

---

constitutionality of alternative civilian service (on the occasion of the recent advisory opinion of the Legal Council of the State)', Y 4 (1993) 1071–1091; Krippas, 'The constitutionality of the exemption from military service on grounds of religious beliefs', EEN 46 (1979) 325–328.

145. *Administrative Appellate Court of Athens 251/2002*: the Constitution or the ECHR do not safeguard an individual right of exemption of those Greeks who are capable of bearing arms from the duty of military draft for reasons of objections of conscience. However, the enactment of unarmed military service or any other mandatory service for those who refuse to fulfil their military obligations on religious or ideological grounds is constitutionally tolerated, as long as grave reasons of public interest apply and the smooth functioning of the armed forces is not harmed.

146. 'Interpretative Clause' added to Art. 4 § 6 Const.: 'The provision of paragraph 6 does not preclude the law to provide mandatory provision of other services, within or outside the armed forces (alternative service), by those having substantiated conscientious objection to performing armed or military duties in general.'

147. CoS 1318/2017; CoS 1210/2018; Chrysogonos/Vlahopoulos, Individual *and social rights*, 197f.

Chapter 3. Organizational Religious Freedom

195. The right of association for religious purposes ('organizational religious freedom'), on the one hand, permits the establishment and operation of legal persons under public or private law for the pursuit of religious purposes, and, on the other hand, secures the self-administration of every creed, according to the provisions of its internal law.

196. As a result, the Constitution recognizes the right of the Roman Catholic, Anglican or any other church or creed to regulate the regime of the internal administration and organization of their legal persons or organs, pursuant to the respective canon law.[148]

197. After the publishing of L. 4301/2014 about religious legal persons, the above relevant constitutional rights are more easily to be implemented under the provisions of that law (*see* Part I. Legal Framework and Sources).

148. Contra *AP 360/1994*, which ruled that the Roman Catholic Church in its totality as well as its organizational subdivisions can acquire the legal personality that is provided for not in its canon law, but only in Greek law and as long as the relevant provisions are implemented. Greece was subsequently condemned by the ECtHR in the case 'Catholic Church "Panagia ton Chanion"' (143/1996/762/963, 16.12.1997), in which it was recognized that the previously mentioned ecclesiastic community has a sui generis legal personality. The Greek State later enacted Art. 33 of L. 2731/1999, stipulating that: 'The legal persons that have been in effect by way of article 13 of the Introductory Law of the Civil Code include the institutions of the Catholic Church that were established or operated in Greece prior to 23.2.1946.' On this issue, *see also* Papageorgiou, 'L. 4301/2014 on the organization of the legal form of religious communities and the establishment of religious legal entities', Arm. 70 (2016) 573–584. *See also* Asimakis, *Legislation and jurisprudence for the catholic church in Greece*, Thessaloniki 2014; *Codex juris canonici*, Athens 2020.

Part III. Legal Status of Religious Communities

Chapter 1. The Formal Status of Religious Communities

198. The special legal regime governing the creeds of the Greek territory lies in direct conjunction with:

(a) the provisions of the Constitution relating not only to the 'prevailing' Orthodox Church but also to the protection of the religious freedom of all 'known' religions;[149]
(b) the international treaties that have been signed, safeguarding the religious freedom of all Muslims and Roman Catholics residing in Greece;
(c) the special legislation regulating the organization, administration and institutional operation of certain specified religious communities;
(d) the by-laws/regulations governing their internal affairs, provided they have been ratified according to law;
(e) the provisions of L. 4301/2014 on the legal form of religious communities and the establishment of religious legal entities.[150]

199. The main organizational subdivisions of the Orthodox Church[151] as well as the Israelite communities[152] are recognized directly by the law as legal entities in public law. The remaining religious communities function, as a rule, as legal entities in private law. In this case, the creeds form associations (as long as they have at least twenty members), foundations or civil not-for-profit partnerships, pursuant to the relevant provisions of the Civil Code. The by-laws of those associations must also have been ratified by the relevant court. Furthermore, according to L. 4301/2014, the religious minorities may establish one particular category of legal persons, the so-called religious/ecclesiastical legal entities in private law.

149. *See* Part I.
150. Papageorgiou, 'L. 4301/2014 on the organization of the legal form of religious communities and the establishment of religious legal entities', Arm. 70 (2016) 573–584.
151. Laws 590/1977, 4149/1961 and 4301/2014.
152. *See* L. 2456/1920 'On Israelite Communities' and its amendments by Laws 4837/1930, 367/1945, 3817/1958.

§1. The Orthodox Church

I. The Orthodox Church of Greece

A. Central Organization

1. Synodical Bodies

200. The highest ecclesiastical authority of the Church of Greece is the Holy Synod of the Hierarchy (HSH): it is composed of the 'Archbishop of Athens and all Greece' as its President and the active bishops, who shepherd and administrate metropolises (Article 3 SCCG): these are the metropolitans who have been lawfully elected, ordained and consequently appointed to their metropolises by presidential decree, without having subsequently lost their position or prelacy because of a judicial dispute.[153]

201. The HSH decides on all issues concerning the Church (Article 4 SCCG), but mainly in what concerns:

- the observance of doctrinal and canonical issues;
- the matter of ecclesiastical unity with the Ecumenical Patriarchate and the other Orthodox Churches;[154]
- the relations of the Church of Greece with the followers of other doctrines;
- the spiritual issues relating to the clergy and the laity;
- the ecclesiastical order, holy communion and rituals;
- the exercise of the institution of ecclesiastical 'economy';
- the issuance of regulatory decisions pertaining to the internal organization and administration of the Church.

202. Furthermore, the HSH:

- exercises the highest supervision and reviews the actions of all ecclesiastical administrative organs and legal persons;
- elects the Archbishop of Athens and the metropolitans;
- exercises all the competencies deriving from the holy canons and the other ecclesiastical statutes.

203. The HSH convenes (Article 6 SCCG) regularly on the 1 October of every year, and extraordinarily when it is convened by its President on his own initiative

153. Papageorgiou, *Ecclesiastical law*, 239ff; Papastathis, 'On the ecclesiastical synodical system', in: *ibid.*, *Nomocanonical studies*, 85–92; Troianos, 'Die Synode der Hierarchie als höchstes Verwaltungsorgan der einzelnen Autokephalen Orthodoxen Kirchen', Kanon 2 (1974) 192–216.

154. CoS (Plenary Session) 944/2020: the act of the Holy Synod recognizing the right of the Ecumenical Patriarch to grant autocephalous status, as well as the prerogative of the Archbishop of Athens to deal further with the matter of the recognition of the Church of the Ukraine, does not constitute an executive administrative act by an ecclesiastical authority but an act of purely spiritual character.

or by decision of the Permanent Holy Synod (PHS) or following an application of at least one-third of its members. The President of the HSH is the Archbishop of Athens, and the vice president is the metropolitan who has seniority as regards his prelacy.

204. The HSH is in quorum, when its present members are more than half of the total number of its members. Its decisions are taken by majority rule. If there is a tie vote and the voting is public, then the vote of the President prevails. However, in matters of fundamental importance (such as the exercise of ecclesiastical economy[155]), a majority of at least two-thirds of the total number of the HSH's members is required (Article 6 § 3 section d' SCCG). Details about the proceedings, the discussions, the decision-making and the taking of minutes are included in the by-laws of the HSH (Reg. 1/1977, as they were amended and completed by Reg. 214/2010).

205. The Permanent Holy Synod (PHS) is a permanent administrative organ of the Church of Greece, which is comprised of the Archbishop of Athens as a permanent member and President, and twelve active metropolitans. The metropolitans are chosen according to their seniority in prelacy and on a rotating basis – six of them from the Autocephalous Church and six from the metropolises of the so-called New Lands for a one-year term of service (Articles 3 § 1 and 7 § 1 SCCG). The aforementioned composition of the PHS is stipulated not only in Term B' of the Patriarchal and Synodal Act of 4.9.1928 but also (and in accordance with the Constitution) in the Patriarchal Tome of 29.6.1850 (*see* Part I).

206. The main competencies of the PHS are:

- the execution of the decisions taken by the HSH;
- the rendering of advisory opinions for every ecclesiastical law under consideration;
- the treatment of current ecclesiastical affairs;
- the collaboration with the State on issues of ecclesiastical education and the continuing education of the clergy (Article 9 SCCG).

Moreover, the PHS exercises (during the period that spans until the convocation of the HSH, namely for one year) every other ecclesiastical administrative power, which does not belong exclusively to the HSH.

207. The PHS convenes:

- regularly from Tuesday until Friday during the first two weeks of every month; during the third week, it convenes as a Synodical Court;

155. In general *see*: Papageorgiou, *Ecclesiastical law*, 75ff; Troianos, *Lectures in ecclesiastical law*, 38ff; Irene Tsagri, 'The legal nature of the ecclesiastical economy', EEN 39 (1972) 876–879; Jérôme Kotsonis, *Problèmes de l'économie ecclésiastique*, Thessaloniki 1971.

– extraordinarily, following the initiative and the invitation of its President or following the petition of at least seven synodal members, which is submitted to the President and which explicitly mentions the reasons for the extraordinary convocation.

208. The PHS constitutes a quorum if its present members exceed half of the total number by one member, that is, if the present bishop, together with the President, makes eight. Decisions are taken by majority rule, whereas, in case of a tie and a public vote, the vote of the President prevails (Article 7 § 1 section B' SCCG). The Bylaws of the PHS (Reg. 2/1977, as this was amended) contain details about the proceedings. The SCCG also provides for the operation of Synodical Committees, aiming at the study and elaboration of matters relating to the HSH, the facilitation of the work of the PHS and the enforcement of the decisions of these two organs (Article 10 SCCG).

2. Central Ecclesiastical Organizations

209. The *Apostolic Deaconry of the Church of Greece*: it constitutes a legal entity of public law (Article 1 § 4 SCCG), which operates under the supervision of the PHS, aiming at the more effective organization and execution of the missionary and educational work of the Church (Article 40 § 1 SCCG).

210. The *Inter-Orthodox Center of the Church of Greece:* it too constitutes a legal entity of public law, which operates under the supervision of the PHS. Its purpose is to promote the inter-Orthodox and inter-Christian relations of the Church of Greece.

211. Ecclesiastical Central Service of Finances (ECSF): it operates under the direct supervision of the PHS, according to the statutes of Regulations 267/2015 and more recently 317/2020. It aims at the administration, management and effective use of all (movable and immovable) ecclesiastical property. The Administrative Committee of the ECSF is composed of three prelates, a monastery abbot and three laypersons of high prestige, with knowledge and experience in economic and legal issues.

212. Service of Fiscal Control of the Church of Greece (SFCG): it was established with Reg. 210/2010, aiming at exercising fiscal (preventive and repressive) control over the financial management of all ecclesiastical legal persons.

213. The *Communication and Education Service of the Church of Greece (CESCG)*: it aims at examining the pastoral problems of the contemporary social environment under the lens of the Greek Orthodox tradition and the advancement of ecclesiastical tradition (Reg. 307/2018).

214. The Office of the Church of Greece in the European Union, the Council of Europe and UNESCO. It is responsible for European cultural, juridicial, administrative and financial aid matters.

215. The Building Service and Central Council of Ecclesiastical Architecture of the Church of Greece (Reg. 247/2013, Article 32 of L. 4495/2017). Its purpose is to control and review ecclesiastical architectural matters.

216. The Synodal Office of Pilgrimage Tours of the Church of Greece (Reg. 281/2015, Article 15 of L. 4582/2018). It aims to check the religious tourism in places of ecclesiastical pilgrimage.

B. Peripheral Organization

1. Archdiocese and Metropolises

217. The Church of Greece is administratively subdivided into the Archdiocese of Athens and the following metropolises (Article 11 SCCG):

(i) Of the *Autocephalous Church of Greece:* (1) Aitolia and Akarnania; (2) Argolis; (3) Arta; (4) Attica; (5) Gortyn and Megalopolis; (6) Mani; (7) Dimitrias and Almyros; (8) Zakynthos; (9) Ileia; (10) Thebes and Levadia; (11) Thera, Amorgos and Islands; (12) Thessaliotis and Fanariofarsala; (13) Kaissariani, Vyron and Hymettus; (14) Kalavryta and Aegialis; (15) Karysteia and Skyros; (16) Kerkyra and Paxoi; (17) Cephallonia; (18) Corinth; (19) Cythera; (20) Larissa and Tyrnavos; (21) Lefkada and Ithaca; (22) Mantineia and Kynouria; (23) Megara and Salamina; (24) Messinia; (25) Mesogaia and Lavreotiki; (26) Monemvasia and Sparta; (27) Nafpaktia and Eurytania; (28) Nea Ionia and Philadelphia; (29) Nea Smyrni; (30) Nicaia; (31) Paronaxia; (32) Patra; (33) Piraeus; (34) Peristeri; (35) Syros, Tinos, Andros, Kea and Milos; (36) Trikki and Staga; (37) Trifylia and Olympia; (38) Hydra, Spetses and Aegina; (39) Fthiotida; (40) Fokida; (41) Chalkida; (42) Karpenissi (Article 11 § 2 section b' CCCH); (43) Glyfada (Article 6 § 2 of L. 3027/2002); (44) Ilion, Acharnes and Petroupolis (L. 3822/2010); (45) Kifissia, Amarousio and Oropos (L. 3822/2010).

(ii) Of the *Ecumenical Patriarchal Throne:* (1) Alexandroupolis; (2) Verroia and Naoussa; (3) Grevena; (4) Didymoteichos, Oerstias and Soufli; (5) Drama; (6) Dryinoupolis, Pogoniane and Konitsa; (7) Edessa, Pella and Almopia; (8) Elassona; (9) Eleftheroupolis; (10) Zichna and Nevrokopi; (11) Thessaloniki; (12) Ierissos, Mount Athos and Ardamerio; (13) Ioannina; (14) Kassandreia; (15) Kastoria; (16) Kitros and Katerini; (17) Langadas, Liti and Rentina; (18) Limnos; (19) Maroneia and Komotini; (20) Methymna; (21) Mytilini, Eressos and Plomari; (22) Neapolis and Stavroupolis; (23) Nea Krini and Kalamaria; (24) Nikopolis and Preveza; (25) Xanthi and Perithorio; (26) Paramythia, Filiata and Giromerion; (27) Polyani and Kilkis; (28) Samos and Ikaria; (29) Servia and Kozani; (30) Serres and Nigrita; (31) Sidirokastro; (32) Sisanio and

Siatista; (33) Philippi, Neapolis and Thasos; (34) Florina, Prespes and Eordaia; and (35) Chios, Psara and Oinousses.

218. The foundation, merging or dissolution of metropolises is effectuated by law, whereas the territorial jurisdiction, the name and the seat of every metropolis presuppose a decision by the HSH, publishable in the Official Government Gazette.

219. The Archdiocese of Athens and every metropolis constitute a special legal entity of public law (Article 1 § 4 SCCG), subdivided into numerous territorial districts, the parishes. The archbishop and the metropolitans hold the hieratic rank of bishop. They comprise ecclesiastical authorities with the powers of administration and pastoring of the faithful (clergy and laity) in the respective ecclesiastical eparchy.

2. Metropolitan Council

220. This is a seven-member administrative organ which operates in the seat of the archdiocese and of every metropolis, aiming to assist the respective prelate in his work (Article 35 SCCG, as it has been substituted by Article 51 § 1 L. 4301/2014). When it convenes, it is presided over by the respective metropolitan in the context of the competencies provided for by Reg. 263/2014. Its main authorities relate to the operation of churches and parishes. Moreover, the metropolitan council drafts the budget and the annual report of the metropolis, it acts as a service council for vicars and deacons and it signs their wage forms.[156]

3. Parishes and Ecclesiastical Councils

221. Every metropolis is subdivided into several parishes. The parish is populated by the Orthodox Christians who reside in its district and have the respective parish church as their centre of worship. Thus, the parish with its parish church comprises the basic unit of organization of ecclesiastical life (Article 36 § 1 SCCG, CoS 940/2017). It is recognized as a legal entity of public law (Article 1 § 4 SCCG), and its boundaries are determined by the decision of the local metropolitan council.

222. The parish is founded by presidential decree, which is issued after the recommendation of the Minister of Education and Religious Affairs, as long as the following requirements apply (Article 36 SCCG & Article 3 Reg. 8/1979-1980):

(a) a number of residents, which varies according to the size of the towns/cities from three hundred to six hundred families, whereas in the villages and communities up to fifty families;
(b) an application by at least half of the number of the aforementioned families;

156. Papageorgiou, *Ecclesiastical law*, 253ff.

(c) the concurring opinion of the respective metropolitan council; and
(d) an advisory opinion from the respective municipal council.

223. The parish is dissolved or it merges with a neighbouring parish by presidential decree, as long as the number of families required for its establishment has decreased. The regions alongside the Greek borders constitute an exception since in what concerns them, the abolition or merging of parishes is not allowed (Article 36 § 5 SCCG).

224. The detailed organization and operation of all churches, parish or nonparish, are governed by the provisions of Regulations 8/1979-1980, 263/2014 and 305/2018, according to which the parish is governed by the vicar and the ecclesiastical council, who represent its legal entity both judicially and extrajudicially. The ecclesiastical council consists of five members and is comprised of the vicar as President and four laypersons as members, who are selected and appointed by the metropolitan council, following the recommendation of the metropolitan.

225. The members of the ecclesiastical council must:

(a) not have been convicted of a felony or a misdemeanour for offences such as theft, fraud, forgery, and extortion;
(b) be fairly educated;
(c) not be in judicial dispute with the church;
(d) not be held responsible for paying any monetary amount in their capacity as members of the ecclesiastical council;
(e) not owe money to the church; and
(f) be faithful and devoted children of the Church (Article 7 §§ 2–3 Reg. 8/1979–1980).

226. Furthermore, the election of council members who are related to each other and to the presiding vicar is prohibited, and so is the election of persons who at the same time have the capacity of member of an organ/organization of local self-administration which is in legal conflict with the church or has a salaried employment relationship with the church. The service of the members of the ecclesiastical council lasts for three years, always beginning on the 1 January of the year for which they have been appointed.

227. The property of ecclesiastical council members constitutes a rank that is honorary and without pay. It ceases when the council member resigns or is relieved of his duties, if the member ceased to reside in the vicinity of the parish, or if he is discharged, always by decision of the metropolitan council (Article 7 §§ 7–11 Regs 8/1979–1980, 263/2014).

228. The main responsibility of the ecclesiastical council is the drafting of the budget, and the annual report of the church. Every act of the ecclesiastical council is valid only after its approval by the respective metropolitan council. If the latter does not decide within two months from the submission, the act is executed.

4. Other Categories of Churches

229. Chapels and country churches: they by definition fall under the jurisdiction of the parish churches and, since they lack a legal personality (Article 1 Reg. 8/1979–1980), they cannot be the subjects of rights and obligations. The unified treatment of these two types of churches demonstrates that there is no legal difference between them and that their distinguishing feature lies in their urban (for chapels) or agrarian (for country churches) environment. In addition to the chapels which belong to parish churches, there are also those belonging to charitable foundations, educational institutions, and correctional facilities.

230. Pilgrimage Churches: in this category, we find those churches which, regardless of their prior legal regime and because of their special religious significance, reverted to public worship and were constituted as a distinct legal entity, subject to a specific regulatory regime. Since L. 590/1977 (SCCG) took legal effect, pilgrimage churches are legal entities of private law since they are not included in the ecclesiastical legal entities of public law which are enumerated in Article 1 § 4 SCCG. The vicars of pilgrimage churches are appointed by the metropolitan, after a recommendation on the part of the administration of the establishment to which the church belongs.

231. Private churches: they belong to natural persons, aiming to serve their religious needs and those of their families (Article 13 Reg. 8/1979–1980, Article 32 § 15 L. 4495/2017). When they are open to public worship, they are sealed by command of the metropolitan or are expropriated in favour of the closest parish or shrine church.[157] However, the public operation of the private church is allowed on the day of its celebration (Article 13 Reg. 8/1979).

232. Cemetery churches: they are distinguished into parish and non-parish cemetery churches. If they are parish cemetery churches, they operate in accordance with the provisions regulating parish churches (Article 14 § 1 Reg. 8/1979–1980); otherwise, we need to distinguish between cemetery churches in cities and towns having a population that is smaller or larger than fifty thousand inhabitants. In the first case, cemetery churches are governed by the closest parish church (Article 1 of L. 547/ 1977, Article 14 § 2 Reg. 8/1979–1980), while in the second, by the organizations of local self-administration. The positions of the vicars, cantors and sacristans in these churches are determined by decisions of the respective municipal councils. The vicars' positions are filled by decision of the respective metropolitan, whereas the positions of the cantors and the sacristans by decision of the mayor (Articles 1 and 2 of L. 547/1977).

157. CoS 264/2020: a private church which is used for public worship comes under the management and administration of the nearest parish church.

5. Vicars

233. *Vicars* serve the worshipping and spiritual life of parishioners, aiming at the spiritual and material progress of the parish. Each vicar presides over the respective ecclesiastical council. Vicars are distinguished into regular and extraordinary: married presbyters are appointed as regular vicars, whereas unmarried presbyters may be appointed as extraordinary vicars by exception. Their regime of service is today governed by the provisions of Reg. 305/2018. Today there are over eight thousand vicars serving in Greece. These vicars are divided into more specific employment categories, based on the criterion of their educational qualifications. They receive their wages and their pensions from the Greek state, but without being considered public servants.[158]

6. Cantors: Sacristans

234. The regime of cantors, their service and wages, is governed by the provisions of Reg. 176/2006. They are appointed by decision of the respective metropolitan, following the recommendation of the ecclesiastical council and a justified opinion of the Committee for the Evaluation of Cantors. Cantors leave their service with the completion of the 70th year of their age, which may be extended until their 75th year by decision of the respective metropolitan and consequently until their 80th year, if this is requested in writing by the cantor and there is a concurring opinion by the respective ecclesiastical council.

235. The legal relationship of sacristans with the church, where they serve, is governed by Article 53 of Reg. 2/1969. They are appointed and discharged by justified decision of the metropolitan, following an opinion by the ecclesiastical council. Sacristans leave their service upon completion of their 65th year of age.

236. Cantors and sacristans do not fall under the force of collective employment agreements. If they provide their services as their only means of livelihood and under full working hours, then the time during which they remain in service is considered pensionable. In addition, this time is also considered as constituting their years of previous employment for vicars and employees of the public sector and of legal entities of public law.

7. Monasteries

237. They are religious establishments whose purpose is to train the men or women dwelling in them according to the institutions of monastic tradition and life of the Orthodox Church (Article 39 § 1 SCCG, Reg. 39/1972). The monasteries of

158. *See* CoS 210/2020 on service status of parish priests.

the Church of Greece are recognized as legal persons of public law (Article 1 § 4 SCCG) and are founded or dissolved by presidential decree, which is published in the Official Government Gazette.[159]

238. Monasteries are usually distinguished into:

- *men's or women's,* using the criterion of the sex of those who dwell in them;
- *cenobitic or idiorrhythmic*, depending on whether the monks live together and are entitled to own private property;
- *episcopal or synodical stavropegic,* depending on the organ (local bishop or Synod) that exercises spiritual, administrative and canonical supervision;[160]
- *dominant or dependent:* the former enjoy administrative self-existence, whereas the most common form of a dependent monastery is the dependency (*metochi*), which has no legal personality and is subject directly to the dominant monastery.

239. The supervision of the monasteries consists in the approval of the tonsure of new monks, in the ordination of the Abbot after his election, in the examination of the canonical offences of the monks, in the review of the legitimacy of financial administration and more generally in the surveillance of the operation of each monastery according to the holy canons (Article 39 §§ 2 and 6 SCCG, Article 6 Reg. 39/1972). The patriarchal and stavropegic monasteries of the Ecumenical Patriarchate, as well as the dependencies of the Holy Sepulcher and of Mount Sinai, are exempted from the supervision of the regional prelate (Article 39 § 8 SCCG).

240. The internal organization and administration of each monastery are determined by its by-laws, which are drafted by the Abbot's council and put into effect when it is published in the official review 'Ekklisia' (Article 39 § 4 SCCG). If the monastery has no internal by-law, then the provisions of the Royal Decree of 28 July 1858 are implemented (Article 27 § 1 L. 4301/2014).

241. The administrative organs of every monastery are its Abbot and the Abbot's council, whose number of members is determined depending on the number of monks of every monastery by its internal by-laws. The Abbot and the members of the Abbot's council are elected by the brotherhood of the monastery if this has at least five monks.[161] If not, they are appointed by the decision of the local metropolitan. The Abbot who is elected by the brotherhood serves a lifelong term of service, but he can lose his position if he is convicted by an ecclesiastical court. The members of the Abbot's council serve a term that is determined by the internal by-laws of the monastery. If there are no internal by-laws, then they serve for five years (Royal Decree of 1858).

159. CoS 299/2016; CoS 1075/2019; CoS 14/2020.
160. Papastathis, *Nomocanonical studies*, 189–195; Papageorgiou, *Ecclesiastical law*, 269ff.
161. CoS 1393/2017; CoS 511/1983, EDDD 27 (1983) 189; CoS 1952/2000, NoV 49 (2001) 760.

242. The hermitage constitutes a special type of monastic establishment, as legal entity of private law (Article 50 § 2 of L. 4559/2018). Hermitages usually have the form of foundations and they operate according to their internal charter.[162]

C. *The Administration*

1. Acquisition and Loss of the Capacity of Church Member

243. The capacity of member of the Orthodox Church is generally acquired by way of a valid baptism, which is performed in one of the local Orthodox Churches. More specifically, a person becomes a member of the Church of Greece when on the one hand he or she has been baptized and on the other hand when he or she has acquired a residence within its territorial ecclesiastical jurisdiction.

244. Baptism is conducted in accordance with the Orthodox doctrinal teachings, namely by triple immersion in the holy baptismal water and a simultaneous invocation of the Holy Trinity. In an application of 'ecclesiastical economy', when the interested party is ill, baptism is conducted by the pouring of water over the candidate's head or by sprinkling of water. Baptism constitutes a sacrament, and it is administered by a clergyman in the rank of presbyter or bishop. The baptized person declares his request, which should be free of defects (duress, mental illness or any other disturbance of one's spiritual capacities, such as drunkenness). Error or misrepresentation does not have an impact on the validity of the baptism because of its ceremonial and sacramental character. However, baptism nowadays is performed during the candidate's preschool age.

245. It is possible that the stage of catechism precedes baptism. During catechism, the candidate is taught the principles of doctrinal faith and participates, to a certain degree, in the holy ceremonies.

246. Baptism is proven by certification of the clergyman who conducted the sacrament or by any other means. A licence from the bishop is not required to conduct a baptism. A valid baptism is not repeated, unless its effectuation is uncertain.

247. The selection and acquisition of one's first name are not connected to baptism. It constitutes an act relating to the care of the child as a person, and as such, it has to do with child custody. For this reason, both parents should decide about the

162. Chrysogonos, 'The constitutional protection of the holy monasteries in private law (hermitages/hesyxastiria) and the L. 4559/2018', NoV 68 (2020 1773–1790.

name of their child (Article 1518 CC).[163] The name that is registered on the child's birth certificate may be altered by judicial decision, unless it was given during the sacrament of baptism.[164]

248. The loss of the capacity of church member comes about by means of an explicit statement addressed to the respective ecclesiastical authority or by way of a person's indoctrination into another religion or creed. In every case, the exit from the church constitutes a right for every one of its members *(the right to change religious beliefs),* which is safeguarded in the Constitution in the context of the individual right of religious freedom (Article 13 C. & Article 9 ECHR). Finally, the loss of the capacity of church member occurs by necessity as a result of the imposition of the penalty of formal excommunication or 'anathema'. This penalty is imposed when grave ecclesiastical offences (such as cases of a sect or schism) are committed, and it results in the convicted person's complete removal from the body of the church. But it is always possible to return to the church, without the need for a new baptism; of course, it is required to follow a particular canonical procedure.

2. Clergy

a. Ranks of Priesthood and of the Clerical State

249. The most common meaning of the term 'clergyman' refers to the three higher ranks of priesthood: the deacon, the presbyter and the bishop, hieratic ranks that are acquired with the commission of the sacrament of 'ordination'. However, there are also three lower ranks, namely the subdeacons, the readers, and the cantors, who acquire this capacity by way of 'the laying on of hands', which is a simple ceremony and not a sacrament.

250. Ordination and the laying on of hands are conducted only by a bishop and their repetition is not allowed, unless they were not effectuated in a valid manner. Their performance is attested not only by the way of special documents, but also with any other lawful appropriate documentation. The capacity of Orthodox clergyman is uniform for all Orthodox Churches.

251. The performance of ordination and the laying on of hands are valid when certain requirements relating both to the Minister performing them and to the candidate are met cumulatively. The Minister conducting them should have: (a) the power to solemnize (to hold rites), (b) local authority and (c) personal authority.

252. The power to solemnize exists when the ordaining minister is a bishop, who lawfully acquired and holds his rank as bishop. For the lawful acquisition of the

163. Georgiadis/Stathopoulos, *The civil code*, Vol. VIII: *Family law (Articles 1505-1694)*, Athens 2007, 253–303.

164. *See also* ECtHR *Stavropoulos v. Greece* (52484/18/25.6.2020): the birth certificate must not contain information from which the religious beliefs of the child or his/her parents can be deduced.

bishop's rank, an ordination is required by three (or if necessary at least two) bishops, who preserve the 'apostolic succession'.[165] The term 'apostolic succession' refers to the dispensing of holy grace through an unbroken succession of ordinations by pre-existing bishops, a succession that is traced back to the Apostles. The interruption of apostolic succession, which is due to an 'ordination' by a person who did not hold the bishop's rank, impedes the further passing on of holy grace and, consequently, leads to the nullity of all subsequent sacramental acts or ceremonies. This nullity is incurable, even by way of exercising ecclesiastical economy, because of the doctrinal nature of apostolic succession. Furthermore, the ordination is not valid if the ordaining bishop had lost his episcopal state because of dethronement.

253. The bishop is locally competent as long as he conducts the ordination or the laying on of hands within the boundaries of his eparchy.[166] The bishop is personally competent when the clergyman or monk, who is being ordained, is already a clergyman or monk in a monastery of his eparchy.[167]

254. As for the person being ordained, a series of prerequisites should also apply cumulatively for him. These prerequisites are separated into positive and negative ones (also known as 'impediments'). Furthermore, it is necessary that a particular position is vacant for the clergyman.[168] The bishop who performs the ordination examines the fulfilment of the prerequisites relating to the person of the candidate through his own personal moral and disciplinary responsibility. As for the ordination into the bishop's rank, this investigation is conducted in the context of the procedure for inclusion in the registry of persons eligible for prelacy. The requirements are as follows.

255. Positive requirements:[169]

(a) The property of membership in the Orthodox Church.
(b) The candidate should be male.
(c) The completion of a certain age limit for each rank, which is 18 years of age for readers, 20 years of age for subdeacons, 25 for deacons,[170] 30 for presbyters (elders)[171] and 34 for ordination into the rank of bishop.
(d) Educational qualifications analogous to the rank into which the ordination will take place. These qualifications also constitute the criterion for the introduction of a clergyman into a specific category of wages.

256. Impediments (negative requirements).[172] The ordination is disallowed if the candidate:

165. Papageorgiou, *Ecclesiastical law*, 199; Troianos, *Lectures in ecclesiastical law*, 145ff.
166. Canon 35 (Canons of the Apostles), Canons 13 and 22 (Synod of Antioch).
167. Canon 16 of the First Ecumenical Synod, Canon 15 of the Synod of Sardica.
168. Canon 6 of the Fourth Ecumenical Synod.
169. Troianos, *Lectures in ecclesiastical law*, 163ff; Papageorgiou, *Ecclesiastical Law*, 198ff.
170. Canon 14 of the Synod in Trullo and Canon 16 of the Synod of Carthage.
171. Canon 14 of the Synod in Trullo and Canon 11 of the Synod in Neocaesarea.
172. Troianos, *Lectures in ecclesiastical law*, 164f; Papageorgiou, *Ecclesiastical law*, 200ff.

(a) is suffering from a mental illness or has a physical handicap that prevents him from exercising his hieratic duties;
(b) has conducted marriage which contravened the holy canons or had premarital sexual relations. For ordination into the bishop's rank, the celibacy or widowhood of the candidate is required;
(c) morally reprehensible behaviour, according to the judgment of the bishop who will be ordaining him;
(d) the lapse of a minimum time period since the ordination into the previous rank.

257. The loss of the clerical status occurs only in a compulsory manner, through dismissal from the clerical state, because resignation from priesthood is not allowed. Dethronement from prelacy and priesthood comes about with the imposition of a final sentence of dethronement or defrocking on the part of an ecclesiastical court, in which case the former clergyman returns to his former state of origin, namely that of laity or of monkhood. The acts committed by defrocked clergymen are null and they themselves are criminally liable if they continue to appear as clergymen (Article 175 § 2 P.C.: the offence of usurpation of the authority of a minister of the Eastern Orthodox Church or any other known religion in Greece). The defrocked clergyman reacquires the clerical state only with the granting of a pardon, without requiring but also without allowing his reordination.

b. Election of the Archbishop of Athens

258. When the see of the Archdiocese of Athens becomes vacant, the senior in priesthood metropolitan among the active metropolitans undertakes the duties of prolocutor. If he refuses or is otherwise impeded, the next metropolitan in line takes over, on the basis of the same criterion. Within five days from the day of the see's vacancy, the Permanent Holy Synod is convened under the chairmanship of the prolocutor, and it determines an extraordinary convocation of the Holy Synod of the Hierarchy, on a date that cannot be further than twenty days from the day of the see's vacancy.

259. All active metropolitans of Greek national origin are eligible for the position of archbishop, as well as those who are listed in the registry of candidates eligible for prelacy (Article 12 § 3 SCCG). The election is effectuated in one single session without any intermission, which is conducted in the Cathedral Church of Athens. The Minister of Education and Religious Affairs is present. The Minister must have been invited in writing at least forty-eight hours prior to the election; otherwise, the procedure may be nullified. If the Minister, although invited, does not attend, the assembly is considered valid. The HSH is in quorum if at least two-thirds of its members are present. The voting takes place by secret ballot, and it begins with the youngest member of the HSH.

260. The candidate receiving the absolute majority of all electors is elected the Archbishop of Athens. If during the first vote no candidate has the required majority vote, the voting is repeated immediately and without any interruption. If during the second vote, an absolute majority is again not reached, then the voting is repeated in the form of a run-off election, for a third and final time, and the candidate who is elected is the one to concentrate the most votes. In the event of a tie vote during the third voting session, the archbishop is elected by lots among those who received an equal number of votes (Article 15 §§ 2–3 SCCG).

c. Election of Metropolitans

261. When a metropolitan throne becomes vacant, the senior metropolitan among neighbouring metropolitans assumes the duties of prolocutor. The filling of the vacant metropolitan throne is performed by the HSH, within six months at the latest from the day of the vacancy. The filling of a vacant metropolis is effectuated either with the transfer of an active metropolitan from another metropolis of the Church of Greece or by election. In case of an election, those eligible for election are the ones listed in a special registry of candidates. The inclusion in this register presupposes Greek citizenship or Greek nationality, celibacy or widowhood, a degree from a School of Theology and an age of at least 34 years (Articles 17–22 SCCG).[173]

262. The election of a metropolitan is conducted by secret ballot in two phases. Initially, the members of the HSH write down three candidates on the ballots. From these candidates, the first three in votes continue to run for the second vote. In this second vote, the name of only one of the three candidates is written down on the ballot. The candidate who receives the highest number of votes is elected metropolitan.

d. Loss of the See of Archbishop or Metropolitan

263. This is in essence a person's dismissal from the administrative authority of archbishop or metropolitan (but not of prelacy itself), which comes about only in the following cases:

(a) by irrevocable decision of an ecclesiastical court, which imposes the sentence of dethronement, lifelong suspension or defrocking;
(b) by resignation from the see;
(c) because of incapacity in the performance of his duties, following the decision of a special committee (Article 34 §§ 3–6 SCCG);
(d) because of his permanent removal by decision of the PHS.

e. Special Legal Regime of the Clergy

264. In many cases, clergymen enjoy a special (and by definition privileged) treatment on the part of the Greek legal order. This special treatment in certain cases raises reasonable doubts as to the compatibility of such arrangements with Article 4 Const., which enshrines the general principle of equality. However, it should not be

---

173. Marinos, *Relations between church and state under the constitution of 1975 and the new statutory charter of the church of Greece*, 164–173.

overlooked that this principle on the one hand mandates the equal or similar treatment of all citizens who find themselves under the same or similar circumstances, and on the other hand, it allows the differential legal treatment of categories of persons, as long as they are subject to special circumstances which convincingly justify this different, dissimilar treatment.

265. Then again, under the perspective of the Constitution, the implementation of any privileged arrangement that is enacted for the clergy of the prevailing religion must also be extended to the religious ministers of other known religions, as this is prescribed by the constitutional principle of religious equality (Article 13 Const.). Who these persons are shall be judged in accordance with the provisions of the internal religious law of each religious community.

266. Private Law:

(a) The clerical state constitutes an impediment for the performance of religious marriage. If the clergyman loses his clerical state because of a final judgment of conviction by an ecclesiastical court, he may thereafter contract religious marriage as a layperson. Finally, the provisions of the Civil Code are implemented as concerns the divorce procedure for clergymen.
(b) Married clergymen inherit according to the general statutes of the Civil Code.
(c) Under canon law, the capacity of clergyman is incompatible with the undertaking of any commercial activity.[174] This fact does not influence the validity of commercial acts, but it does entail the initiation of disciplinary proceedings against the clergyman.

267. Penal Law:[175]

(i) *Abuse of minors to lewd acts* (current Article 342 PC): an adult who has sexual intercourse with a minor who has been entrusted with supervision or custody, even temporarily, shall be punished as follows: (a) if the victim has not reached the age of 12, with imprisonment of at least ten years; (b) if the victim has reached the age of 12 but not 14, with imprisonment; (c) if the sufferer has reached the age of 14, with imprisonment of up to ten years. An adult who makes gestures, suggestions or narrates or depicts or presents sexual acts to a minor who has been entrusted to supervise or guard him, even temporarily, shall be punished by imprisonment of at least six months.
(ii) *Violation of professional confidentiality* (Article 371 PC): clergymen, lawyers, notaries public, medical doctors, etc., are punished with a monetary penalty or with imprisonment of up to one year if they disclose private confidential information that they received because of their capacity. Under

174. Canons 3 of the Fourth Ecumenical Synod and 20 of the Apostles.
175. L. 4619/2019 abolished the crime of 'abuse of ecclesiastical office' (ex-Art. 196 PC), according to which the religious minister who during the exercise of his duties or in public and using his capacity was provoking or inciting citizens to hostility against state power or against other citizens had to be punished by imprisonment of up to three years.

the established case law, it has become accepted that the protection of this type of confidentiality is not limited only to what was said in the context of the sacrament of confession, but that it extends to include anything that someone has confided to a clergyman because of his capacity.

(iii) The performance of engagement separately from marriage as well as the performance of marriage without the licence of a bishop *are punishable by a sentence of imprisonment of up to one year* (Article 49 §§ 2–3 SCCG).

268. Procedural Law:

(i) When clergymen are summoned as litigants or as witnesses before criminal or civil courts or when they undertake a public service, they are not sworn in, but they give an affirmation invoking their priesthood or prelacy. This affirmation has the place of an oath with consequences of perjury if the clergyman knowingly provides a false affirmation.

(ii) Clergymen are not examined as witnesses for whatever they learned during the sacrament of confession (Article 339 Case 1 of the CCProc and Article 212 § 1 of the CCrimProc).

(iii) Personal detention, as a means of a writ of execution for the satisfaction of monetary claims, is not imposed against the clergymen of every known religion (Article 1048 Case d of the CCProc).

(iv) No licence by the principal ecclesiastical authority is required in order for a clergyman to appeal to courts (Article 57 § 4 SCCG).

269. Constitutional – Administrative Law. Just like all other citizens, clergymen also enjoy the individual rights that are enshrined in the Constitution and in the international treaties ratified by Greece. However, religious ministers of all creeds cannot be elected as mayors, councillors, regional governors or regional councillors (Article 70 1 L. 4604/2019). Moreover, a restriction of their right to establish associations (Article 12 § 4 Const.) may be imposed by law, but this is precisely the case with all employees of legal persons under public law.

270. Taxation Law. Members of the clergy are subject to the same taxation obligations as all other Greek citizens. But case law has accepted that any monetary amounts received by priests through the voluntary contributions of the faithful during the performance of ceremonies are not taxed.[176]

3. Monks

a. Definition and Differentiations

271. Monks are persons who have decided to devote themselves to the worship and service of God, offering in the context of a special ceremony (by the name of 'tonsure') vows for voluntary poverty, abstinence and obedience to their spiritual

176. Papageorgiou, *The tax regime of religions: Tax equality and religious freedom*, 137ff.

leader. This definition concerns only the monks of cenobitic monasteries, but not idiorrhythmic monks: the monks belonging in this latter category may have personal property.[177]

b. Acquisition of the Monastic Capacity

272. Admission into the monastic state is effected by way of the religious ceremony of tonsure. In tonsure, four locks of hair of the novice monk are cut off in a cruciform pattern and the novice takes three vows of: poverty, chastity and obedience. The tonsure takes place in the monastery in which the monk shall dwell.

273. The stage of postulancy precedes tonsure. Postulancy may last for a period of up to three years (15 L. 3414/1909). However, the abridgement of this time period or even the exemption from postulancy is permitted, by decision of the competent metropolitan, if special circumstances apply or if the candidate is a graduate or a senior undergraduate of an Orthodox School of Theology. The postulant should be at least 17 years of age; he should be celibate or a widow and childless, or if there are any children born to him, these children must have already completed their 18th year of age. If the postulant is married, then the written consent of his wife (or the husband in the case of a nun) is required for his or her acceptance (Article 9 Reg. 39/1972).

274. Tonsure presupposes the adulthood of the postulant, a vacant post in the monastery and a declaration of the will of the postulant which will be free from any defects (Article 5 L. 3414/1909, Article 9 Reg. 39/1972). As for the other criteria, anyone can be tonsured as a monk since there are no prerequisites based on education, nationality, origin or physical condition. Tonsure is performed by an elder (who is habitually the Abbot of the monastery), and it is corroborated by a written certification of the local metropolitan. The latter is based on a solemn affirmation of the Abbot's Council that the particular monk is registered in the 'monachologion', which is the official list of monks dwelling in the monastery (Article 4 L. 3414/1909, as this was amended by Article 1 of LD 1918/1942). This document of certification constitutes full (but not exclusive) evidence; however, rebuttal and counter-evidence by means of other documents are allowed.

275. 'Hieromonks' (or priest monks) are those monks who also possess the capacity of clergyman, a fact that has consequences (as we will find out) as to their rights of property.

276. The monastic state is considered a lifelong one, and it is not lost by resignation or by any other manner. Nonetheless, the constitutionally safeguarded right to religious freedom (Article 13 Const.), which also includes the right to change religious beliefs towards any direction, requires us to acknowledge that the decision to withdraw from monastic life cannot have any negative legal consequences.

---

177. Generally, *see* Panagiotakos, *System of ecclesiastical law during its enforcement in Greece*, vol. D: *The law of monks*, Athens 1957.

c. The Special Legal Regime of Monks

277. Monastic tonsure constitutes an impediment to marriage by religious ceremony. Furthermore, choosing a monastic life without the consent of one's spouse constitutes a reason for the irretrievable breakdown of the marital relationship and hence grounds for divorce.

278. Monks are not exempted from the obligation of military service (Article 13 § 6 L. 3421/2005). The monks or novice monks of Mount Athos comprise an exception because of the special regime applying there (Article 77 § 2 L. 3883/2010).

279. Property rights regime. Upon his tonsure, the monk loses his property, which *ipso jure* devolves to his monastery. From this property, all legal shares in favour of his heirs apparent are subtracted, as this is regulated on the basis of the general provisions of inheritance law in the Civil Code.

280. By exception of the vow concerning landlessness and lack of property, monks may acquire assets even after their tonsure (Article 99 of the Introductory Law to the Civil Code, which maintained in effect the pre-existing provisions of Articles 4, 17, 18, 19, 27 L. 3414/1909, Article 7 L. 4684/1930, Article 1 LD 1918/1942).

281. More particularly, any assets that they acquire by way of inheritance, bequest or donation, devolve to their monastery, while the monks themselves only maintain half of the usufruct. The monks attain ownership without any restriction to all assets that they acquire through their own individual work or any other cause.

282. As it is evident from the above-mentioned analysis, it is possible that the monk at the time of his death has individual property, as a result of his revenues (which accumulated from having one half of the usufruct) or from another lawful cause (e.g., the purchase of a plot of land with money deriving from the work of the monk as a hagiographer). Therefore this property devolves by 50% *ab indiviso* to the respective monastery of the monk and by 50% to the legal entity of the Church of Greece. The will of the monk is valid only if through it he disposed of his property or a part of it to other brothers or to novice monks of the same monastery.

283. According to the case law, hieromonks are exempted from the aforementioned special provisions, and their succession is permeated by ordinary (general) inheritance law as long as they reside outside the monastery, serving as vicars, preachers, teachers, etc. For the same reason, as it is self-evident, the same holds true for those hieromonks who were defrocked and were dismissed from their clerical state.

284. Pursuant to Article 33 SCCG, the holy vestments and the personal library of prelates devolve to the legal entity of the respective metropolis, as long as the deceased had not left a will of a different content.

285. It is at this point clarified that the aforementioned analysis relates to the monks of the monasteries of the Church of Greece. Different provisions govern the property regime of the monks of Mount Athos, of Crete and the Dodecanese (*see* following paragraphs).

4. Administrative Power over Persons

a. Prelates and Other Clergy

286. The Holy Synod of the Hierarchy exercises the highest supervision over all clergymen and monks, as well as on the ecclesiastical legal persons of the Church of Greece (Article 4 Case f' SCCG). However, the supervision exercised by the Permanent Holy Synod is considerably more effective because of its character as a permanent body. Finally, metropolitans exercise administrative authority over the clergy and the monks of their eparchy, whereas the monks are subject to the close supervision of the administrative organs of their monastery (the Abbot and the Abbot's council).

287. Prelates may be absent from their see within Greece for a time period that is longer than ten days (or for absence abroad regardless of time duration) after receiving a licence from the PHS (Articles 9 § 1 and 56 § 1 SCCG). The PHS also investigates the filings of complaints against prelates. If the complaint comes from a clergyman, it is served to the local metropolitan who within fifteen days transfers it to the PHS. If the complaint is filed by a layperson, it is served directly to the PHS.

288. The other clergymen are subject to the supervision and review of their respective metropolitan, who is the one to provide them with the relevant licence to travel within the Greek territory or abroad (Article 56 § 2 SCCG).[178]

b. Ecclesiastical Clerks

289. The legal regime of the (paid and unpaid) clerks serving in the numerous ecclesiastical legal entities is governed by the provisions of Regs 5/1978 and 315/2010 ('The Code for Ecclesiastical Employees').[179] Although the extensive provisions of the said legislative act regulate many employment issues of ecclesiastical clerks (such as their qualifications, the procedure of their appointment, promotion, transfer, and transference, their leaves, and disciplinary responsibilities), any issue that is not explicitly mentioned in Reg. 5/1978 is (according to Article 154 § 5 of the said Reg.) resolved by supplementary implementation of the respective provisions of the general Employee Code (L. 3528/2007).[180]

---

178. CoS 2336/1980.
179. Troianos/Papageorgiou, *Religious legislation: Special legislation – bibliography – case law*, 697–855.
180. Kondylis/Ktistaki/Tziraki, *Employees code*, Athens 2018.

5. Ceremonial Competence

290. The clergy in Greece is acknowledged with the double capacity to perform sacraments or other religious ceremonies on the one hand and to teach the faithful on the other hand.

291. According to the doctrinal teachings of the Church, there are seven sacraments: baptism, anointment, holy Eucharist, ordination or priesthood, confession, unction and marriage. The sacraments are valid as long as the clergyman performing them has this capability under ecclesiastical (and canon) law.

292. The sacrament of 'Eucharist' (or 'Holy Communion') is conducted by a bishop or a presbyter, whereas its transfer may also be performed by a deacon. Any members of the Church who have been administered the penalty of temporary excommunication may not participate in this particular sacrament.

293. When unction is performed, parts of the body of the faithful are anointed with holy oil with the purpose of healing ailments.

D. Ecclesiastical Justice

1. Introduction

294. The mission of the judiciary in the Orthodox Church of Greece is to examine ecclesiastical offences – committed by clerics or laymen – and to impose the relevant forms of censure or penalties.

295. An ecclesiastical offence is an act or omission by a member of the Church, which results in violation of one or more of the ecclesiastical canons or failure to comply with the lawful orders of the competent ecclesiastical bodies. Study of ecclesiastical offences falls within the field of substantive ecclesiastical penal law.

296. These provisions are the same for all local Orthodox Churches but certain differences can be found in the procedural provisions. When ecclesiastical procedure contains a regulatory lacuna, the provisions of ordinary penal procedural law apply *mutatis mutandis.*

2. Substantive Law: Ecclesiastical Offences

297. The conditions for an ecclesiastical offence are:

(a) the existence of a specific act;
(b) that that act is wrong;
(c) that that act can be imputed to the perpetrator; and

(d) that a punishment exists for the act.

The following acts are considered to be the most important ecclesiastical offences.

298. Apostasy: this is considered to be divergence from the Christian faith, which manifests itself by adherence to another religion, or acceptance of atheism or secularism. The reasons which lead to this act are irrelevant. The Church may impose the penalty of 'major excommunication' on the apostate [Articles 4 (i) and 6 (3) SCCG]. Of course, from the viewpoint of civil law, apostasy is nothing more than a manifestation of the right to religious freedom.

299. Heresy: this is denial of the fundamental dogma of the Orthodox faith, without changing religion. The penalty imposed is major excommunication.

300. Schism: this is severance of administrative ties with the church and establishment of or secession to another separate ecclesiastical organization. The 'schismatic' (compared to the apostate) remains a Christian and is not considered to be a heretic, provided the dispute relates merely to administrative issues rather than issues of dogma. The schism between the Orthodox and the Roman Catholic Church is considered to be a *schism of faith* because their dogmatic differences are of minor importance. Schismatic clerics are punished with discharge from the priesthood and the laity are punished with major excommunication.

301. Simony: this entails performing rites and in general providing ecclesiastical services in return for consideration which is as a rule, but not always, financial in nature. Clerics who commit this crime are punished with discharge from the priesthood and major excommunication, while the laity are punished with major excommunicated. A cleric who has committed simony and who at the same time is also an 'employee' (*in the sense of civil servant:* Article 13 Case a PC) is also deemed to have committed the crime of bribery (Articles 235–236 PC).

302. Sacrilege: this is stealing items dedicated to God, no matter where they are located. Any cleric who commits the crime of sacrilege will be punished with discharge from the priesthood, while monks or members of the laity will be excommunicated. Sacrilege is also punishable as 'major larceny' under ordinary penal law (Article 374 Case a PC) for which the punishment is imprisonment for up to ten years for the person who purloins items dedicated to the worship of any known religion. The question of whether an item is dedicated for the purpose of religious worship is a matter to be determined by the internal law of the relevant religious community.

3. Ecclesiastical Punishments

303. *Excommunication:* this penalty may be imposed on all members of the Church. There are two types of this punishment: minor and major excommunication.

304. *Minor excommunication* is imposed in relation to the sacrament of penance or confession and results in the person concerned temporarily being deprived of the right to receive the holy Eucharist. The purpose of this penalty is to exert moral pressure on any person who committed an ecclesiastical offence so that he conforms. If that is achieved, the penalty may be removed.

305. *Major excommunication* (or *anathema)* entails permanent (but not always final) severance of the person being punished from the body of the Church. This penalty is imposed very rarely, due to its major ecclesiastical and social gravity. For the same reason, major excommunication is today only imposed by the Church of Greece following a decision by the Holy Synod. This decision is taken by a qualified majority of two-thirds of all members of the Synod (Article 4 Case i and Article Case 3 SCCG).

306. In the past, major excommunication was imposed as a penalty to condemn viewpoints, which were deemed to be heretical. However, social reactions against the imposition of that penalty were always particularly intense. Major excommunication may, though, be revoked by the body which imposed the penalty where it is ascertained that the reasons for imposing it have ceased to exist.

307. *Discharge:* this penalty is only imposed on clerics at all levels and entails removal of their priestly role and placement of the cleric in the category he was in before he was ordained (i.e., monk or layman). Sacraments or rites which are performed by a cleric who has been 'defrocked' have no effect. In this case, the person performing those sacraments or rites not only commits a new ecclesiastical offence but will also be criminally prosecuted for impersonating an officer of the Eastern Orthodox Church (Article 175 PC) or misappropriation of the uniform if he continues to wear the clothing of a cleric (Article 176 PC and Article 56 of the SCCG).[181]

308. *Demotion:* when this penalty is imposed, the bishop is demoted in the priestly rank.

309. *Suspension:* when this penalty is imposed, the cleric is prohibited for performing rites or carrying on administrative duties, for such time as the penalty is in effect. Sacraments performed by a suspended cleric are valid, but the cleric himself

181. CoS 1111/2015: the penalty of discharge has a spiritual character as long as it does not affect the clergy's official relationship with the church. CoS 3385/2017: the penalty of discharging a clergyman constitutes a spiritual act and cannot be reviewed by the Council of State.

in performing them is committing a new, more serious ecclesiastical offence, insubordination. Under the current legislation, the maximum duration of the penalty of suspension is five years for unmarried priests and deacons, seven and a half years for married ones.

310. Loss of seniority in the hieratical ranking: this penalty entails the cleric being placed in the last position in the ranking among other clerics of the same grade.

311. Dethronement: this penalty may only be imposed on bishops and entails removal of their administrative powers. Since the bishop who receives such a penalty continues to be in the priesthood, he may rightfully perform rites, but must have the permission of the local bishop to do so.

312. Fine: this penalty is imposed on married clerics, and entails depriving them of their salary or pension for a specific time period.

313. Transfer: this entails moving the cleric or monk from the parish or monastery where he was serving or living.

314. Rebuke: this penalty can be imposed on clerics at all grades (and is known as *censure*, when imposed on prelates) or on monks.

315. It should be stressed that the ecclesiastical judge has a great degree of latitude when determining which ecclesiastical penalties are to be imposed, and at his discretion he must weigh up various issues, including:

(a) the severity of the ecclesiastical offence;
(b) the personality of the perpetrator;
(c) mitigating circumstances which may exist in relation to the accused (previous honourable life, noble sentiments, major poverty, the fact that the offence was committed under grave threats or was required by a person he was obliged to obey or on whom he was dependent, etc.);
(d) the fact that the offence was committed as a continuation of some previous inappropriate behaviour of the accused;
(e) heartfelt regret by the perpetrator and at attempt by him to redress the damaging consequences of his acts, etc.

316. Where the perpetrator commits the same offence again, that is grounds for imposing a more severe penalty.

4. Ecclesiastical Courts

317. L. 5383/1932 – a quite old and outdated piece of legislation in many respects, which is still in force, but with a plethora of amendments – specifies that the following ecclesiastical courts operate within the Church of Greece.[182]

318. Episcopal Court: one such court sits in each local metropolis and is comprised of the local metropolitan (bishop), acting as presiding judge, and two priests who are appointed to serve for a three-year term in office by the PHS on a proposal from the metropolitan.

319. Only the metropolitan has a casting vote, while the priests are simply entitled to express any differing view they may have in the minutes (Articles 2 and 5 L. 5383/1932).

320. The Episcopal Court tries ecclesiastical offences committed by clerics (priests and deacons) and monks within the metropolis, no matter where those offences were committed. It is also competent to try offences which were committed by any cleric or monk within the boundaries of the metropolis.

321. The Episcopal Court tries any offences which can be punished with the following penalties:

(a) rebuke;
(b) deprivation of salary or pension for up to three months or a fine;
(c) suspension for up to one and a half years for married clerics and up to one year for monks;
(d) confinement for up to fifteen days for married clerics and up to three years for unmarried clerics; and
(e) removal from office (Articles 10–11 L. 5383/1932).

322. However, if the offences committed are more serious and are punishable with more severe penalties, the Episcopal Court will declare that it has no competence to try the matter and will refer the case to the First Instance Synodical Court.

323. First Instance Synodical Court: this court is comprised of the top-ranking metropolitan – a member of the Holy Synod, who acts as presiding judge – and another four members of the PHS, drawn by lots at the first meeting in each synodical period (Article 13 L. 5383/1932). The members of the court remain in office for the duration of the synodical period.

182. It must be underlined that according to the standard jurisprudence of Council of State (*see*, for example, CoS 2518/2018), if the penalties imposed by the ecclesiastical courts affect the service relationship between clerics or monks and the Church or another ecclesiastical legal person, as well as the rights arising from this relationship, then ecclesiastical courts take the form of disciplinary councils. Generally *see* Papageorgiou, *Ecclesiastical Law*, 332ff.

324. The First Instance Synodical Court tries:

- at first instance, offences of priests, deacons and monks which the Episcopal Court is not competent to try; and
- at appellate level, appeals against the judgments of the Episcopal Court (Article 17 L. 5383/1932).

325. *Appellate Synodical Court*: this court is comprised of the Archbishop of Athens, who acts as presiding judge, and six metropolitans from the Synod, who are not members of the First Instance Synodical Court. This court's term in office is also one year and coincides with the synodical period (Article 14 L. 5383/1932). The Appellate Synodical Court tries appeals against judgments of the First Instance Synodical Court (Article 18 L. 5383/1932).

326. *First Instance Prelatic Court:* this court is comprised of all members of the PHS, other than the Archbishop of Athens, and is under the presidency of the most senior metropolitan (Articles 20–22 L. 5383/1932). As a first instance court, it tries the offences of prelates and may impose the penalties of:

(a) censure;
(b) suspension from all rites;
(c) dethronement; and
(d) discharge from the priesthood (Article 23 L. 5383/1932).

327. *Appellate Prelatic Court*: this court consists of the Archbishop of Athens, acting as presiding judge, and the fourteen most senior metropolitans, who are not members of the PHS. Seven of them come from the Autocephalous Church of Greece and the other seven from Metropolises of the New Lands (Articles 24, 25 and 26 L. 5383/1932). It tries appeals against the judgments of the First Instance Prelatic Court.

328. *Synodical Court:* this court is comprised of one-third of serving metropolitans (of whom there must be at least fifteen) appointed by lot from among all members of the prelacy (but all metropolitans who were on the PHS when the offences being tried were committed are excluded: Articles 28–29 L. 5383/1932). It tries at first instance and appeals the offences which the President and members of the PHS committed when performing their duties. It may impose all penalties which are commensurate with the rank of prelate (Article 30 L. 5383/1932).[183]

329. *Other jurisdictional bodies:* in addition to the ecclesiastical courts, various administrative ecclesiastical bodies are recognized as having judicial-type powers, such as:

183. Generally *see* Papageorgiou, *Ecclesiastical law*, 335f.

(a) the Holy Synod of the Hierarchy of the Church of Greece, which can impose the penalty of major excommunication (Article 4 Case i SCCG) and try objections to entry/non-entry of names in the list of persons eligible for election to the prelacy or deletion from that list (Article 21 § 3 and 22 § 3 SCCG);
(b) the Permanent Holy Synod, which can initiate criminal proceedings against prelates (Article 143 L. 5383/1932, Article 9 § 1 Case h SCCG) and decide on deletion of persons eligible for election to the prelacy from that list or not (Article 22 SCCG);
(c) the local metropolitan who among other things:
   (i) can initiate ecclesiastical criminal proceedings against clerics or monks within his jurisdiction;
   (ii) impose the penalty of suspension for up to thirty days for minor offences committed by clerics (after the accused is given the opportunity to provide a written or oral statement of defence) and up to six months, if the offence caused a scandal (Article 11 L. 5383/1932).

5. Overview of Ecclesiastical Procedural Law

330. Pretrial Procedure – Investigation: the pretrial procedure commences when ecclesiastical criminal proceedings are initiated either ex officio or following a criminal complaint. The criminal complaint relating to priests, deacons and monks must be filed with the secretary of the metropolis, while a criminal complaint against prelates must be filed with the secretariat of the PHS.

331. After criminal proceedings are initiated, the metropolitan either orders an investigation under oath or, if he considers that the offence is not serious, he may impose a penalty of suspension of up to thirty days on the accused after the accused is given the opportunity to provide a written or oral statement of defence. However, if the crime caused a scandal, the penalty of suspension of up to six months will be imposed (Article 11 & 100 L. 5383/1932).

332. The investigating judge will make every effort to identify the truth by using all evidence which is admissible under ecclesiastical procedural law: he may examine witnesses and the accused, carry out on-site inspections, examine documents and order the preparation of expert opinions (Article 106 L. 5383/1932). If it is necessary to carry out a house search or to seize exhibits, documents or items, the investigating judge will contact the local public prosecutor to request his assistance.

333. After the investigation is completed, the investigating judge will submit the case file and his written proposal to the metropolitan or, in the case where the accused is a prelate, to the PHS.

334. The competent investigating judge then has three possible courses of action he can choose from:

(1) he can cease any further prosecution of the case if he ascertains that there is insufficient evidence;
(2) he can order additional investigation; or
(3) he can refer the case to be tried by the competent court in each case.

335. Evidence: in ecclesiastical procedural law, evidence includes witness testimony, documents, on-site investigations, expert opinions and the statement of defence made by the accused (Articles 56–94 L. 5383/1932).

336. As in ordinary procedural law, the ecclesiastical judge freely weighs up all evidence, subject to the express restriction that the conviction of a cleric cannot be based on the testimony of a single witness *(testis unus testis nullus).* It also precludes the imposition of the obligation on the accused to take an oath.

337. Certain persons are considered to be unfit to give testimony, such as those who are not yet 14 years old, the mentally challenged, anyone convicted of perjury by an ecclesiastical or ordinary criminal court, certain relatives of the accused, and clerics in relation to everything they know deriving from the sacrament of confession (Article 68 L. 5383/1932).

338. By carrying out an on-site investigation, the ecclesiastical jurisdictional organ acquires a direct understanding of a specific true fact (Article 87 L. 5383/1932) and the provisions of ordinary criminal procedural law apply *mutatis mutandis* (Articles 180 et seq., CCrimProc).

339. The preparation of an expert opinion can be ordered when specialized knowledge is required to better understand certain facts, knowledge which the investigating judge or trial judge usually do not have. The opinion prepared by the expert can be written or oral (Articles 88–94 L. 5383/1932).

340. Main proceedings: the hearing before the ecclesiastical courts is conducted with limited public access; in other words, only clerics or monks can appear before the court (Article 118 § 2 L. 5383/1932 as in force following Article 11 § 2 L. 1700/1987). However, oral proceedings are also limited before ecclesiastical courts: the accused is invited to make an oral statement of defence but in all other respects the documents in the case file prepared in the pretrial stage are simply read out (Article 118 § 3 L. 5383/1932).

341. The accused is entitled to be represented by counsel who may be a cleric or attorney-at-law (Article 119 L. 5383/1932 as in force following Article 11 § 1 L. 1700/1987).

342. The judgments of ecclesiastical courts are taken by absolute majority. In the case of a tied vote, the opinion which is most lenient on the accused prevails (Article 95 L. 5383/1932). At the Episcopal Court in particular, only the metropolitan has a casting vote, while the vote of the two priests is simply advisory in nature (Article 5 L. 5383/1932).

343. Judicial remedies:

(a) A *stay of default judgment* may be ordered where the accused who is not in court has not been lawfully summoned to appear or was prevented from appearing in court, due to force majeure or other insuperable barriers. The request for a stay of default judgment must be lodged within ten days of service of the judgment on the accused. It will be tried by the same court which issued the judgment in the absence of the accused. If the grounds cited in the application are deemed to be well founded, the judgment will be quashed and the case once again tried from the outset (Articles 125–131 L. 5383/1932).
(b) An *appeal* may be lodged against the judgments of the Episcopal Court, the First Instance Synodical Court (where trying cases at first instance) and the First Instance Prelatic Court. An appeal is lodged in the same way as a request for a stay of default judgment. Both the deadline for appeal and for lodging it suspend the effect of the judgment, unless a penalty of suspension has been imposed. When hearing the appeal, the court may confirm it, modify it or send the case back to first instance, but may not put the accused in a worse position (Articles 133–149 L. 5383/1932).
(c) *Appeal to the Ecumenical Patriarch* (Article 44 § 2 SCCG). This appeal can be lodged within thirty days from service of the judgment of conviction if the penalties of suspension, dethronement or discharge from the priesthood are imposed. The case file must be sent to the Ecumenical Patriarchate within another thirty days. The deadline for lodging this appeal and sending it do not suspend the effect of the judgment.
(d) A *petition for review* (Article 4 Case j SCCG) can be lodged against a final judgment of any ecclesiastical court, which imposes any penalty on priests, deacons and monks. It is tried by the HSH and primarily seeks to address legal defects in judgments.

344. Enforcement (Execution) of Judgments: final judgments of the ecclesiastical courts (i.e., judgments which are not subject to a stay of default judgment or appeal) are enforceable throughout the entire territory of the Church of Greece.

345. If the person convicted refuses to comply with the judgment or commits the offence again, the judgments shall be enforced with the assistance of the local police, following a written order from the local prelate.

346. Enforcement of the judgment shall cease:

(a) upon the convicted person's demise;
(b) if the crime was characterized as non-criminal by a later law; or
(c) if the penalty is commuted. In the latter case, the penalty may be reduced or even fully removed. This will be done by presidential decree, issued on a proposal from the Minister of Education & Religious Affairs after an opinion is obtained from the local metropolitan and the PHS. A vital condition for this is that the person convicted has already served half of his sentence.

347. Relationship between ecclesiastical and criminal proceedings: when the same act constitutes an offence both in ecclesiastical law and in ordinary criminal law, the two proceedings before the ecclesiastical and ordinary criminal courts will be conducted in parallel, without the outcome in one affecting the commencement or conduct of proceedings of the other (Article 156 L. 5383/1932).

348. If criminal proceedings are proceeding against a cleric or monk, the local metropolitan (or the PHS, if the accused is a prelate) can request that the judicial authorities notify them of the case file and provide copies after the accused has made his statement of defence (Article 157 L. 5383/1932).

349. The ecclesiastical court can suspend its proceedings, against the cleric or monk, which are pending before it until the parallel criminal proceedings are finished (Article 57 § 3 SCCG and Article 158 L. 5383/1932).

350. The judgment of any of the courts will not exert any influence on the outcome of the same case before the other court (Articles 161–162 L. 5383/1932). However, if the cleric is convicted on the basis of a final judgment to imprisonment by an ordinary criminal court, the public prosecutor will immediately notify that judgment to the President of the Holy Synod and the competent ecclesiastical court will without delay declare the cleric discharged from the priesthood (Article 160 L. 5383/1932).[184]

351. In all events, the judgments of the criminal courts (irrespective of whether they acquit or convict the accused) will be notified by the public prosecutor to the metropolitan who is in charge of the cleric or monk (or the PHS if the judgments relate to a prelate) (Article 57 § 3 SCCG and 161 L. 5383/1932).

352. Relationship between ecclesiastical and disciplinary proceedings: one cannot preclude the same act being punished as an offence not only by the ecclesiastical courts but also by disciplinary bodies. This can occur when the cleric who committed the act also serves as a civil servant or an employee of a body governed by public law.

353. Under Article 98 of the 'Ecclesiastical Employees Code', the two procedures are independent of each other. The disciplinary judge, however, can suspend the disciplinary proceedings on exceptional grounds if parallel ecclesiastical criminal proceedings are pending.

354. A final judgment of an ecclesiastical court is binding on the disciplinary judge only in relation to the existence or non-existence of the true facts involved, but does not prevent the disciplinary body from issuing a decision to the contrary.

184. *See* CoS 3003/2014.

6. Critical Remarks: The Ecclesiastical Justice in Greece, as a Serious Deficit in the Constitutional Relations Between State and Orthodox Church

a. The Anachronistic Legal Framework

355. It is obvious from what has been written that the administration of justice in the Greek Orthodox Church, which is still governed by the provisions of L. 5383/1932, is quite anachronistic. The ecclesiastical trial is not 'fair', given that it is organized in an unequal manner and its nature is solely repressive. The institutional framework of L. 5383/1932 should be replaced by a legal instrument in line with the procedural provisions of the Greek Constitution and the European Convention for the Protection of Human Rights and Fundamental Freedoms.

356. During the last two decades, in particular, the public in Greece has been exposed to many cases of ecclesiastical criminal justice, which, due to their particular importance, have crossed the boundaries of the ecclesiastical world, giving rise to public debate. Apart from the substantive part of these cases (i.e., the investigation of complaints as to the actual disciplinary offences committed by clergymen), the interest of the public and of many legal practitioners has focused on the procedural rules governing the administration of ecclesiastical criminal justice.

357. The noteworthy criticisms expressed to this day by many Greek scholars in the areas of constitutional, ecclesiastical and criminal law with regard to the institutional framework governing the relations between the State and the Orthodox Church in Greece have primarily focused on the unconstitutional organization and operation of the so-called ecclesiastical courts. These are special bodies of the Church, established by L. 5383/1932, 'On ecclesiastical courts and the procedures therein', in view of hearing the offences of clergymen and monks and imposing the corresponding sanctions.[185] As it has been already said, these bodies include 'Episcopal Courts', 'Synodical Courts', and 'Courts for Bishops and Members of the Holy Synod'.

b. Regulations of Law 5383/1932 Contravening the Constitution

358. With a few exceptions, both theory and case law agree that the organization and the operation of ecclesiastical courts do not meet the fundamental procedural guarantees provided for by the Greek Constitution and the European Convention for the Protection of Human Rights and Fundamental Freedoms (ECHR) regarding the administration of justice.

185. Article 1 L. 5383/1932: 'On ecclesiastical courts in general. In view of maintaining ecclesiastical discipline and sanctioning clergymen and monks who violate their duties and commitments, the following ecclesiastical courts shall be established: (a) Episcopal Courts, (b) First and Second Instance Synodical Courts, (c) First and Second Instance Bishop Courts, (d) Synodical for Metropolitans Court. In accordance with this law, "clergymen" shall mean bishops, priests, deacons and subdeacons. "Monks" shall also include nuns.'

359. Thus, the rulings of such ecclesiastical bodies can neither be considered as fair and just nor as guaranteeing the fundamental rights of the defendant clergyman or monk. Among the various problematic provisions of L. 5383/1932, this criticism primarily focuses on the following matters.

360. The focus is on the composition and operation of the three-member Episcopal Courts, because in such courts:

(a) the presiding judge is the metropolitan who happens to be the hierarchical superior of the defendant clergyman;
(b) the same metropolitan also exercises the functions of prosecutor-examining judge in the same case;
(c) the other two members of this sui generis court are not only clergymen falling under the hierarchical authority of the metropolitan-presiding judge, appointed in practice by him as members of the court, but also, in accordance with L. 5383/1932, only have an advisory and not a decisive vote (only the metropolitan-presiding judge has such a decisive vote).[186]

361. Thus, the defendant and the other 'judges' of the Episcopal Court fall under the absolute and centralized authority of the metropolitan-presiding judge, who is also their hierarchical superior. In order to understand the quality of justice delivered by the aforementioned ecclesiastical body, it should be noted that only in rare occurrences do the presiding judge and its members have the slightest legal knowledge.[187] Thus, it is probably unnecessary to point out that the aforesaid metropolitan-presiding judge becomes completely uncontrolled in a manner reminiscent of rather dark moments of the Middle Ages and the Holy Inquisition.

362. Moreover, as contrary to the principle of fair trial must be seen:

- the problem of lack of full publicity in the hearings, as provided for by Article 93 § 2 C. for ordinary courts;[188] and

---

186. Article 2 § 1 L. 5383/1932: 'The Episcopal Court shall convene at the Metropolitan See and in the Metropolitan's office. It shall be made up by the relevant Metropolitan as presiding judge and two acting priests of the Metropolitan See district as regular members … who may only be appointed and dismissed by the Holy Synod, upon proposal of the relevant Metropolitan'; Art. 5: 'The Metropolitan shall have the only decisive vote at the Episcopal Court. The priests, members of the court, shall only have an advisory vote, but they shall be entitled to have their dissenting opinion entered in the court's record.'
187. It should be emphasized that, in order to ensure the fair administration of justice, the Greek Constitution provides (Art. 87 § 1 & 88 § 1 Const.) that the courts shall be composed of regular judges, who shall enjoy functional and personal independence and who shall be appointed for life. As appropriately noted by Professor of Criminal Law, Androulakis, *Fundamental concepts of the criminal trial,* Athens 2007, § 38: 'In any event, the criminal judge, in particular, should be *functionally* and *personally* (Art. 87 § 1 Const.) independent and, in addition, to the extent possible, *internally* independent, i.e., fair and unbiased.'
188. Androulakis (§§ 221 et seq.) notes that in the past the secrecy of the courts' hearings could cover any kind of judicial arbitrariness and abuse.

– the refuse of the Church – until recently – to provide the defendant clergyman or monk with the possibility of fully and substantially defend himself. Lately, the accused clergymen obtained the right to appoint an authorized lay attorney-at-law at the ecclesiastical court.

363. Only in 1987 (i.e., after fifty-six years) did the Greek State decide at last (ignoring the pressuring reactions of the Church administration) to adopt Article 11 of L. 1700/1987, recognizing for defendant clergymen or monks their unalienable constitutional right (given that they remain Greek citizens) to appoint an attorney-at-law as counsel to defend them before ecclesiastical courts. At the same time, this provision made a hesitant step forward by introducing the restricted publicity of the hearings of ecclesiastical courts, allowing them to be attended (only) by clergymen and monks.[189]

364. However, until recently, the administration of the Greek Orthodox Church officially refused to apply Article 11 of L. 5383/1932, insisting on supporting the (anachronistic and, in any event, unconvincing) view that the aforementioned (abolished) provisions of L. 5383/1932 should be understood 'within the sacrament of Church' because they were an expression of the 'spiritual character and purpose' of the holy canons.[190]

365. On the other hand, the Council of State[191] has, in many cases, annulled the rulings of ecclesiastical courts[192] for refusing to apply Article 11 of L. 5383/1932.[193] In one of them (CoS 1294/2003), it appropriately ruled that 'the possibility of a person under disciplinary prosecution to obtain, as long as he so wishes, the

189. Thus, Arts 118, 119 and 140 of L. 5383/1932, allowing the defence of a clergyman only by another clergyman-counsel (but not by a lay attorney-at-law) and completely prohibiting any publicity of the ecclesiastical trial, were abolished.

190. Document of PHS no 396/1999 addressed to the Minister of National Education and Religious Affairs, E. 76 (1999) 51–52.

191. The Council of State, being the Supreme Administrative Court in Greece, may annul the decisions of administrative authorities for violation of the law (Art. 95 Const.). *See* CoS 2205/2020, 390/2020 and 723/2020: the acts of the ecclesiastical authorities that are of a spiritual nature are not subject to cassational review by the Council of State.

192. It should be emphasized that, through the landmark judgment no 825/1988, the Council of State (Plenary Session) turned away from its previous case law, now accepting that, when ecclesiastical courts impose sanctions which are not only 'spiritual' but also directly affect the clergyman's employee status (such as salary deprivation, pecuniary penalty, and suspension), they have the character not of courts but of administrative bodies ('disciplinary councils'), and therefore their rulings are scrutinized by the Council of State. In order to understand this reasoning by the Council of State, it should be specified that L. 536/1945 and 469/1968 established the remuneration of the Orthodox Church priests and deacons by the Greek State. Today, it is estimated that the number of clergymen remunerated by the State is approximately 8,570, with a decreasing trend, given that some unwillingness has been noted regarding entering the ranks of the clergy.

193. Relevant judgments of CoS 4595/2014, 3824/2012, 644/2010, 3490/2009, 988/2006, 1023/2006, 1190/2006, 988/2006 (according to which: 'the possibility for clergymen, where prosecuted for disciplinary offences, to appoint before any ecclesiastical court, as their counsel, also a lay authorized attorney-at-law is an expression of their right to be heard, Arts 20 § 2 of the Constitution and 6 § 3 of the ECHR'), CoS 1123/2005, 4120/2005, 1294/2003, 2928/1996 and many others.

assistance of an authorized attorney-at-law as his counsel before the competent disciplinary council is an expression of his right to be heard. Such right is enshrined in the provision of Article 20 § 2 Const., as interpreted in conjunction with the provision of Article 6 § 3 ECHR. Therefore, the Constitution does not allow the legislature to exclude this possibility in proceedings before ecclesiastical courts'.

c. Points of Criticism

366. Serious reservations can be expressed with respect to the accuracy of the aforementioned official position of the Church administration, according to which the ecclesiastical trial, as performed in accordance with the provisions of L. 5383/1932, has a 'spiritual' and 'sacramental' character.

367. The aforementioned view limits itself to a general and vague reference to 'Canon Law' as its foundation, omitting however to name the specific holy canons upon which it believes it is based. However, in my view, such references should either be seriously documented, in order to be more convincing, or be completely avoided.[194] Furthermore, said view insists on shrouding with a 'sacramental' veil the numerous legal problems of the ecclesiastical trial, while ignoring the fact that, if the Church wishes:

(a) to be united with the Greek State;
(b) to constitute – both itself and its organizational subdivisions – legal persons governed under public law;[195] and
(c) to have its clergymen assimilated to civil servants both as regards their status and their salary, the Orthodox Church should itself be institutionally in line with the requirements of the Constitution, good administration and the rule of law (i.e., just like all other public bodies).[196]

368. It is quite obvious that those who have faced the ecclesiastical courts as defendants, i.e., ordinary priests, deacons and monks, do not agree at all with the view on 'sacramental spiritualism' of such courts. On the contrary, the association representing them, the 'Holy Association of Greek Clergymen', has repeatedly expressed strong criticisms regarding the operation of ecclesiastical justice,[197]

194. This tactic – which is unfortunately very common in the Orthodox Church – raises reasonable doubts about the real knowledge of canon law. In addition, it undermines in general the validity of any reference to the holy canons, which are used as a corpus from which it is possible to derive 'confirmation' of any predefined position.
195. In accordance with Art. 1 § 4 of L. 590/1977 (SCCG), the Autocephalous Church of Greece and its organizational subdivisions (metropolitan sees, parishes and parochial churches, monasteries, etc.) are legal persons of public law. Due to this quality, ecclesiastical legal persons have become public authority bodies. Today, many scholars claim that the Orthodox Church has become a 'State' Church, having lost a large part of its autonomy.
196. This antinomy ('State' Church – self-government) is one of the symptoms of the current status of the relations between State and Church in Greece today.
197. *See* denouncement under the title: 'Double standard applied by Bishops', in newspaper *Eleftherotypia* (27-1-1999), according to which: 'In ecclesiastical courts, the metropolitan is both prosecutor and examining judge or assigns the investigation to a priest who blindly obeys him.'

denouncing, *first,* that it is administered unequally towards metropolitans and the rest of the clergy, aiming at the authoritarian discipline of the latter (which are the weak party), and, *second,* that they themselves would prefer, instead of the 'sacramental-spiritual' (i.e., uncontrolled) character of ecclesiastical courts, the organization and operation of such courts in accordance with the guarantees provided by the 'secular' Constitution.

369. It is interesting to note what a prominent ecclesiastical law expert wrote,[198] rather eloquently, on the same subject:

> Contrary to all notions of elementary justice, the defendant clergyman is deprived of the right to appoint an attorney-at-law to defend him, but has to accept as his counsel an elderly, as a rule, priest, who is afraid of losing the favours of the metropolitans 'judges'. As a consequence, he may become a defendant himself after a while, for not showing his superiors due respect/ submission. It is a common secret that our ecclesiastical justice has always been administered very rigorously only to deacons, priests and monks.

370. So let us be more realistic. One cannot fail but notice that the aforementioned document issued by the PHS expresses the views of its bishop members (metropolitans), who come to ecclesiastical courts almost always to occupy the seat of presiding judge, and only rarely to seat in the defendant's dock. Suffice it to say that, while in the last two decades hundreds of ordinary clergymen have been condemned by ecclesiastical courts without having been allowed an attorney-at-law, at trials with no publicity and no respect for the fundamental constitutional guarantees, only two (!) cases regarding complaints against bishops have reached the ecclesiastical courts.

371. In one of them,[199] while obstinately refusing up to that moment to apply Article 11 of L. 1700/1987 regarding the rights of the rest of the ordinary clergy, the Holy Synod, on the contrary, allowed this metropolitan to be defended by an attorney-at-law as well as restricted publicity of the hearing of the case.

372. In the second case, the defendant before the same ecclesiastical court was the former metropolitan of Attica charged with numerous violations of the criminal legislation and for having caused public scandals. However, as can be noticed from the procedure followed by the ecclesiastical court as well as the voluminous relevant legal literature, in spite of the very serious charges he faced, that have been widely discussed, said bishop was treated by many of the members of the court in a favourable manner that would have been completely unthinkable for an ordinary clergyman.

---

198. Panagopoulos, *Ecclesiastical law*, Athens 1980, pg. 489.
199. Extensive coverage has been exposed by the newspaper *The News*, 20 Jan. 1999, pp 20–21).

d. Conclusions: Suggestions

373. Therefore, the ecclesiastical trial should also comply with the guarantees of 'fair trial'. Ecclesiastical courts should effectively operate as bodies administering justice and not as means to repress and oppress the lower clergy. To this end, it has become imperative to replace the anachronistic L. 5383/1932 by a modern legal instrument, in line with the Greek Constitution[200] and the ECHR.[201]

374. In my view, these requirements are adequately covered by the 'Draft law on ecclesiastical justice', prepared in 1987 by Professor of Ecclesiastical Law at the Law Faculty in University of Thessaloniki Charalambos Papastathis.[202] Said draft has been submitted for further elaboration on 5 May of the same year to the 'Committee for studying the relations between State and Church', set up by decision of the then Minister of National Education and Religious Affairs, Antonis Tritsis.

375. Unfortunately, the Committee did not have the time to complete its work, including the elaboration of the aforementioned draft, whose main innovations can be described as follows:

(a) Setting up of a special body of ecclesiastical judges, consisting of priests and deacons, participating with full rights in the composition of ecclesiastical courts.
(b) The metropolitan acting as examining judge shall not be a member of the court trying the defendant clergyman.
(c) A judge from ordinary justice shall also participate in all ecclesiastical courts, to be nominated with a three-year mandate.
(d) The defendant's counsels (attorneys-at-law or clergymen) shall be present in all procedural acts of the trial (pretrial proceedings and main proceedings).
(e) The hearing of ecclesiastical trials may be attended by clergymen, monks and relatives of the defendant (limited publicity).
(f) Defendants before ecclesiastical courts shall enjoy all guarantees and rights provided for by the common procedural law before the State's criminal courts.

376. However, it would appear that the time is not ripe yet for the Church administration to abandon its authoritarian perception of ecclesiastical courts as a repression mechanism against ordinary clergymen or monks. This can be deduced from the decision of the Holy Synod of the Church of Greece, adopted in October 2009, according to which, although a Special Lawmaking Committee has been established for drafting a new law on ecclesiastical justice, *not one ordinary clergyman or monk was invited to participate in said Committee.* And this, in spite of the fact that, as already explained, the law under elaboration – provided it shall

200. One should not overlook the fact that clergymen and monks maintain, including after their ordination or tonsure, the quality of citizens, with all constitutional rights and obligations that it entails.
201. In accordance with Art. 28 § 1 Const., the ECHR supersedes the provisions of any domestic law, therefore also L. 5383/1932.
202. Ch. Papastathis, 'Draft law on ecclesiastical justice', Arm Scientific Yearbook 19 (1998) 49–77.

become one day a law of the State after its adoption by the Greek Parliament – will certainly be applied almost exclusively to said ordinary clergymen.

377. Therefore, our hopes lie with the Greek Parliament and the Council of State, that, being the institutional expressions of the legislative and judicial powers, should never allow the validation or implementation of a legal instrument on ecclesiastical justice, not in line with the fundamental procedural guarantees provided for by the Constitution and the ECHR, such as should be implemented by any modern rule-of-law state.

II. The Semi-autonomous Orthodox Church of the Island of Crete

A. Statutory Regime

378. The Orthodox Church of the Island of Crete is administratively semi-autonomous, subject to a canonical dependence on the Ecumenical Patriarchate of Constantinople (Article 1 L. 4149/1961, 'Statutory Charter of Church of Crete', SCCC).[203] This sui generis ecclesiastical regime – which today only applies to the aforementioned regional Orthodox Church – is characterized by a limited degree of self-administration vis-à-vis the Patriarchate, which does not however reach the status of 'autonomy'. The provisions of L. 4149/1961 specify in greater detail the content of the relationship between the Church of Crete and the Ecumenical Patriarchate.[204]

B. Administrative Organization: Provincial Synod

379. The Church of Crete consists of the Archdiocese of Crete, whose seat is in the city of Heraklion, and eight metropolises (Dioceses), which all are recognized as legal persons in public law. The archbishop and the metropolitans (bishops) are members of the Provincial Synod of Crete, which meets in Heraklion. The Synod is convened by the archbishop regularly, at least three times a year, and on an extraordinary basis following a decision of its chairman or following a request by the majority of its members or by the government (Articles 2–3 L. 4149/1961).

380. The metropolitans are elected by the Provincial Synod, using procedures similar to those which apply to the Church of Greece. The Archbishop of Crete, however, is elected by the Synod of the Ecumenical Patriarchate, chosen among

---

203. Troianos/Papageorgiou, *Religious legislation: Special legislation – bibliography – case law*, 1351–1407.

204. The foundation of this regime is the convention signed by the Ecumenical Patriarchate and the Cretan Polity on 14 Oct. 1900. Although attempts were made to enact a more recent version of the Charter which would address the shortcomings of L. 4149/1961, this has not been possible thus far. *See* generally Papageorgiou, *The orthodox church of Crete: Institutions and administrative organization under its statutory charter (L. 4149/1961)*, Chania 2001; *ibid.*, 'Le cadre nomocanonique des relations du Patriarcat wcumenique avec TEglise semi-autonome de Crete', Contacts, 133–148.

three active metropolitans of the Church of Crete (Article 19 L. 4149/1961, as it has been modified by Article 52 L. 4310/2014).

381. Pursuant to the authorization of Article 43 § 6 of L. 3848/2010, the Provincial Synod of Crete may by way of its decisions, which are approved by the Synod of the Patriarchate, issue ecclesiastical regulations and administrative acts of regulatory content, published in the Official Governmental Gazette. These acts regulate the internal affairs of this regional church, such as the organization and the operation of the Provincial Synod, of the archdiocese and the metropolises, as well as of the various ecclesiastical legal entities (churches, parishes, monasteries and so on).

382. Up today have been published Regulations 1/2013 'on vicars and deacons', 2/2014 'on composition, convening, operation and responsibilities of metropolitan councils', 3/2015 'on the organization, responsibilities, composition, operation of the Church Architecture Council of Crete and Dodecanese and the Building Service Of Crete', 4/2015 'Code of ecclesiastical employees of the Church of Crete', 5/2015 'on the publication of the official bulletin 'Apostle Titus' of the Church of Crete', 6/2015 'Synodical Office of the Holy Provincial Synod of the Church of Crete', 7/2015 'on Holy Temples and Parishes'.

C. *Churches and Monasteries*

383. The regime governing the churches and the operation of metropolitan and ecclesiastical councils which at different times applies to the Orthodox Church of Greece is implemented by analogy to the Church of Crete (Article 54 L. 4149/1961).

384. The monasteries of the Church of Crete can be divided into two categories, depending on the organ exercising spiritual supervision:

(1) monasteries which are supervised by the local metropolitan; and
(2) patriarchal stavropegic monasteries, which are supervised by the Patriarchate of Constantinople.

385. The monasteries are governed by a monastic council, which is comprised of the Abbot and two councillors (Articles 101–106 L. 4149/1961). The Abbot is elected by the brotherhood of the monastery or is appointed by the local metropolitan, whereas the councillors are elected by the brotherhood. The Abbot and the councillors serve for a four-year term, but they can be removed before that term ends if they are convicted by a court of law.

386. The monastic state (or monkhood) is acquired by an adult by way of tonsure, after an initiation period of three years. A novice monk may, before his tonsure, dispose of his assets by acts *inter vivos* or by way of a last will and testament. The monastery shall only acquire whatever property the monk donates to it and whatever the monk acquires as a product of his labour after the tonsure. From that amount, the monastery will acquire one-third, while the rest shall remain under the ownership of the monk. He may freely dispose of property he owns either by way of acts *inter vivos* or by means of a last will and testament (Article 124 L. 4149/1961). However, if the monk dies intestate, his entire estate will devolve to the monastery, apart from the lawful share which his family members are entitled to by law.

D. *Ecclesiastical Justice*

387. The ecclesiastical offences committed by priests, deacons and monks are tried in the first instance by the First Instance Episcopal Court. It is comprised of the local metropolitan and two presbyters, who are appointed for a three-year term of service by the Synod. More serious offences are tried by the Appellate Episcopal Court (Article 62 L. 4149/1961), comprised of the Archbishop of Crete and two metropolitans, who are appointed for a term of one year by the Synod. This court also hears appeals against the judgments of the First Instance Court.

388. The Provincial Synod tries the following offences as a First Instance Synodal Court (Article 65 L. 4149/1961):

(a) offences committed by metropolitans, entailing a penalty of suspension for up to six months; and
(b) offences committed by presbyters and deacons, which entail the penalty of defrocking;
(c) on the appellate level, it hears appeals against the judgments of the Appellate Episcopal Court.

389. Lastly, the Synod of the Ecumenical Patriarchate tries:

(a) in the first instance, all offences of the Archbishop of Crete and all offences of metropolitans, which entail a penalty that is heavier than a six-month suspension;
(b) on the appellate level, appeals against the judgments of the First Instance Synodal Court.

390. As concerns the civil procedures adopted by the Church of Crete (judicial remedies, stays of judgment, appeals, and enforcement of judgments), the provisions which at various times apply for the Church of Greece are primarily implemented.

III. The Ecclesiastical Provinces (Eparchies) of the Dodecanese

391. According to the Treaty of Paris, signed on 10 February 1947, the Dodecanese islands, which until then had remained under Italian rule, were annexed to Greece.

392. The six ecclesiastical provinces (eparchies) of the Dodecanese (five metropolises and the patriarchal exarchy of Patmos)[205] are still subject to the direct spiritual and administrative jurisdiction of the Ecumenical Patriarchate, a fact which has become constitutionally accepted (*see* Article 3 § 2 Const.). Pursuant to Article 22 § 2 L. 4301/2014, the metropolises, the temples and the monasteries of the Dodecanese are legal entities under public law.

393. The six metropolitans of the Dodecanese are elected by the Holy Synod of the Ecumenical Patriarchate, a body in which they also participate.

IV. The Monastic State of Mount Athos

A. *Historical Developments*

1. Byzantine Period (Ninth Century-AD 1430)

394. Organized monasticism on the peninsula of Mount Athos first emerges in the mid-ninth century. Special weight must be given to the sigil (signet) granted in AD 883 by the Byzantine Emperor Basil A' the Macedon (867–886). This sigil granted the Athonite monks, for the first time in history, self-administration, tax exemption and territorial sovereignty over Mount Athos.[206] The sigil, which was ratified by succeeding emperors with respective documents,[207] established thereafter a *regional privileged regime of self-administration*[208] in the peninsula of Mount Athos.

395. The arrival of Athanasios Trapezountios, the monk at Mount Athos, signals for the citizens of Athos (hereinafter 'Athonites') a turning point from archaic solitary life to a developed form of communal monasticism (cenobitic). At about AD 963, Athanasios, relying upon the financial support of Emperor Nikiforos Fokas (963–969) and using as his basic model the Stoudhios monastery in Constantinople, founded the Megisti (Great) Lavra monastery. This incident alone initiated the

205. Nikitaras, *Patriarchal exarchy and holy monastery of Patmos*, Katerini 2005.

206. Papachryssanthou, *Actes du Protaton, Edition diplomatique, Archives de l'Athos VII*, Paris 1975, 156; *ibid., Athonite monasticism: Principles and organization*, 23ff.

207. Such as Leo VI the Wise (886–912) in AD 908 and Roman A' the Lecapin (919–944) in AD 934.

208. As it is very accurately stressed out, the very publication of an imperial sigil presupposes that the Athonites comprise a totality (a legal entity), which through an organization, albeit a simple one, acts on behalf of all monks. And there is no doubt that it is the representatives of this organization who are in possession of that sigil and, as it is stated in the document itself, present it to the authorities when there is a need to do so (*see* above Papachryssanthou).

establishment of many other great monasteries in the upcoming centuries (Iviron, Vatopediou, Aghiou Pavlou, Xiropotamou, Dohiariou, Esphigmenou, etc.).[209]

396. Shortly afterwards, Athanasios drafts the 'Typikon' (i.e., the internal by-laws) of the Megisti Lavra monastery, subsequently appending to it two more documents, of similar institutional content: the 'Diatyposis' and the 'Hypotyposis'. These regulatory manuscripts laid the foundations for the communal organization of Mount Athos.

397. Nevertheless, the reformative initiatives of Athanasios were not fully accepted by the majority of his contemporary Athonites, who felt that these changes would only lead the Athonite community to secularization. For that reason, they asked for the intervention of Emperor Ioannis A' Tsimiskis (969–976) who in return sent Efthymios (the Abbot of Stoudhios monastery) to Mount Athos in AD 972, with direct orders to settle the dispute.

398. Efthymios then summoned an assembly of Abbots and representatives of the monks, which resulted in the drafting of the first Typikon[210] of Mount Athos. This Typikon, consisting of twenty-eight articles (also known by the name of 'Tragos' because of the goatskin parchment on which the original manuscript was inscribed), was ratified by the imperial seal.[211]

---

209. *See*: Tome I. – *Actes de Lavra 897-1178,* par G. Rouillard et P. Collomp, 1937. Tome II. – *Actes de Kutlumus,* par P. Lemerle, 1945. Tome II2 – *Actes de Kutlumus,* nouvelle edition remaniee et augmentee par P. Lemerle, 1988. Tome III. – *Actes de Xeropotamou,* par J. Bompaire, 1964. Tome IV. – *Actes de Dionysiou,* par N. Oikonomides, 1968. Tome V. – *Actes de Lavra. I. Premiere Partie: des origines a 1204, Partie: des origines a 1204,* par P. Lemerle, A. Guillou, N. Svoronos, D. Papachryssanthou, 1970. Tome VI. – *Actes d'Esphigmenou,* par J. Lefort, 1973. Tome VII. – *Actes du Protaton,* par D. Papachryssanthou, 1975. Tome VIII. – *Actes de Lavra. II. De 1204 a 1328,* par P. Lemerle, A. Guillou, N. Svoronos et D. Papachryssanthou, 1977. Tome IX. – *Actes de Kastamonitou,* par N. Oikono- mides, 1978. Tome X. – *Actes de Lavra. III. De 1329 a 1500,* par P. Lemerle, A. Guillou, N. Svoronos et D. Papachryssanthou, 1979. Tome XI. – *Actes de Lavra. IV. Etudes historiques – Actes serbes – Complements et Index,* par P. Lemerle, A. Guillou, N. Svoronos et D. Papachryssanthou, avec la collaboration de S. £irkovi£, 1982. Tome XII. – *Actes de Saint Panteleemon,* par P. Lemerle, G. Dagron et S. £irkovi£, 1982. Tome XIII. – *Actes de Docheiariou,* par N. Oikonomides, 1984. Tome XIV. – *Actes d'Iviron. I. Des origines au milieu du XIe siecle,* par J. Lefort, N. Oikonomides, D. Papachryssanthou, avec la collaboration d'Helene Metreveli, 1985. Tome XV. – *Actes de Xenophon,* par D. Papachryssanthou, 1986. Tome XVI. – *Actes d'Iviron. II. Du milieu du XIe siecle a 1204,* par J. Lefort, N. Oikonomides, D. Papachryssanthou, avec la collaboration de Vassiliki Kravari et d'Helene Metreveli, 1990. Tome XVII. – *Actes du Pantocrator,* par V. Vassiliki Kravari, 1991. Tome XVIII. – *Actes d'Iviron. III. De 1204 a 1328,* par J. Lefort, N. Oikonomides, D. Papachryssanthou, V. Kravari, avec la collaboration d'Helene Metreveli, 1994. Tome XIX. – *Actes d'Iviron. IV. De 1328 au debut du XVIe siecle,* par J. Lefort, N. Oikonomides, D. Papachryssanthou, V. Kravari, avec la collaboration d'Helene Metreveli, 1995. Tome XX. – *Actes de Chi- landar I, Des origines a 1319,* par Mirjana Zivojinovic, Ch. Giros, V. Kravari, 1995. Tome XXI. – *Actes de Vatopedi I,* par J. Bompaire, J. Lefort, V. Kravari, Ch. Giros, 2001. *See also*: www.college- de-france.fr/chaires/chaire23 /'pub_archives_athos.htm.

210. The 'Typika' of Mount Athos were published by Meyer, *Die Haupturkunden fur die Geschichte der Athoskloster,* Leipzig 1894 (reprint: Hakkert, Amsterdam 1965).

211. The 'Tragos' original prototype is today preserved in the archives of the Holy Community of Mount Athos (Karyes).

399. The 'Tragos' regulated a series of crucial administrative and organizational issues while at the same time establishing cenobitic monasticism as well as the self-administration of Mount Athos monasteries. In the ensuing time period, the cenobitic regime was generally expanded throughout Athos, whose peninsula consequently fell under the ownership of the monasteries.

400. During the Byzantine era, the self-administration of Mount Athos was exercised:

- at *first instance* by the monasteries and their Abbots;
- at *second instance* by the central administrative bodies, such as the First Monk *(Protos*: elected by the Abbots of the monasteries), the Synaxe of the Elders *(Gerondes)* or Abbots, exercising administrative duties jointly with the Protos, and the Steward *(Oikonomos),* who was charged with police duties and was elected annually by the Protos and the Synaxe (Assembly) of Gerondes.

2. The Period of Ottoman Rule (1430–1912)

401. The Sultans recognized the self-administration of Mount Athos, without interfering in its internal affairs.[212] Nevertheless, the previous regime of financial favouritism was not continued during the post-Byzantine era. The enforcement of heavy taxation duties on the part of the Ottoman administration, in conjunction with many appropriations or disasters, led the monks to an endless struggle in order to respond to their new unbearable financial burdens.

402. It was by Article 62 § 8 of the Berlin Treaty (1878) that the rights and privileges of Athonite monks were secured irrespectively of their nationality.[213]

3. Recent Years (1912-Today)

403. Article 5 of the Bucharest Treaty (1913) and consequently Articles 13, 27 and 84 of the Sevres Treaty for the Protection of Minority Rights in Greece (1920), which was ratified by the Lausanne Treaty (1923),[214] rendered Mount Athos a part of Greek sovereignty. But in parallel to that, as it is specifically determined by the content of the above-mentioned Article 13 of the Sevres Treaty, in conjunction with Article 62 of the Berlin Treaty (1878), the rights of non-Greek monasteries were

212. Papachrysanthou, *The administration of Mount Athos (1600-1927): A brief historical overview*, Athens 1999.

213. The relevant provision stipulated: 'Les moines du Mont Athos, quelque soit leur pays d' origine, seront maintenus dans leurs possessions et avantages anterieurs, et jouiront, sans aucune exception, d' une egalite de droits et prerogatives': Antonopoulos, *La condition international du Mont Athos,* in: *Le Millenaire du Mont Athos, 963-1963. Etudes et Melanges* 1 (Chevetogne 1963) 381–405; Economides, *Le Mont Athos et le droit international,* 47ff.

214. Papastathis, *Nomocanonical studies*, 55–65; Antonopoulos, *La condition international du Mont Athos, supra*, 395–397.

secured as well [St. *Panteleimon* (Russian) – *Zografou* (Bulgarian) – *Hilandariou* (Serbian), etc.], including the rights of all non-Greek nationality ('foreign') Athonite monks.

404. In May 1924, a committee of Athonite monks drew up a Draft Charter of Mount Athos, consisting of 188 articles. The Draft Charter respectively, after it was amended in some of its sections by the Ecumenical Patriarchate, was subsequently completed and ratified by the Greek State by way of the LD of 10/16.9.1926.

405. The constitutional protection of Mount Athos was consolidated initially by Articles 106–109 of the provisional Constitution of 1926, whose content was included, almost verbatim, in Articles 109–112 of the Constitution of 1927, in Article 103 of the Constitution of 1952 and, finally, in Article 105 of the current Constitution of 1975 (1986/2001/2008/2019).

B. *Nature and Resources of Mount Athos Law*

1. General Remarks

406. A fundamental characteristic of Athonite law is the composition of its content from statutes originating from different branches of the law, such as:

(a) *Constitutional law,* which by Article 105 Const. determines the limits of the privileged self-administration of Mount Athos within the Greek state. At the same time, it regulates a series of significant affairs, such as:
  - the structure of the exercised state and ecclesiastic supervision;
  - the (closed) number of Athonite monasteries and their hierarchy;
  - the drafting procedure of the Statutory Charter of Mount Athos (SCMA);
  - the citizenship of Athonite monks; and also
  - the exemption of Mount Athos territory from expropriation by the State.

(b) *Administrative law,*[215] as to the system of internal administrative organization of Mount Athos – in the first and second degree.

(c) *Public international law,*[216] as to the statutes of international treaties and conventions that may apply on Mount Athos.

(d) *Civil, penal and civil procedural and penal procedural law*, concerning the special civil and penal treatment of the monks and monasteries of Mount Athos.

(e) *Canon law*, which strongly affects the daily life of the monks and monasteries of Mount Athos.

---

215. Papastathis, *The status of Mount Athos in hellenic public law and the European Community*, 55ff.

216. Antonopoulos, *La condition international du Mont Athos*, 381ff; Papastathis, *The nationality of Mount Athos monks of non-Greek origin*, 75ff; Economides, *Le Mont Athos et le droit international*, *supra*, 47–53.

2. The Constitutional Protection of the Mount Athos Regime

407. The constitutional foundations of this privileged system of Mount Athos may be found in Article 105 Const., which, comprising a distinct chapter of the Third Part of the Constitution ('Organisation and Functions of the State', section 6: 'Administration'), is as follows:[217]

Regime of Mount Athos (Aghion Oros)

Article 105

1. The Athos peninsula extending beyond Megali Vigla and constituting the region of Mount Athos shall, in accordance with its ancient privileged status, be a self-governed part of the Greek State, whose sovereignty thereon shall remain intact. Spiritually, Mount Athos shall come under the direct jurisdiction of the Ecumenical Patriarchate. All persons leading a monastic life thereon acquire Greek citizenship without further formalities, upon admission as novices or monks.
2. Mount Athos shall be governed, according to its regime, by its twenty Holy Monasteries among which the entire Athos peninsula is divided; the territory of the peninsula shall be exempt from expropriation. The administration of Mount Athos shall be exercised by representatives of the Holy Monasteries constituting the Holy Community. No change whatsoever shall be permitted in the administrative system or in the number of Monasteries of Mount Athos, or in their hierarchical order or in their position to their subordinate dependencies. Heterodox or schismatic persons shall be prohibited from dwelling thereon.
3. The determination in detail of the regimes of Mount Athos entities and the manner of operation thereof is effected by the Charter of Mount Athos which, with the cooperation of the State representative, shall be drawn up and voted by the twenty Holy Monasteries and ratified by the Ecumenical Patriarchate and the Parliament of the Greeks.
4. Faithful observance of the regimes of Mount Athos entities shall in the spiritual field be under the supreme supervision of the Ecumenical Patriarchate, and, in the administrative, under the supervision of the State, which shall also be exclusively responsible for safeguarding public order and security.
5. The afore-mentioned powers of the State shall be exercised through a governor whose rights and duties shall be determined by law. The law shall likewise determine the judicial power exercised by the monastic authorities and the Holy Community, as well as the customs and taxation privileges of Mount Athos.

408. The thematic content of Article 105 Const. may be categorized as follows:

217. Papastathis, 'Le statut du Mont Athos', L' Annee Canonique 46 (2004) 141–158.

(i) Designation of the geographical boundaries of Mount Athos (paragraph 1).
(ii) Recognition of the 'ancient privileged regime' (paragraph 1).
(iii) Recognition of Mount Athos as a 'self-governed section' of the Greek State, whose sovereignty shall remain intact (paragraph 1).
(iv) Spiritual supervision by the Ecumenical Patriarchate (paragraph 1.4).
(v) Immediate acquisition of the Greek citizenship by all persons admitted – as novices or monks – into an Athonite monastery or its subordinate dependencies.
(vi) Self-administration of Mount Athos by the twenty monasteries and the Holy Community (paragraph 2).
(vii) The designation of Mount Athos territory as not subject to any expropriation by the State and as divided among the twenty monasteries (paragraph 2).
(viii) Prohibition of any amendments to the internal administrative system of Mount Athos (paragraph 2).
(ix) Prohibition of any amendment concerning the number and the order of hierarchy among monasteries and their subordinate dependencies (paragraph 2).
(x) Prohibition imposed on heterodox or schismatic persons to dwell on Mount Athos (paragraph 2).
(xi) Determination of the procedure in which the Charter of Mount Athos is drafted, enacted and ratified (paragraph 3).
(xii) Administrative supervision by the Greek State, which is also charged with maintaining public order and security on Mount Athos (paragraph 4).
(xiii) State supervision authority is exercised by the Governor, whose powers are specifically determined by special legislation (paragraph 5).
(xiv) Judicial power is exercised by the monastic authorities and the Holy Community (paragraph 5).
(xv) Referral to the ordinary (common) legislator. All customs and tax privileges on Mount Athos are determined by law (paragraph 5).

3. Charter of Mount Athos

409. The constitutional legislation of Mount Athos is considered to be the unified legislative corpus comprised by the *Statutory Charter of Mount Athos* (188 articles, enacted in 1924) and the *Legislative Decree of 10/16.9.1926,* 'The Ratification of the Statutory Charter of Mount Athos' (forty-four articles).

410. It is clarified that, because the two aforementioned legislative acts (SCMA and LD/1926) comprise law of local force and of a special and extraordinary nature, their revision or abrogation requires specific and special subsequent regulation.

4. Regulatory Provisions

411. Even more particular issues are resolved by the Regulatory Provisions that are enacted by the Extraordinary Twenty-Member Synaxe (Assembly) of Mount Athos, implementing:

(a) the general authorizing statute of Article 6 of LD/1926; and
(b) the specific authorizing statutes of Articles 40 (concerning the exploitation of forests on Mount Athos) and 42 LD /1926 (for the maintenance of libraries, manuscripts, relics, icons, etc.).

412. The said Regulatory Provisions – which cannot contravene the SCMA – are ratified and placed in effect by the Minister of Foreign Affairs. If their content is spiritual, they must be approved by the Ecumenical Patriarchate (Article 6 LD/1926).

5. Monastic Rules

413. The internal rules governing the organization and administration of the monasteries and the sketes, which are ratified by the Holy Community and the ruling monasteries respectively (Article 144 SCMA), are also considered sources of Athonite law.

6. Common Declaration 4/1979

414. An attempt to secure the privileged regime of Mount Athos was also made in the context of European legislation.[218] More specifically, before Greece joined the EEC (1979), by means of the 6th Directive of the European Community Council on 17 May 1977 (77/388/EEC), Mount Athos was expressly characterized as exempt from the scope of implementation of value-added taxation.

415. In 1979, Common Declaration no. 4 was appended to the Final Act of the Accession of Greece to the European Communities, stating:

> Recognizing that the special regime granted to Mount Athos, as safeguarded by article 105 of the Greek Constitution, is justified exclusively on spiritual and religious grounds, the Community shall ensure that these grounds are taken into consideration during the implementation and further elaboration of the provisions of community law, especially concerning the customs and taxation exemptions, as well as the right of residency (pg. XVII, of the Final Act of Accession of Greece in the EEC, 1979).[219]

416. As it is pointed out, the Common Declarations have a political-programmatic and not a legally binding character (as, for example, do the Protocols). For this reason, it cannot be assumed that the regime of Mount Athos enjoys full protection in the context of the European Union.

---

218. Scandamis, 'La Communaute Europeenne et le Mont Athos', 120ff; Papastathis, 'The status of Mount Athos in hellenic public law and the European Community', 55–75.
219. Evrigenis, 'Reflexions theoriques sur la Declaration Commune relative au Mont Athos', 13ff; Yataganas, 'Declaration commune relative au mont Athos (intervention)', 83–84.

417. Finally, in Declaration no. 8 'Concerning the status of the churches and of non-denominational unions' of the Treaty of Amsterdam,[220] Greece made reference to (reminded) the above-mentioned Common Declaration no. 4 concerning Mount Athos, as it had been added to the Final Act of the Treaty for the accession of Greece to the European Union.

C. *The Administrative System of Mount Athos*

1. The Self-Administration of Mount Athos

418. The unique, in terms of their long history and universality, religious and cultural institutions of Mount Athos constitute an adequate justificatory basis for the privileged granting of self-administration to Mount Athos. It should be pointed out that this regime of self-administration does not entail a curtailment of the Greek State's sovereignty on the Athonite peninsula.

419. According to Article 9 SCMA, the monasteries are self-administered. They are all governed according to their internal rules (by-laws) that are enacted by them and approved by the Holy Community, which supervises their implementation.[221]

420. In the context of Athonite self-administration, certain Athonite bodies have been granted powers, which normally belong to the domain of the exercise of public authority. These are indicatively the following:

(a) The recognition of legislative power to the Extraordinary Twenty-Member Synaxe (Assembly). This body is assembled pursuant to Article 43 SCMA and it is empowered (implementing the legislative authorization granted by Article 6 LD/1926) to enact Regulatory Provisions in the framework set by the SCMA. Following their enactment, the Governor is notified of these provisions which are then ratified by the competent Minister, unless their content is purely spiritual, in which case they are approved by the Ecumenical Patriarchate, as the foremost ecclesiastical authority of Mount Athos.
(b) The exercise of judicial power on the part of Athonite bodies (Monastic Authorities, the Holy Community, the Holy Epistasia) for the resolution of private disputes or even penal cases (Articles 7–35 LD/1926, Articles 41–83 SCMA).
(c) The power of the Monastic Authorities or the Holy Community to draft public documents, under the condition that they are ratified by the Holy Epistasia (Article 37 LD/ 1926).

220. Ratified by L. 2691/1999.
221. CoS (Plenary Session) 1267/1966.

2. Monastic Authorities

421. There are twenty monasteries on Mount Athos ('numerus clausus', Article 105 paragraph 1 Const.), ranked in hierarchy as follows: (1) Holy Monastery of The Megista Lavra, (2) HM Vatopaidi, (3) HM Iveron, (4) HM Chilandari (Serbian), (5) HM Dionysiou, (6) HM Koutloumousiou, (7) HM Pantocrator, (8) HM Xeropotamou, (9) HM Zografou (Bulgarian), (10) HM Docheiariou, (11) HM Karakalou, (12) HM Philotheou, (13) HM Simonopetra, (14) HM Aghiou Pavlou, (15) HM Stavronikita, (16) HM Xenophontos, (17) HM Gregoriou, (18) HM Esphigmenou, (19) HM Aghiou Panteleimonos (Russian), (20) HM Konstamonitou.

422. The development of the aforementioned 'ranking' is rooted in historical reasons and is only honorary since all Athonite monasteries are equal from a legal and administrative standpoint.

423. Article 84 SCMA divides the monasteries into 'cenobitic' and 'idiorrhythmic', based on the criterion of the monks' ability to own private property. However, since 1992, all Athonite monasteries operate according to the cenobitic regime, while eight of the *sketes* (monastic dependencies subordinate to the prevailing monasteries, which are twelve in total) to this date follow the idiorrhythmic system of monastic organization. It should be pointed out that the CCHM permits the conversion of an idiorrhythmic monastery into a cenobitic one, but not the inverse.

3. Organization and Administration

424. The internal administrative bodies of the (cenobitic) monasteries are the Abbot, the Council of Elders ('Gerondia' or 'Synaxe of the Gerondes') and the Committee (Article 111 SCMA).

425. An *Abbot* has life tenure and he is elected by secret ballot by those members of the monastery's brotherhood who have completed six years from their tonsure. The Abbot is par excellence responsible for the spiritual life of the monastery and of the brotherhood members. He is also empowered to represent the monastery in or out of court.

426. The *Gerondia* (also known as the *Synaxe of the Elders* or the *Synaxe of the Prelates*) is the most significant collective administrative body of the monastery, with the decisive competence to handle all matters of a more general nature (Article 90 SCMA).

427. Finally, the *Committee* is a two or three-member body, elected annually by the members of the Gerondia (the Elders) (Article 119 SCMA). The Committee, together with the Abbot, is charged with the duty of executing the decisions made by the Elders.

4. Holy Community

428. This is a central, collective and permanent administrative body of Mount Athos, whose powers are legislative, administrative and judicial. It is based in Karyes (the capital of Mount Athos) and it is comprised of the twenty representatives of the monasteries (Article 24 SCMA). They represent their monasteries by executing their direct guidelines, excluding the judicial cases, on which they act upon conscience.

429. The Holy Community holds regular sessions three times a week and in extraordinary session should matter arise, based on special arrangements of its internal constitution. A majority decision therefore is to be submitted before the Governor of Mount Athos,[222] for verification and execution.

5. Holy Epistasia

430. This is a four-member body, charged with executing the decisions of the Holy Community (Articles 28–40 SCMA). In addition, the Holy Epistasia also performs certain civic duties (police, judicial, municipal), whereas it maintains the right, in cooperation with state police authorities, to deport any troublemakers.[223]

6. Extraordinary Synaxes (Assemblies)

431. These are:

(a) *The Extraordinary Twenty-Member Synaxe,* which is comprised of the twenty representatives of the monasteries. It constitutes the supreme legislative and judicial body on Mount Athos (Article 43 SCMA) and meets twice annually, after Easter and on 20 August.
(b) *The Extraordinary Double Holy Synaxe* (forty members) and the *Extraordinary Great Triple Holy Synaxe* (sixty members), whose composition and operation do not comply with the SCMA or LD/1926, but is based upon the tradition derived from Mount Athos institutions. These bodies are convoked in order to take action on issues that are crucial for the history of Mount Athos.

222. CoS (Plenary Session) 339/1976.
223. *See* in general Karakoulakis, *The holy epistasia of Mount Athos,* 16–23.

D. The Exercise of Supervision

1. Governor

432. The Governor of Mount Athos represents the State's supervision on it. The person appointed for this position by the Ministry of Foreign Affairs should be a personality with integrity, administrative experience and a profound knowledge of all issues pertaining to Mount Athos.

433. The organization and the duties of Mount Athos Governance, which resides in the capital city of Karyes, are regulated by P.D. 227/1998,[224] pursuant to which the Governor exercises limited administrative authority, within the boundaries of Mount Athos:

- either during the decision-making stage, provided that he is summoned to participate in the meetings of the Holy Community;
- or after the decisions have been reached, by reviewing the legitimacy of the decisions taken by the Holy Community and all monastic authorities.[225]

434. If it comes to the attention of the Governor that a body exercising constitutional self-administration on Mount Athos (Holy Community, Holy Epistasia, Monastic Authorities) has violated an SCMA provision of administrative nature, then he reports the violation in writing to the Holy Community, requesting the implementation of legitimacy. In the case of disagreement, the Governor turns to the Ministry of Foreign Affairs, and he complies with its decisions.

2. Ecumenical Patriarchate

435. The supervision exercised by the Ecumenical Patriarchate[226] is of a spiritual nature and it is manifested by the following restricted number of powers:

(a) the participation of the Patriarchate in the administration of justice on Mount Athos;
(b) the ratification of all Regulatory Provisions of a spiritual character that are enacted by the Extraordinary Twenty-Member Synaxe (Article 6 LD/1926);

224. More recently *see* Art. 29 L. 3566/2007, as it has been already substituted by Art. 43 L. 4633/2019.
225. *AP 1290/1989*: all decisions issued by the Holy Community must be submitted to the Governor; this obligation concerns only the 'administrative aspect' of Athonite regimes; CoS (Plenary Session) 621/1979: the decision of an Athonite monastery, to sell or rent its property, shall be reported to the Governor prior to its enforcement, so that he may examine its legitimacy.
226. CoS 736/2005; CoS 4/1996: the Constitution prohibits the residency in Mount Athos of monks who do not recognize (accept) the direct spiritual jurisdiction of the Ecumenical Patriarchate and cease any commemoration of the Patriarch's name. The Holy Community is charged with the duty of expelling these monks; *LCS (Plenary Session) 1093/1976*: a Mount Athos monk, who questions the jurisdiction of the Ecumenical Patriarch in his letter-writing, is lawfully expelled from Mount Athos by decision of the Holy Community.

(c) the obligation to notify the Patriarchate of any election, removal, resignation or dismissal of an Abbot, any member of the Committee or any member of a Monastic Synaxe (Article 117 SCMA and Article 36 LD/ 1926);
(d) the issuance of certain licences (Articles 173 & 185 SCMA).

E. The Law of Persons

1. The Status of Athonite Monks

436. He who wishes to dwell on Mount Athos as a novice or monk must necessarily be a Christian Orthodox and he must not have committed the offence of schism. An Athonite monk acquires full status with the lawful completion of his tonsure in a monastery or in a Mount Athos dependency or by registration in the monastery's register *(monachologion).* At the same time, the same general requirements stipulated for every monk under the canon law of the Orthodox Church must apply, such as the successful completion of their trial period (one to three years) and the novice monk reaching adulthood (Article 93 § 1 SCMA).

437. Every novice is free to leave the monastery or any other monastic dependency in which he dwells at any point in time, as long as he has not ceased to be a layman, nor has he taken his monastic vows.

438. In contrast, the expulsion (or dismissal) of a monk from his monastery constitutes a canonical penalty, which is imposed when he commits a grave offence under canon law. A monk's expulsion does not bring about the loss of his status as monk – which under Orthodox canon law is permanent – but only does away with the property of being a member of a particular monastic brotherhood.

2. The Canonical Institution of 'Avaton'

439. Prohibition on entry for women to Mount Athos (called *avaton* in Greek language) is expressly stipulated in Article 186 SCMA and Article 43b LD/1926, which prescribe a non-convertible prison sentence of two months up to one year.[227]

227. It is clarified that the 'avaton' not only of women in general but also of men in areas of monastic practice (both in the Eastern and in the Western Church) constitutes an ancient monastic institution. Its main purpose is the unhindered devotion of the practising monks or nuns to the ideals of monastic life. The implementation of the avaton was stipulated in a series of provisions of State or ecclesiastic Byzantine law, such as (indicatively), the holy canons 47 of the Ecumenical Synod 'in Trullos', 18 of the 7th Ecumenical Synod, etc.

440. Although until today several cases concerning the violation of the 'avaton' have reached the penal courts of Thessaloniki, after the initiation of prosecution proceedings, these have not issued condemning sentences, ruling in all cases that there was either a state of emergency or an ignorance of the law (for foreign female defendants).

441. The Mount Athos institution of 'avaton' has been often criticized as unconstitutional. The main line of argumentation is on the one hand that it contravenes the fundamental and constitutionally enshrined principle of equality of the sexes (Article 4 § 1 Const.) and on the other hand that it constitutes a restriction on the freedom of movement and circulation (Article 5 § 3 Const.). The other camp holds a different view, arguing that:

(a) the Mount Athos avaton is fully safeguarded by the Constitution (Article 105) but it also constitutes an expression of the Athonites' right of religious freedom (Article 13 Const.);
(b) any amendments to the provision contained in Article 186 SCMA fall under the exclusive jurisdiction of the Athonites;
(c) the freedom of movement is not absolute, but it is subject to the restrictions imposed by legislation (cf. Common Declaration 4/1979); and
(d) the avaton is also protected by Article 17 Const., according to which the full and exclusive (and not subject to any kind of expropriation) territory of Mount Athos belongs to its twenty monasteries, which consequently reserve the exclusive right to allow or block entry to it for any party.

3. Acquisition and Loss of Greek Citizenship

442. According to the provision of Article 105 § 1 section c' Const., all those who have been admitted as novices or monks to Mount Athos instantly acquire Greek citizenship (*privilege of nationality*).[228] If the foreign novice or monk leaves Athos, then he too is subject to the provisions regulating the loss of Greek citizenship and applying for any non-Greek citizen.

---

228. However, according to CoS 2101/1991, a necessary requirement for the entry of a foreign national into the Mount Athos region, if his solemn purpose is to live in a monastery and to be admitted as a monk, is the issuance of a special licence by the Greek State (the Governor of Mount Athos). The same court decision holds that the tonsure of a foreign national without the previous authorization of the Ecumenical Patriarchate does not entail the instant acquisition of Greek citizenship for the foreign national. Nevertheless, it is evident that the aforementioned judicial opinion is at odds with the unambiguous wording of the constitutional provision in question, which states in an interpretatively crystal clear manner that the novices or monks of Mount Athos instantly acquire Greek citizenship, without any further requirements.

4. Restrictions in Movement: Prohibition of Proselytism

443. The lawful entry to Mount Athos for non-Athonites requires a 'diamoniterion' (stay permit), that is, a special written licence to enter and visit the monasteries and other monastic dependencies. The diamoniterion mentions, *inter alia*, the duration of a visitor's stay in Mount Athos and also contains a request to the monasteries to offer their hospitality to the visitor.

444. The Athonite body authorized to issue such a permit is the Holy Epistasia. If the visitor extends his stay on Mount Athos after his permit has expired, he may be deported by order of the Holy Epistasia.

445. Residency on Mount Athos is prohibited to heterodox or schismatic persons (Article 105 § 2 Const. and Article 5 § 2 SCMA) by penalty of deportation. The status of a person as heterodox or schismatic is decided, in case of doubt, by the Ecumenical Patriarchate.

446. Finally, any form of proselytistic activity is prohibited (religious, ecclesiastic, nationalistic, social, etc.). Here too, the prescribed punishment is deportation from Mount Athos (Article 184 SCMA).

F. Property Law

1. Mount Athos Territory

447. The territory of the entire Mount Athos peninsula is divided among its twenty monasteries (but not in equal portions); it is also exempt from expropriation, which means that any voluntary transaction of sale or forced expropriation of the land is prohibited (Article 105 § 2 Const.). Any other property owned by Athonite monasteries lying outside Mount Athos territory or in any other region of the Greek State is not susceptible to usucaption (acquisitive prescription), under the requirements set down in the provisions of Article 21 LD of 22-4/1926 and 4 Obligatory Law 1539/1938, 'On the Protection of Public Property'.

2. Administration and Management

448. The care for the administration of the property of each monastery belongs to the brotherhood of its monks (Article 13 SCMA), but it is exercised by the Abbot and the Committee (Article 90 SCMA).[229]

229. *AP 783/2000*: the formation of a contract that is binding for a Mount Athos monastery constitutes an act of administration and governance of its estate. Therefore, it falls under the jurisdiction of the Abbot and the Committee, who act jointly. However, it is possible for the Committee to transfer this authority to the former by power of attorney.

449. The Abbot and the Committee are in possession of the treasury and the seal of the monastery, performing all administrative and managerial acts that are provided for in the monastery's by-laws. At the same time, all issues of a more general nature (judicial cases, loans, land exchange, erection or maintenance of buildings, dispatch or purchase of artefacts or land, etc.) are submitted to the judgment of the monastery's brotherhood.

450. Monastic property, wherever it may lie (inside or outside of Mount Athos), is either leased by the monastic authorities or cultivated by self-supervision (if it is agricultural land).[230]

3. The Property of Athonite Monks

451. As concerns this matter, one must distinguish, based on Article 101 SCMA, between:

- cenobitic and idiorrhythmic monks (the former cannot have private property, as can the latter); and
- the property that the monk acquired prior to or following his tonsure.

452. Every Athonite monk reserves the right to donate his property to his monastery prior to his initiation ('koura'). Any personal assets that were not donated by the monk shall remain in his possession, if he is an idiorrhythmic monk. But if he is a cenobitic monk, then – according to the prevailing opinion – the private property that he owned prior to his initiation shall pass on to his heirs since he is not allowed to hold private property after his initiation.

453. Private property that was acquired after the monk's initiation (if he was a cenobitic monk) shall be transferred *ex lege* to his monastery.[231] If the monk is idiorrhythmic, then these assets shall remain in his ownership and possession and he may dispose of them throughout his lifetime in any way he chooses.

454. The property of every monk necessarily passes on to his monastery in the event of his death.[232]

---

230. *LCS 1439/1967*: because of the constitutionally enshrined self-governance of Mount Athos, the State does not have the right to intervene in affairs concerning the administration of monastic property.
231. *AP 831/2013.*
232. *LCS 708/2002*: any property acquired by a Mount Athos monk after his initiation ('koura') will be granted to the monastery of his atonement, in the event of the monk's illegal departure from it. Any possible disposition of this property by last will and testament to another party is void, as is the will and testament itself, in favour of the monastery. The monastery may at any time contest this will and testament, by filing an objection or a lawsuit for a declaratory judgment. However, in the event of an Athonite monk's legal departure from a monastery, he reserves the right to dispose of his property at his own freewill, and consequently, his last will and testament is valid.

455. Finally, a precondition for the monastery to be held responsible for any debts incurred by its monks is a written consent on behalf of the monastery, prior to the signing of the debt (Article 101 SCMA).

4. Tax and Duty Privileges

456. A series of special provisions mandate the exemption of Mount Athos from any tax duty on goods that are imported in its territory, provided that they are destined to be used for the needs of the monks and they do not exceed a particular monetary amount for each monk (Article 167 SCMA).

457. Additionally, monasteries enjoy exemption from many tax duties, such as the estate tax for property within the territory of Mount Athos, value added tax (VAT), and stamp duties.

5. Cultural Heritage and Intellectual Property

458. The vast and priceless cultural heritage which is preserved on Mount Athos (consisting of thousands of manuscripts, books, portable icons, murals, artefacts, vestments, sacred relics, etc.) belongs, as movable and at the same time intellectual property, to the exclusive ownership of the twenty Athonite monasteries.

459. The immense cultural and ecclesiastical value of these treasures necessitated a special legislative arrangement for their preservation, safekeeping and their effective protection, through a series of provisions, such as those found in articles:

- 110 SCMA (it is required by every monastery to keep an accurate record of their treasures) and also in;
- 171 SCMA (any repair or renovation work on ancient murals is prohibited if it damages or distorts them).

G. Administration of Justice on Mount Athos

1. General Remarks

460. Cases which require judicial enquiry also arise on the Mount Athos peninsula – although this does not occur with the equivalent gravity or frequency as in other regions of the Greek territory. Nevertheless, the need for increased legal protection of the sensitive regime of Mount Athos has led to the enactment, in the particular region, of a great number of penal provisions (ordinary and ecclesiastical).

461. Justice on Mount Athos is administered both by secular-state (penal and civil) courts and by local Athonite law-giving bodies (Articles 41–83 SCMA, Articles 7–35 LD/1926).

2. Cases of Ordinary Penal Law

462.

(a) The criminal courts of Thessaloniki[233] are competent to judge all misdemeanours and felonies that are committed in the region of Mount Athos.
(b) Minor offences of common penal law and police violations (of clergy, monks or laymen) are tried:
    (i) by the Holy Epistasia, if the offence took place in Karyes (the capital city of Mount Athos); or
    (ii) by the Elders of the respective monastery, as long as the offence was committed within its territory.

3. Cases of Ecclesiastical Penal Law

463. If the offender is a monk, the following Athonite law-giving bodies are competent to adjudicate:

(a) the Abbot and the Counsels of the monastery of his residence, who may impose lighter penalties (warnings, admonishments, reprimands), for petty offences;
(b) the Abbot along with the Elders, who judge at first instance a grave ecclesiastical offence committed by a monk in their monastery;
(c) the Holy Community, who judges the appeals on the aforementioned decisions;
(d) an Extraordinary Tribunal, comprised of Metropolitans of the Ecumenical Patriarchate and Athonite monks, judges the appeals against the decisions of the Holy Community (Article 9 § 3 LD/1926, Article 43 SCMA);
(e) the Ecumenical Patriarch and the Holy Synod of the Patriarchate judge the appeals against the decisions of the Holy Community for all offences punishable by defrocking.

464. To sum up, Athonite monks who commit any type of criminal act (excluding those offences which fall under the jurisdiction of the common penal court of Thessaloniki) will stand trial:

– at *first instance,* by the competent bodies of his Monastery;
– at *second instance,* by the Holy Community or the special tribunal of Article 9 §3 LD/1926; and
– at *third instance,* by the Ecumenical Patriarch and the Synod.

233. *Court of Appeals of Thessaloniki 477/1993* (distinguished robbery of sacred relics); *Misdemeanors Court of Thessaloniki 523/1977* (violation of the *avaton* of Mount Athos); *Misdemeanors Court of Thessaloniki 1017/1991* (theft of old books from Mount Athos cells).

4. Civil Law Cases

465. As concerns the field of civil law, Athonite courts hold jurisdiction only over those disputes concerning the boundaries of real property between the monasteries or any monastic dependencies within Mount Athos territory. All other disputes of private law come under the jurisdiction of the civil courts of Poligiros and Thessaloniki.

5. Cases of Annulment before the Council of State

466. The Council of State, as the highest administrative court of the land, holds jurisdiction, *inter alia,* over the adjudication of administrative disputes arising from an executable administrative act (or omission) of a state organ or an Athonite administrative authority, deciding about a legal relationship that is governed by the special statutes of Athonite (administrative) law.

467. In fact, the Council of State has since its establishment (in 1929) until today demonstrated a rich relevant production of case law, which has admittedly contributed to a great extent in shaping the content of many important administrative Athonite institutions, such as indicatively:

– the concept and the scope of Mount Athos self-administration;
– the spiritual jurisdiction of the Ecumenical Patriarchate;
– the citizenship of Athonite monks;
– the administrative powers of the monastic authorities on Mount Athos,[234] etc.

6. The Execution of Decisions

468. The following decisions are immediately executable:

(a) the final rulings of the Ecumenical Patriarchate and the Synod, as well as those of the extraordinary court in Article 9 LD/1926;
(b) any first instance penal court decision, unless an appeal was filed against it, in which case it shall be executed after the adjudication of the latter;
(c) all final and unappealable decisions in private law cases. However, even an appealable decision can, upon the request of one party and by decision of the First Instance Court, be held to be enforced temporarily.

469. All executable rulings of Athonite courts are transferred to the Governor for execution, who is empowered to instruct the competent state bodies of Mount Athos (Article 34 LD/1926).

---

234. CoS 2629/1988; CoS 2101/1991; CoS 4/1996; CoS 6/1996; CoS 735/2005.

§2. 'GENUINE ORTHODOX CHRISTIANS' OR 'OLD CALENDARISTS'

I. The Creation and Evolution of the 'Old Calendarist Issue'

470. One of the gravest problems of the Eastern Orthodox Church of Greece – which remains contested since 1924 – is the so-called Old Calendarist Issue that has thus far caused a rupture in the unity of the Orthodox faithful.[235]

471. More particularly, the LD dated 18/25-1-1923, 'On the New Civil Calendar', replaced the Julian calendar which was in force until that date with the more modern and revised Gregorian calendar (introduced by Pope Gregory the XIII).

472. In the immediately following year (1924), the Orthodox Church decided to adjust, by changing thirteen days, the manner of calculation, especially of its fixed feasts, according to the more precise dictates of the Gregorian calendar. Although the mode of calculating the days of the moveable feasts remained unaltered, the change of the liturgical year in accordance with the more recent findings of science met with the opposition of a sizeable portion of the Orthodox flock.

473. Many followers demonstrated their disagreement by separating from the official Church and organizing into distinct religious communities with their own clerical hierarchy, churches and monasteries. Moreover, these same Christians claim, often in an emphatic way, that only they remained 'genuine' Orthodox Christians, in contrast with those who accepted the disputed calendar alteration, arguing that this action adulterated the apostolic faith and tradition of the Orthodox Church.

474. Contrary to the above standpoint, the dominant ecclesiastical view distinguishes between matters of a doctrinal nature, on which most certainly no modification is allowed, and matters which lack the gravity of the doctrinal issues. The calendar's setting of the liturgical year belongs to the latter, which can change based on different historical circumstances. Therefore, because there was no doctrinal impediment as to the calendar issue, following the congruous opinion of the Ecumenical Patriarchate (23 February 1924), the Church of Greece decided to implement the Gregorian calendar effective on 10 March 1924, designating this day as the 23 March and issuing the relevant Circular, dated 1 March 1924.

475. Today, the Old Calendarists are organized into numerous religious communities, with administrative authorities that are independent from each other. It is

235. Analytically, *see*: Marinos, *Religious freedom*, 295–317; Troianos, *Lectures in ecclesiastical law*, 155–157; Papastathis, *Nomocanonical studies*, 185–189; Ware, *Old calendarists*, in: Clogg, *Minorities in Greece: Aspects of a plural society*, 1–23; Papageorgiou, 'Statut constitutional des communautes religieuses des Anciens Calendaristes a l'ordre juridique de Grece', 171–176; Ir. Doens, 'Les Paleoimerologites en Grece et leurs Monasteres', Irenikon 1971, 549f. More generally: Kitsikis, *The old calendarists and the rise of religious conservatism in Greece*, California 1995.

underlined that a defining element of the identity of every Old Calendarist Community is its person-centred character because it is founded and revolves around a particular clergyman (usually a metropolitan). Nonetheless, this fact has given rise to considerable confusion as to the distinction between the many different Old Calendarist groups.

476. The exact number of Old Calendarists is not currently known, but in previous years there were hundreds of thousands of them residing on Greek territory.

II. A Legal Approach of the Old Calendarist Issue

477. The current legal status of the Old Calendarists appears to be quite complicated, with the clear danger of confusing every faction of Old Calendarists not only with the official Church but also with the other Old Calendarist communities.

478. To be more particular, the Constitution recognizes only one Church with the name 'Orthodox Church of Greece', which it further characterizes as 'prevailing' (Article 3 § 1 Const.). On the other hand, every Old Calendarist Community claims for itself the exclusive use of the status of religion, which the provision of Article 3 § 1 Const. characterizes as 'prevailing'. Further, it is widely known that the monasteries of Mount Athos, as well as many other Orthodox Churches (e.g., the Patriarchate at Jerusalem), observe the old calendar for calculating their feast days.

479. It is, however, noteworthy that, during the 76th Session of 23 April 1975 for the enactment of the Constitution that is currently in effect, Ch. Karapiperis, who then served as Deputy Minister of Education and Religious Affairs, submitted a declaration advocating the freedom of worship of the Old Calendarists.[236] This Declaration then had favourable consequences for the religious freedom of Old Calendarists, leading, among others, to the issuance of decision 1444/1991 of the Council of State (Plenary Session),[237] which ruled favourably for the self-administration of the Old Calendarists in respect of the prevailing religion.

480. Some groups of Old Calendarists have been recognized as 'ecclesiastical legal entities in private law' pursuant to the provisions of L. 4301/2014.[238]

---

236. *See* it in Troianos/Papageorgiou, *Religious legislation: Special legislation – bibliography – case law*, 1556.
237. Arm. 52 (1998) 495–496; *Public Prosecutor of Supreme Court (AP) 2/2005*, PDni 8 (2005) 302–305; *Court of Appeal of Thessaloniki 546/2004*, EllDni 46 (2005) 913–915; *AP 162/1996*, EllDni 37 (1996) 1080–1082; *Court of Appeal of Athens 563/2001*, PChr 52 (2002) 254–256; *Multi-Member Court of First Instance of Athens 2823/1999*, D 30 (1999) 871–881: in the context of Art. 13 Const., the Old Calendarists are considered to comprise a distinct religious community; they are recognized as a 'known religion' from a doctrinal point of view; they are protected under state law and they are governed by the rules of their religious community.
238. *See* indicatively *First Instant Court of Thiva 195/2018*; *First Instant Court of Athens 1279/2016 First Instant Court of Thiva* 165/2015.

§3. Muslims

481. More analytically on the legal status of Muslims in Greece, *see* 'Part IV: International, Transnational, Regional Effects on Religious Communities'.[239] Concerning the property regime governing the Muslim *wakfs, see* 'Part VIII: Church Financing'. Finally, in reference to the official status of the Muslim clergymen *(muftis), see* 'Part VI: Labour Law Within Religious Communities'.

§4. Protestants (Evangelicals)

482. According to the view that has prevailed in Greek case law, Greek protestant churches do have a legal personality, but of private (and not of public) law. For the fulfilment of their religious and other goals, the Protestants of Greece form associations or non-profit foundations under civil law. According to L. 4301/2014, 'Organization of legal status of religious communities and associations in Greece', the Greek protestant may establish the so-called religious legal entities.

483. Until today, the Council of State has ruled that the following religious communities of Evangelicals fall under the constitutional precept of 'known religion':

- The Independent Evangelical Church of the Protestant Doctrine (CoS 1322/1963).
- The Church of the Disciples of Christ, which observes the doctrines of the Evangelical Church of the Baptists (CoS 2362/1966).
- The Greek Apostolic Church (CoS 2264/1964).
- The religious community of the Methodists (CoS 756/1952, 1896/1952, 539/1956, 2274/1962).
- The Greek Evangelical Church (CoS 2358/1952, 2058/1957, 851/1961, 2275/1962).
- The doctrine of Protestant Seventh-Day Adventists (CoS 1908/1959, 123/1964, 4054/1973, 2139/1975, 2004/1991).
- The doctrine of the Church of Christian Brothers (CoS 824/1963, 1944/1971).
- The International Church of the Foursquare Gospel (CoS 34/1958, 200/1974).
- The Apostolic Church of Pentecost (CoS 2155/1966, 721/1969, 2226/1969, 1942/1973, 1351/1979).
- The Apostolic Church of God – Evangelical Doctrine (CoS 1842/1992).
- The Christian Apostolic Church of Protestants (CoS 2231/1970).
- The Church of the Christian Brothers (CoS 1944/1971).

---

239. *See* the following studies: Ktistakis, *The holy law of Islam and Muslim Greeks citizens*, Athens-Thessaloniki 2006; Kotzambasi, *The family legal relations of Greeks Muslim men and women*, Thessaloniki 2003; Menaidis, *The religious freedom of Muslims in the Greek legal order*, Athens 1990; Tsitselikis: 'Muslims in Greece', in: Potz/Wieshaider, *Islam and the European Union*, 79–107; *ibid.*, 'Le statut juridique de VIslam en Grece', L'Annee Canonique XLV (2003) 219–242; *ibid.*, 'The legal status of Islam in Greece', Die Welt des Islams 44 (2004) 402–431; Stavrou, 'The legal status of minorities in Greece today: The adequacy of their protection in the light of current human rights perceptions', Journal of Modern Greek Studies 1 (1995) 1ff.

- The Church of Born Again Christians (CoS 749/1987).
- The Free Evangelical Church (CoS 2036/1988, 3096/1988, 2350/1990).
- The Church of Jesus Christ of Latter-Day Saints (CoS 549/1991).
- The Church of God of Prophecy (Evangelical Doctrine, CoS 1465/1992).

§5. Roman Catholic Church

484. According to the Latin Code of Canon Law, the Roman Catholic Church in Greece constitutes a local Church, under the pastoral jurisdiction of the 'Holy Synod of the Catholic Hierarchy of Greece', that is of the Greek Catholic Conference of Bishops *(Episcoporum Conferentia).*[240] On 10 June 1965, the Holy See recognized the particular Synod as a special ecclesiastical legal entity, in accordance with the relevant canon law. The members of the Synod of Bishops include:

- the Archbishop of Corfu and Apostolic Overseer of Thessaloniki;[241]
- the Archbishop of Naxos-Tinos and Apostolic Overseer of Chios;[242]
- the Archbishop of Athens and Apostolic Overseer of Rhodes;[243]
- the Bishop of Syros and Santorini and Apostolic Overseer of Crete;
- the Exarch of the Catholics of *Ritus Graecus;*[244]
- the Exarch of Catholics of Armenian Rite.[245]

485. As the Canon Law of the Roman Catholic Church dictates, the respective ecclesiastical legal entities bear obligations and rights, stemming merely from the fact that they belong to this Church. More analytically on the legal status of the Catholics in Greece, *see* in 'Part IV: International, Transnational, Regional Effects on Religious Communities' and 'Part VIII: Church Financing'. According to the late L. 4301/2014, 'Organization of legal status of religious communities and associations in Greece', the legal persons of Roman Catholic Church in Greece are recognized as 'religious legal entities'.

---

240. Kontidis, *Catholicism*, Athens 2000, passim; Salachas, *The legal status of the catholic church in the Greek territory*, 55ff, 130ff, 160ff, passim; Maghioros, 'L' Eglise Catholique Romaine et l'Etat en Grece: une approche juridicocanonique', L' Annee Canonique 2003, 177–189; Asimakis, *The development of relations between Greece and the holy see (1820-1980): From French protection to the establishment of diplomatic relations*, passim.
241. The Archdiocese of Corfu was created in 1926 and it includes the Heptanese and Epirus. Thessaly, the Northern Sporades, Macedonia, Thassos, Thrace and Lemnos belong to the Apostolic Vicariate of Thessaloniki.
242. With its See in Tinos, the above-mentioned Archdiocese includes the islands of Tinos, Naxos, Paros, Antiparos, Mykonos, Andros and Delos. The islands of Chios, Lesvos, Samos, as well as all other islands of the North Aegean Sea fall under the jurisdiction of the Diocese of Chios.
243. The Catholic Archdiocese of Athens was (re)founded on 23 Jul. 1875, with jurisdiction over Central Greece (Sterea Ellada), Euboea, Skyros, the islands of the Argo-Saronic Gulf, the Peloponnese, Cythera and Anticythera. The Archdiocese of Rhodes originated as a Diocese in 1797 and then was elevated to an Archdiocese in 1928, with power over the Dodecanese.
244. The Greek Catholic Exarchate of Ritus Graecus was created in 1911.
245. The Armenian Catholic Exarchate was founded in 1925.

§6. Jehovah's Witnesses

486. By analogy with the Protestants, the status of Jehovah's Witnesses is not governed by special, international or national legislation. Jehovah's Witnesses are today recognized by case law[246] as a known religion, safeguarded by the Constitution (Article 13). Jehovah's Witnesses are organized in the Greek section of the 'Watchtower Bible and Tract Society', which is considered a non-profit organization, with exclusively religious goals.[247]

§7. Israelites

487. The Israelites of Greece are incorporated in the local Israelite communities,[248] whose status is governed mainly by L. 2456/1920,[249] the RD of 29 March 1949, etc. For more details on the legal status of Greek Israelites, *see* in: 'Part VIII: Church Financing'.

246. Indicatively: CoS 2105/1975, NoV 23 (1975) 1203–1204; CoS 2106/1975, Arm. 41 (1987) 242–244; CoS 2484/1980, NoV 30 (1982) 1344.
247. *Single-Member Administrative First Instance Court of Athens 7491/1982, 7667/1982; Three-Member Administrative First Instance Court of Athens 5755/1984;* CoS 2111/1988.
248. Papastathis, *Nomocanonical studies*, 117–122; Papageorgiou, *Ecclesiastical law*, 137.
249. L. 2456/1920 was amended and revised through a series of subsequent acts, such as L. 4837/1930 and OL 367/1945, LD 301/1963, L. 1657/1951, LD 301/1969 and others. *See* the relevant legislation in Troianos/Papageorgiou, *Religious legislation: Special legislation – bibliography – case law*, 1737–1758.

Chapter 2. The Autonomy of Religious Communities

488. During the last few decades, the issue of the autonomous organization and institutional operation of the creeds in the Greek territory – comprising perhaps the most crucial manifestation of the right to religious freedom – has preoccupied Greek legal theory and case law with a steadily increasing interest.[250] The dialogue begins with the existing constitutional framework for the relations between the State and the religious communities in Greece, ending nearly always with the expression of scepticism, certainly not as to the undisputed need to safeguard religious self-governance, but as to the *(de lege lata* or *de lege ferenda)* scope of its limits.[251]

489. At this point, we should call attention to the fact that the right to religious self-governance manifests itself in two primary forms.

490. According to the first, the followers of a creed or doctrine may form religious communities or establish legal entities with religious goals, in the context of the constitutionally safeguarded right of assembly (in this instance, for religious purposes). These collectivities may assume legal entities of public law, legal entities of private law or 'religious legal entities' (*see* the late L. 4301/2014, 'Organization of legal status of religious communities and associations in Greece').

491. In the second form, every creed is entitled to organize the administration of its internal affairs according to the special provisions of its respective Law (canon law or law of any other form).

492. The significance of this entire issue inevitably leads to the development of a more broadly conceived discussion, whose main parameter is the need to delineate more clearly the public presence and activity of every creed. The influence of the case law of Greek courts, as well as of that of the European Court of Human Rights (Strasbourg), should be considered pivotal in this investigation. The formative impact of case law on the limits and the content of religious autonomy and self-administration cannot be ignored, nor of course overrated, given the not infrequent turns of case law, even of that which is considered to be well established. In fact, the frequent and multilevel application of the principle of proportionality (Article 25 § 1 Case d Const.) on the part of the aforementioned law-giving bodies gives rise to new perspectives in the entrenchment of the autonomy of creeds.

493. The influence of the provisions contained in Article 43 paragraph 2 of the Greek Constitution in matters of religious self-administration is also quite important, as these provisions open up wide normative horizons towards this direction.

---

250. *See* in general the interesting studies in Robbers, *Church autonomy: A comparative survey*, Frankfurt am Main 2001.
251. On the whole issue, *see* Papageorgiou, *The limits of ecclesiastical self-administration. I: Regulatory jurisdiction*, Thessaloniki 2012. *See also* Papastathis, *Religious self-administration in the hellenic republic*, in: Robbers, *Church autonomy: A comparative survey*, 425–450; Marinos, *Religious freedom*, 117f.

494. We are referring here to the well-known direct constitutional recognition of the possibility to grant by statute special legislative authorizations, among others, also to religious legal entities, to issue 'general regulatory decrees'. The significance of the latter for the content of religious self-administration is monumental: with their issuance, religious communities are empowered to expand and to enrich, in an immediate, direct and legally practical manner, every aspect of the organization and functioning of their administrative authorities or their legal entities.

495. The regulatory decrees, by virtue of special delegation granted by statute in laws of the Greek Parliament, are primarily concerned with the organization, administration and operation of central or peripheral ecclesiastical or religious authorities, bodies or legal entities, the organization of the monasteries and of monastic life in general, the official status of ecclesiastical employees, the organization of ecclesiastical education, the administration of ecclesiastical justice, the governance and management of overall ecclesiastical property.

496. More specifically, the activation of these legislative delegations has already led to the creation of approximately fifty regulations of the Orthodox Church, which have covered – with greater or lesser success – wide-ranging institutional fields of its internal administrative organization.

497. For example, some characteristic regulations include the following:

- Regulation 1/1977, 'On the proceedings of the Holy Synod of the Hierarchy of the Church of Greece'.
- Reg. 2/1977, 'On the proceedings of the Permanent Holy Synod of the Church of Greece'.
- Reg. 5/1978, 'Code for Ecclesiastical Employees'.
- Reg. 8/1979–1980, 'On Holy Churches and Parishes'.
- Reg. 210/2010, 'Department for the Financial Audit of the Church of Greece'.
- Reg. 247/2013 and Article 32 of L. 4495/2017, 'Building Service and Central Council of Ecclesiastical Architecture of the Church of Greece'.
- Regs 267/2015 and 317/2020, 'Ecclesiastical Central Service of Finances'.
- Reg. 281/2015, Article 15 of L. 4582/2018, 'The Synodal Office of Pilgrimage Tours of the Church of Greece'.
- Reg. 305/2018, 'Vicars and Deacons'.
- Reg. 307/2018, 'The Communication and Education Service of the Church of Greece'.
- Reg. 317/2020, 'Organization of the Ecclesiastical Service of Finance of the Church of Greece'.
- Reg. 318/2020, 'Leases, sales and management of the property of the Church of Greece', and so on.

498. Greek case law and legal theory have repeatedly handled the issue of the extent to which the Constitution safeguards the 'holy canons' of the Orthodox Church, that is, of the statutes of ecclesiastical origin which organize and regulate its internal life. The entire issue was perceived to be of great magnitude because of the repercussions that any interpretative version would have on the field of self-administration of the Church.

499. Today it is widely accepted that: (a) all the holy canons of doctrinal content are constitutionally guaranteed and (b) the holy canons which have merely administrative content are constitutionally safeguarded only if they concern fundamental administrative institutions of the Church. Consequently, it is possible to repeal or amend all other simple administrative holy canons by regular law of the Greek Parliament.[252]

500. Lastly, through legislative authorization provided in Article 1 of L. 2456/1920, 'On the Israelite Communities', the local synagogues were permitted to found an Israelite community, which shall constitute a legal entity of public law and shall be governed by its own internal organization of administration and operation.

252. CoS 5057/1987, NoV 36 (1988) 801–806: all holy canons which are of administrative content and do not concern doctrine and worship may be amended according to the ordinary legislative procedure, in alignment with the needs of society and always in the joint interest of Church and State. *See also* Orfanoudakis, 'The holy canons and the Constitution (a counter-argument or the "other" interpretative approach', Arm. 35 (1981) 82–83.

Chapter 3. Fundamental Rights and Religious Communities

501. As it was already mentioned in the chapter on the entrenchment of religious freedom (Part II), the religious communities residing on Greek territory bear the duty, in the context of the constitutional and legal limitations of religious freedom, to respect the fundamental human rights and freedoms of their members. Put differently, the constitutional protection of the fundamental human freedoms constitutes the limit of protection of the internal law of the creeds. Consequently, the religious dictates of a church or creed, which do not respect the relevant constitutional provisions, are illegal and may be annulled by Greek courts.

Chapter 4. Contractual Religious Freedom

502. As it is known, the law, the concordat and the ecclesiastical convention are the most common abiding forms chosen by the states to regulate their relations with the religious communities in their territory. In the Greek public order, one encounters, almost exclusively, the law and the convention, the latter ratified by an act enacted by the Parliament.[253]

503. Furthermore, issues related to various religious communities in the Greek territory, such as those of the Muslims, the Catholics or the Israelites, are protected by international conventions (*see* Part IV), which, however, also need to be ratified by an act enacted by the Greek Parliament in order to become an inseparable part of the domestic law and supersede any contradicting provision of law (Article 28 § 1 Const.).

504. Finally, the relations of the Greek State with the religious communities need to be attuned both to Article 13 of the Const., which safeguards religious freedom in all its expressions, and to the ECHR.[254]

505. On the contrary, up-to-date no concordat with the Holy See or the Catholic Church of the country, or any ecclesiastical convention with a certain religious creed has been concluded, as those commonly concluded between the German Lander with the local protestant churches.[255] In any case, all religious creeds known in Greece have the opportunity to form various urban incorporations, characterized as private law legal entities.

506. Consequently, the standard Act, enacted by the Parliament's Plenary Session, constitutes the only constitutionally permissible opportunity for the settling of the legal issues of all religions within the Greek territory. This way, it is possible for the State to directly and substantially intervene, in a regulatory manner, in the issues of all religious communities. With these laws, the latter secure a more complete self-administration as the cornerstone of the expression of their religious freedom, on the one hand, and, on the other hand, the potential of any state intervention is delimited.

---

253. On the whole issue, *see* Venizelos, *The relations between state and church*, 185f, 194f; Papageorgiou/Papastathis, 'Formes de collaboration conventionelle ou non-conventionelle entre l'État et les communautés religieuses en Grèce', in: Puza/Doe (ed.), *Religion and law in dialogue: covenantal and non-covenantal cooperation between state and religion in Europe*, [European Consortium for Church and State Research, Proceedings of the Conference, Tübingen, 18–21 Nov. 2004], Peeters, Leuven-Paris-Dudley, MA 2006, 65–77.
254. Ratified by LD 53/1974; Sicilianos, *European Convention on Human Rights: Interpretation to articles*, passim.
255. Salachas, *The legal status of the catholic church in the Greek territory*, 55ff, passim; Asimakis, *The development of relations between Greece and the holy see (1820-1980). From French protection to the establishment of diplomatic relations*, passim.

507. Finally, more special issues of all religious creeds can also be regulated with secondary legislative sources such as the decrees, under the condition of previous legislative authorization.[256]

256. More generally, *see* Papastathis, *State and church in Greece*, in: Robbers, *State and church in the European Union*, 118f.

Part IV. International, Transnational, Regional Effects on Religious Communities

Chapter 1. International Law Effects on Religious Communities

§1. General Remarks

508. The Article 28 § 1 Const. stipulates:

> The generally recognised rules of international law, as well as international conventions as of the time they are sanctioned by statute and become operative according to their respective conditions, shall be an integral part of domestic Greek law and shall prevail over any contrary provision of the law. The rules of international law and of international conventions shall be applicable to aliens only under the condition of reciprocity.[257]

509. According to the above constitutional provision, Greece has ratified and accepted as a part of its internal law the most important international conventions concerning religious freedom. In addition to it, some bilateral international public law treaties have become a special part of the corpus of international commitments in the field of religion.

§2. International Texts Relating to the Protection of Religious Freedom

510. As it is known, religious freedom is today protected internationally on both an ecumenical and a peripheral level, in conditions that have established a multi-level system of effective review.[258] The key texts of ecumenical significance are the

257. Chrysogonos, *Constitutional law*, 181ff; Venizelos, *Lessons of constitutional law*, 108, 135, 152, 154; Mavrias, *Constitutional law*, Athens [5]2016, 245f.
258. From the very rich relevant legal literature, *see* especially: Robbers (ed.), *State and church in the European Union*, Germany 32019, passim; Ahdar/Leigh, *Religious freedom in the liberal State*, Oxford 2005; Ferrari/Cristofori, *Law and religion in the 21st century: Relations between states and religious communities*, England-USA 2010; Lindholm/Durham/Tahzib-Lie, *Facilitating freedom of*

Charter of the United Nations (1945),[259] the Universal Declaration of Human Rights (1948)[260] and the two International Covenants for 1966 (the first concerning Civil and Political Rights,[261] and the second for Economic, Social and Cultural Rights[262]). Finally, the protection of the right to religious freedom is sought by the Declarations of the General Assembly of the UNO, first of 1981 on the elimination of all forms of intolerance and of discrimination based on religion or belief, and second of 1992 concerning minorities.

511. Under Article 1 of the Charter of the United Nations (1945, CUN), the UN have also the purpose of promoting respect for human rights and for fundamental freedoms for all without distinction as to race, sex, language or religion. However, in human rights issues, the CUN provides only causes for cooperation among states, not containing statutes of self-enforced implementation or a list of internationally recognized human rights. This deficient protection was covered by the formation of the United Nations Commission on Human Rights (1946), with the participation of experts and of Member States of the UNO. During its annual session in Geneva, the Commission examines the condition of human rights around the globe, makes recommendations and decides on the need for penalties or improvements. The progeny of the Commission's proceedings were the Universal Declaration of Human Rights (1948), the Declaration on Religious Freedom (1981) and the two International Covenants (1966).[263]

512. As was previously mentioned, the Universal Declaration of Human Rights (1948) was adopted by the General Assembly of the United Nations and it constitutes the first significant achievement of the United Nations Commission on Human Rights (UNCHR). Although the international binding force of the UDHE is the subject of controversy, its universal political and ethical reputation is indisputable. Religious freedom is cited in:

– Article 2, which recognizes that every person (without distinction of race, colour, language, religion, etc.) has the right to invoke the freedoms of the UDHR;

---

religion or belief: A deskbook, The Netherlands 2004; Renucci, *Article 9 of the European Convention on Human Rights: Freedom of thought, conscience and religion*, Strasburg 2005; Robbers (ed.), *Church autonomy: A comparative survey*, Frankfurt am Main 2001; Uitz, *Freedom of religion in European constitutional and international case law*, Strasbourg 2007.

259. It has been ratified by L. 585/27.29-9-1945.

260. Although it has not yet been ratified by the Greek Parliament (as provided by Art. 28 § 1 Const.), however, the UDHR is considered a part of international customary law.

261. L. 1532/1985, 'Ratification of the International Covenant on Economic, Social and Cultural Rights'.

262. L. 2462/1997, 'Ratification of the International Covenant on Civil and Political Rights'.

263. On 20 Dec. 1993, the General Assembly of the UN decided to set up an Office of the High Commissioner on Human Rights in Geneva, with the purpose of coordinating the actions for the protection of human rights within the institutional framework of the United Nations. The High Commissioner holds the rank of deputy Secretary-General of the United Nations and presides over the Center for Human Rights. In addition to the High Commissioner, there are a number of principal organs in the United Nations that undertake various activities to protect human rights (such as the General Assembly, the Security Council and the United Nations Secretariat).

- Article 18, according to which every person has the right of freedom of thought, conscience and religion. This right includes the freedom to change religion or beliefs, as well as the freedom to manifest religious beliefs, individually or in community with others, in public or in private, in teaching or worship;
- Article 26, which declares that education should promote tolerance and friendship among all nations, racial or religious groups, and that parents have the prior right to choose the kind of religious education that shall be given to their children;
- Article 29, underlining that in the exercise of his rights and freedoms, every individual shall be subject only to such limitations as are determined by law solely for the purpose of securing respect for the rights and freedoms of others and of meeting the just requirements of morality, public order and the general welfare in a democratic society.

513. Article 18 of the International Covenant on Civil and Political Rights 1966 (ICCPR) protects freedom of choice and manifestation of religious or other beliefs, individually or in community with others. The same statute establishes as the necessary legal limits to the right of religious freedom the protection of public safety, order, health or morals, as well as the fundamental freedoms of others.

514. Finally, from the International Covenant on Economic, Social and Cultural Rights 1966 (ICESCR), we make particular reference to Article 2 § 1, safeguarding, among other rights, the right to religious equality.

515. The Declaration of the General Assembly of the UN on the elimination of all forms of intolerance and discrimination based on religion or belief was enacted on 25 November 1981. Article 1 of the Declaration reiterates the definitions of Article 18 of the ICCPR. Special weight should be accorded to Article 2, which stipulates that no one shall be subject to discrimination by any person, institution or State on the grounds of religion or other beliefs. According to Article 3 of the Declaration, discrimination between human beings on the grounds of religion or belief constitutes an affront to human dignity and a disavowal of the principles of the Charter of the UN. For this reason, such discrimination shall be condemned as a violation of the human rights and fundamental freedoms proclaimed in the Universal Declaration of Human Rights. Article 4 provides that all states must take effective measures to prevent and eliminate discrimination on the grounds of religion or belief in the recognition, exercise and enjoyment of human rights and fundamental freedoms in all fields of civil, economic, political, social and cultural life. Lastly, Article 6 of the Declaration of 1981 protects the right to freedom of thought, conscience, religion or belief, encompassing the freedom to worship or assemble in connection with a religion or belief, and to establish and maintain places for these purposes; the freedom to write, issue and disseminate relevant publications in these areas; the freedom to teach a religion or belief in places suitable for these purposes; and the freedom to observe days of rest and to celebrate holidays and ceremonies in accordance with the precepts of one's religion or belief.

§3. European Union Law

I. European Convention on Human Rights (1950)

516. The most significant system of peripheral European protection is contained in the European Convention 'for the protection of Human Rights and Fundamental Freedoms' (ECHR).[264] The ECHR was signed in Rome, on 4 November 1950, in the context of the activities of the then newly formed Council of Europe, and is today in effect among its Member States. It is supplemented by thirteen Protocols.

517. The ECHR sets in place an effective mechanism of legal review as regards the implementation of the obligations incurred by the states for the protection of human rights. As the principal characteristics of the ECHR, we should consider on the one hand the proclamation of the so-called first-generation rights (civil and political) and, on the other hand, that these rights are legally protected by mechanisms of international review that provide possibilities for individual appeals.

518. More particularly, the protection of religious freedom and its various manifestations is effected mainly through Article 9, bearing the title 'Freedom of thought, conscience and religion', and stipulating the following:

Article 9

1. Everyone has the right to freedom of thought, conscience and religion; this right includes freedom to change his religion or belief and freedom, either alone or in community with others and in public or private, and to manifest his religion or belief, in worship, teaching, practice and observance.
2. Freedom to manifest one's religion or beliefs shall be subject only to such limitations as are prescribed by law and are necessary in a democratic society in the interests of public safety, for the protection of public order, health or morals, or for the protection of the rights and freedoms of others.

519. In addition, according to Article 2 of the Additional Protocol of Paris (which was enacted on 20 March 1952), no one can be deprived of the right to an education. Moreover, every state, while exercising the duties it undertakes in the field of education and schooling, is obliged to respect the right of parents to secure schooling and education, in accordance with their own religious and philosophical beliefs.

520. Finally, it should be mentioned that certain facets of religious freedom are protected by other Articles of the ECHR, such as Article 5 (right to personal freedom and security), Article 6 (right of access to tribunals), Article 8 (right to respect

264. It was ratified by the Greek State (for a second time) with LD 53/1974. In general *see*: Chrysogonos, The Integration of ECHR in the National Legal Order. The Greek Difficulties in Adjusting to the European Public Order of Human Rights, Athens 2001; Stagos, The Judicial Protection of Fundamental Rights in the Legal Order of the European Community, Thessaloniki 2004.

for private and personal life), Article 10 (freedom of expression), Article 11 (freedom of peaceful assembly and association), First Additional Protocol (protection of property).

521. The ECHR is primarily interpreted and implemented by the competent administrative and judicial organs of every state. But in addition to them, the European Court of Human Rights (ECtHR) in Strasbourg is recognized as the chief organ of review for the implementation of the ECHR. Every state that is a member of the Council of Europe has a justice in the ECtHR. The court adjudicates following an appeal, which can be filed by any (physical or legal) person or groups of persons, as long as he/she is harmed by a violation of the ECHR. It should be pointed out that, in order for an appeal to be considered formally admissible, the legal measures provided for by the internal legal order of the State must have previously been exhausted. The hearing process before the ECtHR is public, oral, written and contested. The Court decides on the violation, with a justified decision that is binding on the states, which is announced to the Committee of Ministers who supervise its enforcement.

522. In applying Article 9, the ECtHR has heretofore interpretatively shaped the following case law principles that are considered as guideposts for the legislations of Member States:[265]

(a) Freedom of thought, conscience and religion constitutes one of the cornerstones of a democratic society. Its religious dimension is included in the most essential elements of the personal identity and world view of the followers. At the same time, religious freedom is a valuable legal good for all atheists, agnostics, sceptics or those who are simply indifferent. It has to do with pluralism, which was conquered with sacrifices throughout the centuries, as the quintessence of a democratic society.
(b) A manifestation of religious freedom is the freedom to manifest religious beliefs (individually or in community, in private or in public). This manifestation can take on several forms, such as worship, education, and the exercise of religious duties of every legitimate form. In any case, not every act that is justified or inspired by a religion or a conviction is protected.
(c) Religious freedom is protected both in its positive and in its negative version, namely as a person's right to belong or not belong in a religion, to practise it or not.
(d) One fundamental assertion is that in a democratic society many religions coexist. Consequently, the protection of religious freedom may be accompanied by limitations that work towards compromising the interests of various religious groups and securing respect for the beliefs of each one.
(e) In such an ordering, the State is obliged to remain neutral and unbiased. The role of national authorities is not to deal with the root causes of (any possible) conflicts by abolishing polyphony, but to make sure that the conflicting groups will respect and tolerate each other.

265. Papageorgiou, *Ecclesiastical law*, 112ff.

(f) The State cannot review the 'legitimacy' of religious beliefs or the manner in which these are expressed. When a religious community appears to be divided, the State cannot take measures that favour one side only or impose a single leadership.
(g) The right of the followers to religious freedom also includes the respect of the right of assembly, without any arbitrary interventions on the part of the State. The autonomy of religious communities is a necessary precondition for securing pluralism in a democratic society.
(h) It should be recognized that religious communities have the possibility of judicial protection for themselves, their members and their property.
(i) The recognition of a prevailing religion (Greece) or even of a State Church (Great Britain, Denmark) does not contravene the statutes of the ECHR, as long as this does not lead to unjustifiable discrimination against individuals who do not belong to them.

523. Here is a list of the most important Greek cases, concerning religious freedom, tried before the ECHR:

- *Kokkinakis (3/1992/348/421, 25-5-1993):* the criminalization of unlawful proselytism (Article 4 of OL 1363/1938) does not violate the ECHR, but the relevant condemning decisions must specify with clarity the unlawful means that were possibly utilized. There is a violation of Article 9 ECHR if it is not proven that the conviction of the applicant was justified by a pressing social need and consequently constituted a necessary measure in a democratic society aiming to protect the rights and freedoms of others.[266]
- *Holy Monasteries (1392/87 και 13984/88, first decision: 9-12-1994 and second decision: 1-9-1997):* the statutes of L. 1700/1987 και N. 1811/1988 violate the right of those monasteries that did not agree to their implementation for the peaceful enjoyment of their possessions. The 'deprivation of possessions' applies here (Article 1 of the Additional Protocol of the ECHR).[267]
- *Manousakis (59/1995/565/651, 26-9-1996):* the freedom of manifestation of religion or of convictions, as this is safeguarded by Article of the ECHR, also includes the right of free practice of religious duties and rites in a temple or house of worship. The restrictions that are laid down regarding the establishment and the operation of a church or house of worship should not permissibly exceed those prescribed by law, when they constitute necessary measures in a democratic society, for reasons of securing public order, morals or the rights of others.

---

266. Lindholm/Durham/Tahzib-Lie, *Facilitating freedom of religion or belief: A deskbook*, 107–108, 149, 160–161, passim; Kyriazopoulos, 'Proselytization in Greece: Criminal offence vs. religious persuasion and equality', 149–245; Kyriazopoulos, 'Proselytization in Greece (Kokkinakis judgment): criminal statute vs. "Nullum crimen nulla poena sine lege certa"', 357–395; Androulakis, 'The punishability of proselytization and its constitutionality', 1031–1032; Christoforidis, 'Proselytization in favor of the prevailing religion', 10–14.

267. Lindholm/Durham/Tahzib-Lie, *supra*, 111, 217; Ramiotis, *The church within the Greek state*, 275ff; Papageorgiou, *Ecclesiastical property and national cadastral, 155ff*; Liapis, *Church property and salaries of the clergy*, 113f; Naskou-Perraki/ Ktistakis, *The Greek cases in Strasbourg*, vol. I (1991–2001), Athens 2006, 251–257.

The adoption of further measures on the part of the Greek government, in accordance with the statues of L. 1363/1938, in order to grant a licence for the operation of a house of worship to the members of a religious minority comprises a violation of Article 9 *ECHR*, because it introduces discrimination against a group of citizens on the grounds of their religious beliefs. The criminal conviction for the establishment or operation of a church or house of worship without state licence contravenes the *ECHR* because it cannot be considered as proportional to the pursued legal purpose or necessary in a democratic society.[268]

- *Efstratiou (77/1996/696/888, 18-12-1996) – Valsamis and others (74/1995/ 580/ 666,18-12-1996):* the compulsory under law participation of children in student parades does not constitute a denial of the parents' right to ensure their children's education and teaching in conformity with their own religious and philosophical convictions (Article 2 of the First Protocol to the ECHR), nor does it constitute a violation of their right to religious freedom (Article 9 ECHR).
- *Georgiadis (Recueil 1997-III/29-5-1997):* the ministers of every known religion are entitled to an exemption from military service.
- *Tsirlis and Kouloumbas* (54/1996/673/859-860, 29-5-1997): *see the aforementioned Georgiadis case.*
- *Pentidis and others (59/1996/678/868, 19-3-1997):* the criminal conviction for the establishment or operation of a temple or house of worship without a state licence (OL 1363/1938, Royal Decree of 20-5/2-6-1939) violates Article 9 ECHR on religious freedom.
- *Catholic Church 'Panagia ton Chanion'* (Virgin Mary of the city of Chania, Island of Crete) (143/1996/762/963, 16-12-1997): *religious communities, regardless of their legal personality, are in any case subjects of rights* guaranteed by the ECHR, which they can exercise in the name of their adherents of members. In the case of the Catholic Church of the city of Chania, there was a restriction to the right of appeal to a court, as safeguarded by Article 6 § 1 ECHR. The applicant, as well as all other Churches that existed in Greece before the entry into force of the Civil Code, has a 'sui generis' legal personality.[269]
- *Tsavahidis (28802/95, 21-1-1999):* religious freedom and inviolability of private life. An appeal for a violation of an individual's religious freedom, arising from the fact that the applicant was under surveillance by the National Information Service on the grounds of his religious beliefs.
- *Thlimmenos (34369/97, 6-4-2000):* the applicant's non-appointment in the public sector because he had a prior conviction as a conscientious objector is contrary to Articles 9 and 14 *ECHR*.[270]
- *Sofianopoulos (1988/02 – 1977/02, 12-12-2002):* the identification card issued by the police constitutes a public document, whose content cannot be determined by the wishes of the interested party. The non-inscription of the citizens' creed among the personal data that is mentioned on their identification cards does not encroach upon their right of religious freedom.

---

268. Lindholm/Durham/Tahzib-Lie, *supra,* 108, 427–429, 432, 436–437, passim; Naskou-Perraki/ Ktistakis, *The Greek cases in Strasbourg, supra,* 327–332.
269. Lindholm/Durham/Tahzib-Lie, *supra,* 154, 219.
270. *Ibid.,* 222, 464, 591.

- *Alexandridis (19516/06, 21-2-2008):* oath-taking of a religious character violates the 'negative' religious freedom of the individual (Article 13 Const., 1 and 2 Lawyers' Code, 9 ECHR).
- *Dimitras* (4283/06, 3237/07, 3269/07, 35793/07 και 6099/08, 3-6-2010): *see* the previously noted *Alexandridis* case.
- K*osmas* (20086/13/29-6-2017): the monasteries of Mount Athos enjoy a special legal status, which protects their real estate. The Monastery had the usufruct as its property title.
- *Molla Sali (20452/14/19.12.2018):* the application of the holy Islamic law (sharia) should not be obligatory for the Greek Muslims of Western Thrace. As for their family and inheritance cases, they can choose the application of civil law by the common courts, and not necessarily the sharia by the muftis.
- *Pantelidou* (10-10-2019): the use of a public building by Old Calendarists as a place of worship is not contrary to the ECHR, even if it is in violation of urban planning legislation.
- *Papageorgiou* (31.10.2019). Violation of Article 2 of the First Additional Protocol of the ECHR concerning compulsory religious education in schools. The Court held that the procedure for exempting children from religious education which consists in the parents' obligation to submit a solemn declaration in writing, ratified by the teacher, stating that their child is not of the Orthodox Christian faith, may risk exposing sensitive aspects of the parents' private life and is likely to deter them from submitting a request for their child's exemption, particularly if they live in a small and religiously compact society. When a Contracting State includes a religious education in its curriculum, it is obliged to offer at least one procedure enabling pupils to be exempted from that course, without requiring the parents to make known their religious or philosophical convictions, which constitute a matter of individual conscience. The Court held that there had therefore been a violation of the rights set out in the second sentence of Article 2 of Protocol No. 1, as interpreted in the light of Article 9 of the ECHR.
- *Stavropoulos* (52484/18/25.6.2020): the birth certificate must not contain information from which the religious beliefs of the child or his/her parents can be deduced.

II. The Final Act of Helsinki (1975)

524. According to the 'Final Act of the Conference on Security and Cooperation in Europe' (as the full title goes), the participating states are obliged to respect human rights and fundamental freedoms, along with freedom of thought, conscience, religion or faith for all. They are also responsible for promoting and encouraging the effective exercise of civil, political, economic, social and other rights and freedoms that originate from innate human dignity and are necessary for a person's free and complete development. In this context, the states that participate in the Covenant are obliged to recognize and respect the freedom of the individual to follow any religion or faith, according to the commands of his or her conscience.

III. Charter of Fundamental Rights (2000)

525. It was drawn up and signed during the proceedings of the European Council, which convened in Nice of France on 12 December 2000. The text of the CFR, because it enhances the role and the rights of European Union citizens, was integrated into the 'European Constitution' so that its provisions become legally binding on the signatory states with the entry into force of the European Constitution.

526. More analytically, the CFR includes:

Art. 10, entitled 'Freedom of thought, conscience and religion', provides that:

1. Everyone has the right to freedom of thought, conscience and religion. This right includes freedom to change religion or belief and freedom, either alone or in community with others and in public or in private, to manifest religion or belief, in worship, teaching, practice and observance.
2. The right to conscientious objection is recognised, in accordance with the national laws governing the exercise of this right.

Art. 21, bearing the title 'Non-discrimination', stipulates that:

1. Any discrimination based on any ground such as sex, race, colour, ethnic or social origin, genetic features, language, religion or belief, political or any other opinion, membership of a national minority, property, birth, disability, age or sexual orientation shall be prohibited, *and*

Art. 22, entitled 'Cultural, religious and linguistic diversity', according to which:

The Union shall respect cultural, religious and linguistic diversity.

527. If we compare the provisions of the CFR with the provisions of the ECHR, we will observe that the former contains all the rights enshrined by the ECHR, with the difference that its statutes are more simple and general than those of the latter.

IV. Treaties of Amsterdam (1999) and of Lisbon (2007)

528. In addition to the three aforementioned systems of protection of human rights and religious freedom in the European continent, we find a reference to the same right in the Treaty of Amsterdam,[271] which amended the Treaty of the European Union and the Treaties establishing the European Communities. Thus, according to the declaration numbered 11 'Declaration on the status of churches and nonconfessional organisations':

271. Ratified by L. 2691/1999.

> The European Union respects and does not prejudice the status under national law of churches and religious associations or communities in the Member States. The European Union equally respects the status of philosophical and non-confessional organisations.

529. Finally, Article 6 of the Treaty of Lisbon (2007)[272] stipulated the accession of the countries of the European Union to the ECHR.

272. Ratified by L. 3671/2008.

Chapter 2. Transnational Law Effects on Religious Communities

§1. Mount Athos

530. The regime of Mount Athos is protected both by the Greek Constitution (Article 105) and by the international treaties of Berlin (Article 62, 1878), of Bucharest (Article 5, 1913),[273] of Sevres (Articles 13, 27 and 84, 1920) and finally of Lausanne (1923).[274]

531. The entrenchment of the privileged Mount Athos regime was also sought after in the context of European legislation. More particularly, a relevant declaration (Common Declaration 4) was annexed to the Final Act concerning the Accession of the Hellenic Republic to the European Communities (1979).[275] Its content was as follows:

> Recognizing that the special status granted to Mount Athos, as guaranteed by article 105 of the Greek Constitution, is justified exclusively on grounds of a spiritual and religious nature, the Community will ensure that this status is taken into account in the application and subsequent preparation of provisions of community law, in particular in relation to customs franchise privileges, tax exemptions and the right of establishment *(page XVIII of the Final Act concerning the Accession of Greece to the European Communities, 1979).*[276]

§2. Muslims

532. The following treaties make specific reference to the religious freedom of the Muslims of Greece:

(i) The Treaty of Athens, signed between the Ottoman Empire and the Kingdom of Greece (4/14-11-1913),[277] which stipulated in its Article 11 that Greece undertook the obligation to respect all religious minorities inhabiting the territories ceded to it, especially the Muslim one.
(ii) Articles 37–45 of the Treaty of Lausanne (1923), by which Greece and Turkey undertook the joint obligation to:

---

273. Papastathis, 'The regime of Mount Athos and of the church in Macedonia after the Treaty of Bucharest', in: The Treaty of Bucharest and Greece, *Foundation for Aimos Peninsula Studies*, Thessaloniki 1990, 191–200.
274. Ratified by P.D. of 29-9/30-10-1923, 'On the protection of minorities in Greece'. *See*: Antonopoulos, '*La condition international du Mont Athos*', Le Millenaire du Mont Athos, *963-1963. Etudes et Melanges* 1 (Chevetogne 1963), 381–405; Papastathis, *The nationality of the Mount Athos monks of non-Greek origin,* 75ff; Economides, *Le Mont Athos et le droit international,* 47ff.
275. Ratified by L. 945/1979.
276. Skandamis, *Mount Athos and the European Communities'*, 271–285; Evrigenis, *Reflexions theoriques sur la Declaration Commune relative au Mont Athos*, 13–17; Yataganas, *Declaration commune relative au Mont Athos (Intervention)*, 83–84.
277. Ratified by L. 4213/14-11-1913.

- provide all their inhabitants with the absolute and complete protection of life and liberty, without distinction of nationality, language or religion (Article 45);
- allow them to freely exercise, in public or private, any creed, religion or belief, as long as its observance is not incompatible with public order and good morals (Article 38); and
- secure equal treatment before the law, without distinction of religion (Articles 39, 40 and 43).

533. It is clarified that the Treaty of Lausanne does not apply to the Muslims of the Dodecanese since these islands were annexed to Greece with the peace treaty which was signed with Italy on 10 February 1947.[278]

§3. The Roman Catholic Church

534. In addition to the other international treaties which generally protect religious freedom, the Roman Catholics inhabiting Greece are also mentioned in the Third Protocol of London, which was signed on 22-1/3-2-1830 between the states of Great Britain, France and Russia.[279,280] In this manner, the force of the canon law of the Roman Catholic Church was introduced to our country as well, regulating the administration and management of the Catholic churches and foundations of Greece, under the precondition that its stipulations do not contravene Greek legislation.[281]

535. According to Article 13 (entitled: 'Recognition of legal personality of the Catholic Church in Greece') of L. 4301/2014, the Catholic Church in Greece, which is based in Athens and governed by the Holy Synod of the Catholic Hierarchy of Greece, is recognized as an ecclesiastical legal person of private law with no further formalities and with no need to follow the procedures laid down in Articles 3 and 12, even if the minimum number of members or religious legal persons stipulated in the previous articles is not met. By the same Article, approximately 240 dioceses, parishes and monasteries of the Catholic Church, that are clearly specified, are recognized as religious legal persons in private law.

278. Ratified by P.D. 423/22-10-1947.

279. Asimakis, *The development of relations between Greece and the Holy See*, 1820–1980. From French protection to the establishment of diplomatic relations, Thessaloniki 2007; Troianos, 'The legal status of the catholic archdiocese of Athens', NoV 31 (1983) 485–487.

280. It became accepted by Greece with a Memorandum (Declaration) of the Greek Senate (4/16 Apr. 1830). *See AP 360/1994*, D 26 (1995) 282–284.

281. *See* lately: *Codex Juris Canonici*, Athens 2020. *See also*: Asimakis, *Legislation and jurisprudence for the catholic church in Greece*, Thessaloniki 2014; *LCS 1229/1955;* contra: *AP 428/1951*, ND 8 (1952) 11–12.

Chapter 3. Regional Law Effects on Religious Communities

536. The VAT, which is the most significant community tax, was introduced to our country with L. 1642/1986, which was ultimately codified by the law which is currently in force, L. 2859/2000. As it is widely known, the VAT is imposed on the purchase prices of goods and services, burdening their end consumer. More particularly, the activities on which the VAT is applicable are: (a) the supply of goods and services, affected for a consideration within the territory of the country; (b) the importation of goods within the territory of the country; and (c) the acquisition of goods within the European Communities, which is carried out for a consideration within the territory of the country.

537. Article 2 § 2 of L. 2859/2000 stipulates that as regards the VAT provisions, the Greek territory is considered as 'the interior of the country', however 'with the exception of the region of Mount Athos'.[282] It should be noted that, before the accession of Greece to the European Communities (1979), Mount Athos had been specifically excluded from the scope of implementation of the VAT, by virtue of Article 3 (Title III: Territoriality) § 3, section 4 of the 6th Directive of the Council of the European Communities of the 17 May 1977 (77/388/EEC).

282. Mount Athos was not the only territory to be exempted from the concept of 'interior' of the Member States as to the implementation of the VAT. Other such territories include certain overseas conquests of France (Martinique, French Guinea, Guadeloupe, St. Peter, Miquelon), Germany (the Island of Heligoland and the region of Buzingen), Spain (the Canary Islands), Italy (the regions of Livigno and Campione d' Italia), as well as Gibraltar which is under the sovereignty of the United Kingdom.

Part V. Religion & Politics

Chapter 1. Religious Influence in Politics

538. In Greece, the considerable influence that decisions by the country's religious leaders can exert on political affairs represents a logical expression of the more general influence that religion exerts on a very large section of modern Greek society.[283] This, of course, does not mean that religious Greeks are guided solely by the political choices – be they direct or indirect, clear or less obvious – of their Church leadership. In the final analysis, all citizens are free to exercise their own personal judgment and even to directly and openly disagree with any of the Church's political decisions.

539. Even so, it should be acknowledged that when the latter is represented by figures of recognized spiritual authority, then the political choices made by the Church's leadership exert a more decisive influence on the Church's members. It should be stressed that this fact is not unconnected with the very high level of corruption and disrepute that exists among the political leaders themselves, which in turn leads the Church's members to place greater trust in their Church leaders and their assessments of the political situation.

540. Some Church hierarchs seek to become directly involved in political affairs, a fact that does not always meet with general social approval.[284] The Orthodox Church itself avoids expressing official support for any political party precisely because it believes that this conflicts with its spiritual role and could cause divisions among its flock.

283. On this issue *see*: Tsironis, *Church in politics (1913-1941)*, 429–434, passim; Zoumpoulakis, *God in town: Essays on religion and politics*, 49ff, 55ff; Zoumpoulakis, *Christians in the public space: Faith or cultural identity?*, 29ff; Close, *Greece (1945-2004): Policy: society-economy*, 160ff; Petrou, *Church and politics in Greece (1750-1909)*, 141–189; Prinzipas/Karagiannis, *Church and hellenism from 1821 till today: An historical overview*, passim; Kitromilides, *New Greek enlightenment: The political and social ideas*, 87ff, passim; Matalas, *Nation and orthodoxy: The adventures of a relationship*, 4ff; Diamantouros, *The origins of the modern state formation in Greek (1821-1828)*, 73ff; Svoronos, *The Greek nation. origin and formation of the new hellenism*, 96ff; Makridis, *The orthodox church in the 20th century: A historico-sociological survey*, 861ff; Manitakis, *The relations of the church with the nation-state under the shadow of the identity*, 163ff, passim.

284. Tsironis, *supra*, 120ff, 171ff, passim; Stefanidis, *In the name of the nation: Political culture, irredentism and anti-Americanism in post-war Greece (1945-1967)*, 40f; Manitakis, *The relations of the church with the nation-state under the shadow of the identity*, 185ff.

541. The Orthodox Church, as well as the country's other religious communities, often takes a public stand on issues of equal concern to the State, such as civil marriage or abortion.[285] No one can deny these religious communities their constitutionally safeguarded right to publicly express their views on issues of general social concern. Religions are entitled to believe that their views can help create a better world and also to proclaim the opinions they hold on various subjects. Moreover, this entitlement stems from the right to individual freedom of opinion and expression. In the context of a democratic society and religious freedom, these rights are safeguarded for all – not only religious people but also those who follow no religion, atheists and agnostics, etc.[286]

542. On the basis of the foregoing, to exclude the views of various church or religious communities from public dialogue, even if this dialogue had political implications, would be a direct violation of the rules governing equal treatment and the democratic functioning of society.[287] Yet, such an extreme stand is taken against the church when the latter's public discourse questions political views or annoys certain sectors of the political establishment that seek to promote their own views to the exclusion of all others. For this reason, I am afraid to say that quite often political fanaticism can prove to be far worse than the religious variety.

543. In connection with the above, it should be made clear that the fact that the majority of ecclesiastical organizations are classified as public legal entities does not make them agencies of the State or political bodies expressing the will of the State. On the contrary, this arrangement aims to provide these ecclesiastical organizations with the maximum statutory protection and the widest powers of self-government.[288]

544. In many cases, decisions of religious importance have political implications and vice versa. Thus, the religious sphere is not always strictly religious but often overlaps the political sphere. In other words, in many cases, a religious matter may become a matter of public or political concern.[289]

545. Thorny issues may arise from the difficulty that Muslims have in understanding that, while religion enjoys complete freedom in the private sphere, the political culture of contemporary Western European societies requires that in the

---

285. Makrides, 'The brotherhoods of theologians in contemporary Greece', The Greek Orthodox Theological Review 33 (1988) 167–187.
286. Argyropoulos, *Freedom of religious conscience and the obligation to declare one's religious affiliation in public documents,* 21ff.
287. Deliyanni-Dimitrakou, *Comparative law and legal pluralism,* 13ff, passim.
288. Papageorgiou, 'The community law on public works and ecclesiastical self-administration: The integration of regulation 55/1974 relating to ecclesiastical works with Directive 2004/18/EC', Arm. 65 (2011) 361f.
289. Makrides, 'Orthodoxy in the service of anticommunism: the religious organization Zoe during the Greek civil war', 159–174. *See also* in general: Madeley, 'Religion and politics', *International library of politics and comparative government, England-USA 2003*, and especially the study of Prodromou, *Paradigms, power and identity: Rediscovering orthodoxy and regionalizing Europe*, 663–689.

public sphere the principle of neutrality should be observed. This is due to the fact that, while Christian communities can distinguish between what is 'secular' and what is 'sacred', such a distinction is not acceptable in the Muslim religion. Even so, this distinction represents a fundamental constitutional rule in contemporary Western democracies, one that safeguards religious freedom and at the same time provides protection against manifestations of religious fanaticism.[290]

546. The religious communities in Greece are not represented as discrete political parties in the Greek Parliament. This, however, does not mean that the members and officials of these religious communities cannot exercise their political rights, namely the right to vote and the right to be elected.

547. On the other hand, the Orthodox Church or any other religious authority can, on the basis of its internal law, place certain restrictions on its clerics if their clerical status is considered to be incompatible with holding public office. If these clerics fail to respect these restrictions on political activity, then the consequences will be felt only in the church and not in the State.

290. *See*, for example, Deliyanni-Dimitrakou, *Comparative law and legal pluralism,* 93–210; Roberta Aluffi Beck-Peccoz, 'Proselytism and the right to change religion in Islam', in: Ferrari/Cristofori (ed.), *Law and religion in the 21st century: Relations between states and religious communities*, 253–259.

Chapter 2. Political Influence in Religion

548. The system of church-state relations that was strictly applied in Greece immediately after its liberation from the Turkish yoke has, to this day, permitted the State to make numerous interventions of either an obvious or inconspicuous kind in the internal affairs of the Orthodox Church, despite the fact that the latter's internal self-government is safeguarded by the Constitution.[291] This extreme form of state dominance over the church has often annulled whatever self-governing powers were held by the Church, turning the latter into an organic extension of the State, completely subordinate to its dictates of government.

549. In collaboration with important ecclesiastical and political figures and other similarly minded bodies, and with the approval of a section of the hierarchy, Maurer drew up the Decree of 23 July/4 August 1833 entitled 'Proclamation of the Independence of the Greek Church'. According to this text, supreme ecclesiastical power was to be exercised by a five-member Synod of Bishops (Prelates), whose members were to be appointed for one year by the government and the King Otto (who was, it should be noted, a Roman Catholic!).[292]

550. The Holy Synod's deliberations were to be compulsorily attended by a representative of the King, the 'Royal Commissioner', without whose approval no ecclesiastical decision could take effect. Thus the ruling Church body came to be very tightly controlled by the state administration, whose policies the Church of Greece had to obediently follow.[293]

551. The 'Statutory Law of the Church of Greece', that was passed in 1923, established the Holy Synod as the supreme ruling body of the Autocephalous Church of Greece, thus consolidating the synodical system of government and stipulating, within the same framework, that bishops were to be directly elected by the Synod. Charters of the Church of Greece were Laws 5187/1931, 5438/ 1932 and 671/1943, as well as LD 126/1932, which was in force during the period of the dictatorship.[294] Shortly after the restoration of democracy in 1974, the law currently in force, Law 590/1977, was passed.

---

291. von Maurer, *The Greek people: Public, private and ecclesiastical law from the beginning of the independence struggle until 31 July 1834*, Athens 2007, passim; Frazee, *Orthodox church and Greek independency (1821-1852),* 119ff.

292. Frazee, *The orthodox church and Greek independence (1821-1852),* 161–213; Troianos/ Dimakopoulou, *Church and state: Relations between them during the period 1833-1852,* 51–58.

293. The newly founded 'Independent Church of Greece' was essentially transformed into a state entity under the oversight of a ministry, while the Head of the Church always had to bear in mind that the Minister of Education and Religious Affairs was his superior; for example, *see* Veremis/ Koliopoulos, *Modern Greece from 1821 up to the present day,* 463.

294. For an analysis of the State interventions that inflicted institutional damage on the Church of Greece during the period of the dictatorship (1967–1973), *see*: Marinos, *Thoughts on the crisis in the Church of Greece,* Church and Law. Theory and Case Law, 604–637, and, *Church-State relations [under the 1975 Constitution and the new Constitutional Charter of the Church of Greece],* 100–116 (on this issue *see* especially Chapter III, *Interventions in Church government attempted during the period 21/4/1967 – 23/7/1974);* cf. Prinzipas/Karagiannis, *The church and hellenism*

552. The post-war period was characterized by a host of arbitrary State interventions in the internal affairs of the Orthodox Church. Some of these were so overt and violent that they were beyond the bounds of any reasonable concept of state control. However, one should not overlook the well-confirmed fact that some of these interventions were welcomed – if not directly encouraged – by certain cliques within the ruling church with the ultimate aim of furthering their own personal interests and ambitions.

553. From the long series of (obvious and inconspicuous) interventions, it is worth mentioning the appointment by the military junta (1967–1973) of a large number of prelates as members of the Permanent Holy Synod, a considerable number of whom provided the necessary ideological 'legitimization' that the colonels' dictatorship needed from the church in order to gain public approval.[295] And yet it was another type of junta that appointed Archbishop Seraphim (1973–1998), the main characteristic of whose reign was a general indifference towards the image and presence of the church in public affairs.[296]

554. The only serious way in which the church hierarchy became involved in public affairs, though it was of short duration, was when it reacted against the implementation of L. 1700/1987 (the so-called Tritsis Law), which unconstitutionally confiscated monastic property.[297] It was of short duration because, after initially calling on the people to take to the streets in dynamic mass rallies, the hierarchy itself immediately backtracked in a sudden and inexplicable manner (one which remains unexplained even today), leaving the monasteries and many faithful members of the Church's flock to fight protracted legal battles to annul the implementation of the same blatantly unconstitutional law.

555. The most recent sharp public confrontation between Church and State occurred in 2001 when the Greek government, following a recommendation by the Greek Data Protection Authority,[298] expressed its intention to remove the reference to religious affiliation from Greek citizens' identity cards. However, this attempt met

---

from 1821 up until the present day: an historical overview, 151–172 ('The period of the dictatorship'). As has been noted: 'The military regime of 21/4/1967 added a comic element to the State's institutional control of the Church. By advertising their relations with the Church at every possible opportunity, the colonels damaged its authority, particularly in terms of exposing the defamation it had suffered over the course of the previous decades. After the 1967 coup, the Archbishop of Athens was forced to withdraw, while another archbishop favoured by the junta was "elected" in his place': Veremis/Koliopoulos, *supra,* 470.

295. Close, *Greece (1945–2004): Politics-society-economy*, 334f.

296. It is no coincidence that enlightened theologians have distinguished this period as one characterized by a doleful silence on the part of the church, a period in which the Orthodox Church 'existed' but was in practice inactive and essentially absent from any serious kind of public activity, which drastically exacerbated the lack of respect that citizens had for the Church and particularly its ruling members. For example, *see*: Zoumpoulakis, *God in town: Essays on religion and politics,* 53ff; Prinzipas/Karagiannis, *Church and hellenism from 1821 till today: An historical overview,* 173ff.

297. Papageorgiou, 'Findings from the ecclesiastical case law of the Council of State of the year 1987', Arm. Scientific Yearbook 17 (1996) 32f.

298. *Greek Data Protection Authority 510/15 May 2000,* ToS 26 (2000) 948: 'identity cards, issue procedure, data included in them; identity cards are public documents that contain data of a personal

with the stout resistance of the dynamic Archbishop Christodoulos, who, among other things, organized two enormous rallies (or laosynaxeis, 'assemblies of the people', as he called them) in Athens and Thessaloniki.[299] On the other hand, this State venture was not supported with much enthusiasm by members of the government and even less by those of the opposition parties, which, evidently in order to avoid any political cost, proposed that a referendum should be conducted on the issue. In the end, any reference to religious affiliation on identity cards, even a voluntary one, was adjudged to be unconstitutional by the Council of State[300] and the whole matter was gradually forgotten.

nature; this data is recorded in an archive kept by the competent public authorities and may be processed by other authorities, services or third parties; consequently, this data falls within the scope of application of L. 2472/1997; the Authority is of the opinion that the fingerprint and references to first name and surname of spouse, occupation, citizenship, residence and religious affiliation exceed the purpose of the data compilation, which is to confirm the subject's identity, and violate the above principles; nor does the subject's consent itself allow any act of processing when the latter is unlawful or contrary to the principle of purpose and necessity'.

299. For the range of views of (mainly) the Church on this issue *see* the collective work *Church and ID cards: a theological and legal consideration of the issue of ID cards,* Athens 2000, published by the Holy Synod of the Church of Greece; cf. Papadopoulou, 'On the creed of identification cards', ToS 26 (2000) 675–723.

300. CoS 2279-2282/2001 *(Plenary Session)*, Arm. 55 (2001) 1111–1135: the data contained in identity cards constitutes data of a personal nature and the recording of such data constitutes an act of data processing; the compulsory recording of religious affiliation on identity cards is contrary to the Constitution. *See* the ECHR judgment of 12 Dec. 2002 in the *Sofianopoulos v. Greece case,* NoV 51 (2003) 801–805: identity cards are public documents, the content of which cannot be determined by the desires of the individual concerned; the non-recording of citizens' religious affiliations among the data contained in identity cards does not contravene their right to religious freedom (Art. 9 ECHR).

Chapter 3. Interaction Between Religion and State on a Political and Legal Level

556. In appraising the political and institutional relations that exist between Church and State, in the form they have come to assume since the time of the rebirth of the Greek nation, we may observe their dynamically dialectical character: the political relations between the two institutions have passed, though of course not in a rectilinear fashion, through all the possible points on a scale ranging from smooth and mutual collaboration, within the framework of the classic concept of 'discrete roles',[301] to direct conflict, for reasons stemming mainly from political choices. A point of constant friction has been not so much the existence of the Church but the manner in which it has operated within the framework of State institutions, as well as its social and political role, in a country where it has been easy, at least in the past, to invest clerics with powers of an ethnarchic nature.[302]

557. The constitutional framework of the relations between the Greek State and the Orthodox Church cannot be said to be particularly stable, as the history of the last few decades has repeatedly shown. And this is because it is influenced to a large extent by both the figures that represent the respective institutions and also the State or Church policy prevailing at any given time. Ultimately, the abstract content of the constitutional provisions that govern the above relations is given meaning by the political, historical and ecclesiastical conditions prevailing at any given moment. For this reason, any attempt to place these constantly changing relations in a cohesive and completely homogenous system carries little conviction or consistency.

558. It is entirely certain that even today the State rules over the Church (the 'State-law rule' system): the State is legally empowered to intervene in ecclesiastical affairs through laws passed by Parliament (Article 72 § 1 Const.). It is, however, a well-known fact that this legislative competence is often accompanied by unconstitutional or extra-institutional interventions that violate the constitutionally safeguarded right of ecclesiastical self-government.[303]

301. Feidas, 'The operation of the discrete roles of church and state and the responsibility of the state', E. 78 (2001) 232–247.
302. As has been aptly observed, from a political standpoint, the Church should be socially active and useful, yet at the same time it should always be under constant State control, whether tight or loose, and basically restricted to the religious sphere. The underlying fear here has been of the possible emergence of tendencies in the Church to make a complete break with the State and the revival of ethnarchic visions. On the other hand, the Church has always sought to overcome the social marginalization in which it has found itself since the Ottoman period, and to play a more vital role in society, beyond the narrow religious sphere; for a more detailed analysis *see* Makridis, *The orthodox church in the 20th century: A historico-sociological survey,* Commemorative volume for Penelope Agallopoulou, 860ff.
303. For example, *see* Papastathis, *Nomocanonical studies,* 65ff, 85ff.

Part VI. Labour Law Within Religious Communities

Chapter 1. Scope of Application of Labour Law

559. As we already know, church or religious entities and organizations are in need of a big number of people, either clergy or laity, for the service and promotion of all kinds of religious, spiritual or broader social objectives. In addition, there are many people who are driven by philanthropic motives and wish to offer their services voluntarily, expecting a merely moral reward.[304]

560. At the same time, a significant number of posts in the broader Greek public sector is expected to be covered by clergy or church officials of the Orthodox Church. Thus, dioceses, parishes, monasteries and religious (charitable, educational, etc.) institutions are served by clergy (bishops, priests and deacons), chanters, vergers and lay church employees, most of whom are paid by the State.[305]

561. Finally, a number of places are provided for the posts of Muslim legal entities (muftis, etc.), which are mainly found in Western Thrace.[306]

562. Due to the fact that in the above-mentioned cases the actual employer is the State, the rules governing the working conditions of these personnel come under the general provisions of civil service law.[307] But if religious bodies (organizations/dioceses/churches/monasteries, etc.) wish to hire personnel on an employment relationship under private law, then, in those cases the common labour law is applied.[308]

304. On all these points, *see* generally Koukiadis/Papastathis, Droit du travail et religion en Gréce, 115ff. More lately, Papageorgiou, *Ecclesiastical law*, 289ff; Troianos, *Lectures in ecclesiastical law*, 307ff, 372ff; Christophilopoulos, *Greek ecclesiastical law,* 129ff; Konidaris, *Lessons*, 65f.
305. From a particular point of view, *see* Liapis, *Church property and salaries of the clergy,* 55ff, passim.
306. *See* below: '2: Muslim Clerics'.
307. L. 3528/2007 (as it is today in force), about the current regime of civil servants. *See also* Kondylis/Ktistaki/Tziraki, *Employees code*, Athens 2018.
308. In general, *see* Lixouriotis, *Individual employment relationships,* Athens 2020.

Chapter 2. Religious Ministers and Labour Law

§1. Orthodox Clergy

563. The organizational, administrative and spiritual needs of the numerous legal entities of the Orthodox Church are served by the clergy, who are divided into bishops, priests and deacons.[309] The clergy are appointed to vacant positions and, as a rule, are paid by the public budget (Article 7 seq L. 4354/2015).

564. Chaplains, in particular, are priests whose mission is to care for the religious and spiritual lives of parishioners, and resolve any issues concerning the spiritual as well as material progress of the parish. Their official status is currently governed mainly by the ecclesiastical Regulations 230/2012 and 303/2018 'On Chaplains and Deacons'.[310] According to this, the chaplain must have been ordained and remain dependent on the local bishop (metropolitan).[311]

565. Depending on the conditions and criteria for their appointment, the chaplains of parish churches are divided into 'regular' and 'temporary' ones. The vacant positions of the parish churches are permanently covered by married priests (regular chaplains), or temporarily by unmarried ones (temporary chaplains), after a decision made by the local bishop.

566. The chaplain carries out the spiritual and administrative tasks always with reference to the relevant bishop, applying the law, the rules and the provisions or directives of the latter (Article 8 Reg. 230/2012). More specifically, chaplains should make sure that they constitute role models for believers. In this context they:

(a) perform, with the required consistency and order, the liturgy and other church ceremonies as well as the sacrament of penance;
(b) provide for the general spiritual or material needs of the parish, support its underprivileged members with organized charity and social welfare initiatives, and cooperate with other charitable institutions of the Diocese;
(c) organize the parish office, handle various relative affairs, prepare and complete the list of parishioners, keep consistently the parish register, acts of ecclesiastical council, baptisms, marriages, celibacy and cadastral certificates, update all archival files and care for the maintenance of holy relics and any other movable or immovable property of the parish;
(d) bear the standard Orthodox clergy attire, avoiding any arbitrary change or appearance without it;[312]

309. As it has been already noted, the members of the Church are divided into three orders, clergy, laity and monks; Troianos, *Lectures in ecclesiastical law*, 142ff, 147ff, 170ff.
310. For an analysis *see* Papageorgiou, *Ecclesiastical law*, 275ff.
311. *See* CoS (Plenary Session) 210/2020 on service status of parish priests.
312. Article 54 SCCG; Decree of 21-1-1931, 'On the standard Greek Orthodox clergy attire'.

(e) are permanently domiciled within the boundaries of the parish and may leave out of them only after being given approval by the local bishop;[313]
(f) carry out the chaplain tasks as those are allocated among the priests, always according to the instructions of the relevant bishop;
(g) are not involved in non-Orthodox mission, neither engage in secular affairs that could disrupt the spiritual unity of parishioners.

567. The chaplain has all the rights deriving from the parish office and his position, as those are defined by the laws (especially L. 590/1977, CCCG) and rules (Article 9 Reg. 230/2012). These rights particularly refer to the:

(a) (lifelong) tenure of the church office;
(b) permanency of the position in the parish, allowing for legal or normal exceptions;
(c) salary, social security and retirement that apply to the exercise of that function;
(d) provision of legitimate monthly leave, sick leave and educational leave (Article 37 § 9 L. 590/1977).

568. The education and training of priests or deacons are covered by the Higher Ecclesiastical Academies, Theological Schools of the Universities of Athens and Thessaloniki, or by other Orthodox Theological Schools (Article 10 Reg. 230/2012). The Orthodox Church of Greece, the Athens archdiocese and the local dioceses (metropolises) may establish special training colleges or clerical schools for the special training and pastoral training of clergy.[314]

569. By filling in an application, priests may leave their service (Article 13 Reg. 230/2012), having reached the age of 70, and served the parish for thirty-five years. They may leave at an earlier time if found unfit for performing their parish duties due to mental or physical illness.[315]

570. Apart from the above-mentioned cases of retirement, the parish priest may be dismissed from his position (Article 15 Reg. 230/2012):

(a) due to an imposed ecclesiastical penalty, in accordance with L. 5383/1932 'On the ecclesiastical courts';
(b) if his conduct is opposed to his official duties, as, for example, an unjustified absence (without permission) from his post for longer than thirty days or failure

313. Article 55 SCCG; CoS 2336/1980: the provisions of Art. 56 §§ 1, 2 L. 590/1977 (CCCG) are contrary to the Art. 5 Const.; Rotis, 'Constitutional order and sacred canons', ToS 7 (1981) 428–439; Orfanoudakis, *The sacred canons and the Constitution (a counter-comment or 'the other' interpretative approach)*, Arm. 35 (1981) 82–83.
314. For more details about the above issue, *see* 'Part IX. Education'.
315. CoS 153/1993: the acceptance of a priest's resignation is mandatory on the part of the bishop; the resignee should be provided with the time needed for considering any withdrawal of resignation, unless reasons of public interest require immediate acceptance.

to comply with a lawful appointment (posting). A standard procedure of bishop's relevant action in such cases is a prior call to the priest so that he is given the opportunity to apologize or provide an explanation;[316]

(c) if the priest is a teacher, who carries out chaplain tasks as well, and he is transferred to another area, so that it is impossible to perform his chaplain duties.

571. The posts of deacons in parish churches are defined by the provisions of LD 1398/1973 and L 673/1977 (Article 20 Reg. 230/2012).[317] To the deacons apply *mutatis mutandis* whatever applies to temporary chaplains. Issues of ranking, payroll, insurance and retirement of the deacons of parish churches are governed by the applicable provisions.[318]

572. Despite the fact that the clergy are paid by the State,[319] they are not considered civil servants (public officials) or employees of public legal entities, but 'public ministers', due to the eminently religious nature of the services they offer.[320] For this reason, restrictions – such as the prohibition of possessing a second work position in the public sector – which apply to all civil servants do not apply to chaplains. Thus, the clergy may simultaneously work as educators or ecclesiastical officials, which constitutes an exception to the general restriction required by L. 1256/1982 (possession of second post).[321]

573. But according to the decision of the Greek Supreme Court (Areios Pagos) 703/1997,[322] the chaplain, as the chairman of the church council, functions as an executive organ of church administration and performs services to the legal entity of public law of his parish. This fact provides him with the status of a 'public official', according to Article 13 paragraph (a) Penal Code, which results in his increased criminal responsibility (Article 262 of the Penal Code).[323]

574. Issues concerning the regime of chanters are regulated by the ecclesiastical Reg. 176/2006, which provides that they are appointed by the local bishop, after a reasoned opinion of the 'Chanters' Evaluation Committee'.[324] According to the

316. Otherwise, there is an infringement on standard procedure, Art. 6 Code of Administrative Procedure, 20 § 2 Const.
317. Troianos/Papageorgiou, *Religious legislation*, 621f, 625f.
318. Papageorgiou, *Ecclesiastical law*, 276ff.
319. L. 536/1945, 'On regulating the remuneration of Orthodox clergy in Greece, the payment method and the way of capping the cost' (OGG A' 226). *See also* L. 469/1968, 'On salary gradation of the Church of Greece clergy' (OGG A 162); *AP 843/1983*, NoV 32 (1984) 474–475.
320. CoS 507/1983, 4045/1983.
321. Papageorgiou, 'Findings from the ecclesiastical case law of the Council of State of the year 1987', Arm. Scientific Yearbook 17 (1996) 35f.
322. NoV 46 (1998) 262–263; of the same content, *see AP 729/1988*, PChr 38 (1988) 856–858.
323. According to the CoS (see lately 1753/2017), priests and monks are not entitled to work as lawyers.
324. Troianos/Papageorgiou, Religious Legislation, *678-693;* Ang. Stergiou, Self-employed and salaried workers in social insurance: towards a typological approach of dependent employment in labour law and social insurance, *160.*

Council of State (Plenary Session) 4078/1979,[325] the services offered by the Church chanters constitute an integral part of worship and are not at all related to administrative work. Therefore, chanters cannot be characterized as 'civil servants' and are not permanent (as it happens with all the rest of the civil servants; *see also* Article 103 Const.).[326]

575. Religious ministers of all creeds cannot be elected as mayors, councillors, regional governors or regional councillors (Article 70 1 L. 4604/2019).

§2. MUSLIM CLERGYMEN

576. The procedure as well as the qualifications for the appointment of *muftis* are defined by the provisions of L. 1920/1991, 'On Muslim religious functionaries'.[327] Vacancies of the muftis are covered by Muslim Greek citizens, who hold a diploma of the higher Islamic theological school (domestic or foreign) or 'Itzazet' diploma holders. In addition, imams who have served for at least ten years may also be appointed as muftis, as long as they are distinguished for their ethos and theological training and for whom there are no appointment impediments according to the Civil Servants Code.

577. The mufti is appointed by a presidential decree, for a ten-year term which may be renewed. This PD is issued in consultation with a committee of Muslim elders and upon the proposal of the Minister of Education and Religious Affairs. The appointee, before taking office, gives the oath of a public official and receives a public salary. Muftis (and some imams) have been trained on their own means in Saudi Arabia, Egypt and Turkey, especially in Mecca or Medina.[328]

578. According to the CoS (Plenary Session) 2100/2019, the muftis are civil servants and occupy the rank of general manager. They exercise religious duties and judicial responsibilities with regard to certain categories of family and inheritance law cases involving Greek Muslims in their jurisdictions.

579. The mufti is dismissed[329] also by a presidential decree of the same minister, in case of:

325. EDDD 24 (1980) 334–335; CoS 3314/1979; CoS 1014/1981; CoS 4602/1988.

326. Dagtoglou, *Constitutional law: Individual rights*, 821ff, 846f; Dagtoglou, *General administrative law*, 19f, 52f, passim. The verges are also appointed and fired by the local metropolitan, *First Instant Court 274/2017.*

327. CoS 466/2003; Antoniou, *Muslim immigrants in Greece: Religious organization and local responses*, 157f; Stavrou, 'The legal status of minorities in Greece today: The adequacy of their protection in the light of current human rights perceptions', 33f; Tsitselikis, 'Muslims in Greece', in: Potz/Wieshaider (eds), Islam and the European Union, 80f. *See also* Menaidis, *The religious freedom of Muslims in the Greek legal order*, 287ff.

328. On this point, *see* Tsitselikis, *Old and new Islam in Greece: From historical minorities to immigrant newcomers*, Leiden 2012, 367ff.

329. CoS (Plenary Session) 869/2018: conditions for dismissal of the mufti from his duties.

(a) reaching the age of 67 years;[330]
(b) an irrevocable conviction of a felony or misdemeanour;
(c) deprivation of political rights for any reason;
(d) a disease that hinders the exercise of his duties, professional incompetence or conduct that was undignified or incompatible with the duties of his position.

580. The muftis are civil servants, holding the position of general manager and receiving appropriate remuneration. In exercising their duties, they have the obligations of public officials according to Constitution and laws (Article 4 L. 1920/1991). The mufti has also the jurisdiction of *qadi,* that is, the judge who is entitled to act as the highest religious teacher and interpreter-judge of *Shari'a.*[331]

581. Imams are graduates of the Thrace *madrasas*, or they may have completed the *imam hatib* in Turkey (comparable to the *madrasas),* or may have completed junior or senior high school education or, in limited numbers, theological university studies in Turkey or in Arab countries such as Saudi Arabia, Syria and Egypt.

582. Nowadays, there are about four hundred Muslim ministers *(muftis, imams, hatibs* and *muezzins).*

330. Article 48 para. 2 of L. 4559/2018.
331. Menaidis, *The religious freedom of Muslims in the Greek legal order,* 348ff.

Chapter 3. Other Church Employees and Labour Law

583. The Church of Greece employs clerical staff in order to cover its organizational and administrative needs. The official rules governing the clerical staff, who work in the legal entities of public law of the Church of Greece, are regulated by the ecclesiastical Reg. 5/1978 'Church Employees Code'.[332] The salary of these church officials is paid from the public budget.

584. Specific provisions of the Church Employees Code define – in a manner similar to what provides the common Employees Code for the civil servants of the public sector in general – the details about qualifications, appointment procedure, promotion, transfer, leaves of absence and disciplinary proceedings of ecclesiastical officials.

585. Furthermore, according to Article 42 § 6 SCCG, clergy who serve as chaplains or deacons may simultaneously hold a position of ecclesiastical official, as long as they meet the legal qualifications.

586. The provisions of Church Employees Code constitute a special law *(lex specialis)*, so they predominate over the general civil service law.[333] The reasons for introducing this special clerical regime are due to the specific character of the ecclesiastical legal persons as to their sought after religious and social aims.[334] However, as it is explicitly provided for in Article 154 § 5 'Church Employees Code' (Reg. 5/1978), for issues that are not covered by a special provision in the above Code, apply additionally the corresponding provisions of the Common Civil Service Code.[335]

332. For the whole text with its amendments, *see* Troianos/Papageorgiou, *Religious legislation*, 697–874. CoS 939/2017, on disciplinary provisions of Reg. 5/1978.

333. About which, *see* a general overview in Kondylis/Ktistaki/Tziraki, *Employees code*, Athens 2018, passim; Spiliotopoulos/Chrysanthakis, *Basic institutions of civil service* law, Athens 92017.

334. The particular conditions, under which church officials have to serve, are reflected, among others, in a series of provisions of Church Employees Code. For example, the Art. 8 § 1 stipulates that: 'Nobody can be appointed as a church official if he is not an Orthodox Christian … '; according to Art. 12: 'Those whose actions or words show disrespect to the Orthodox Christian religion cannot be appointed as ecclesiastical officials.' About the constitutionality of these provisions, *see* Papageorgiou, *The limits of ecclesiastical self-administration. I: Regulatory jurisdiction,* 298ff; Lentzis, 'The European Union law against discrimination on grounds of religion in employment', in Papageorgiou (ed.), *Law and religions: Greece-Europe*, Athens 2020, 79–112.

335. L. 3528/2007; Kondylis/Ktistaki/Tziraki, *Employees code, supra*; Lazarakos, 'The new code of civil, administration servants and legal entities' Employees (Law 3528/2007), ToS 19 (2007) 709–733.

Part VII. Religious Communities and Protection of the Individual

Chapter 1. Protection of Privacy

587. The relevant law currently in force in Greece is L. 4624/2019, 'Principle of Personal Data Protection, measures implementing Regulation (EU) 2016/679 of the European Parliament and of the Council of 27 April 2016 on the protection of natural persons against data processing' (GG A' 137/29.8.2019). The purpose of the above law is to take measures to protect individuals against the processing of personal data. The application of the relevant provisions is overseen by the Greek Data Protection Authority.[336]

588. The provisions of the law apply to – in whole or in part – the automated processing of personal data, as well as to the non-automated processing of such data, which are included or will be included in an archiving system by public or private bodies, unless the processing carried out by a natural person in the context of exclusively personal or domestic activity.[337]

589. Article 44 L. 4624/2019 provides for protected specific categories of personal data that disclose racial or ethnic origin, political views, religious or philosophical beliefs or trade union affiliation, genetic data, biometric data for the identification of an unidentified person, relating to health, data relating to the sexual life or sexual orientation of a natural person.

336. *See ECtHR Stavropoulos (52484/18/25.6.2020)*: the birth certificate must not contain information from which the religious beliefs of the child or his/her parents can be deduced.
337. *See inter alia*: Chrysogonos/Vlahopoulos, *Individual and social rights*, 291ff, 296ff.

Chapter 2. Freedom to Marry

590. According to Article 21 of the Greek Constitution, the family is the cornerstone of the preservation and advancement of the nation, while marriage, motherhood and childhood are under the protection of the State. This constitutional provision does not prevent the Church or other religious bodies from subjecting religious marriage and the family life of their members to the special rules that constitute their internal law, provided that these religious obligations do not conflict with the common law of the State.[338] However, if anyone wishes not to be bound by the ecclesiastical law of marriage, they may engage in a civil marriage, which comes under the complete jurisdiction of the State.[339]

338. *See inter alia*: Ath., *Handbook of family law*, Athens-Thessaloniki 2021; Ath. Papachristou, *Family law*, Athens 2015, passim; Papazissi, *Greek Jews and family law: From Judaic law to the civil law code*, 385–396; Kotzambasi, 'The scope of implementation of the holy Muslim law in the family relations of Greek Muslims', HellDni 44 (2003) 57–72; *ibid.*, The family legal relations of Greek Muslim men and women, Thessaloniki 2003. In general *see* Nasir, *The Islamic law of personal status*, 89ff. *In more details*, *see* Part X: Matrimonial and Family Law, of the present monograph.

339. Papageorgiou, *Ecclesiastical law*, 252ff; Deliyannis, *Le manage religieux et son effcacite civile en droit hellenique, in: Marriage and Religion in Europe*, 121–151.

Chapter 3. Freedom of Expression

591. The right to free expression of clerical or lay staff employed by religious legal entities may be subjected to restrictions out of respect for the doctrinal or moral teachings of a particular religion. If the public opinions of a member of a church or religious community do not conform to or respect these principles, then religious sanctions (and no other kind) may be taken against the member concerned.

592. It is accepted that the special coercive power relationship that governs the relations between clerics or church administrators and their ecclesiastical organizations and whose broader or narrower aims these clerics and administrators have agreed to serve means that the latter are obliged to take on an increased number of duties, with respective restrictions on their individual freedoms.[340] The above clerics or administrators become executors of the will of the legal entity they serve and, among other things, are compelled to:

- 'obey' the service orders of their superiors;
- keep 'confidential' any facts or information that come to their attention in the course of their duties;
- maintain 'political impartiality' or 'political neutrality', in the sense of avoiding any public expressions of a political nature, as well as any public criticism of the actions of organs of the Church.[341]

340. *See*, however, the interesting critical views of Nafpliotis, 'The development of personality in the field of civil servant law', DiDiki 3 (1991), 1031–1039, according to which the restrictions imposed on the rights of civil servants are contrary to Art. 5 § 1 Const. Nafpliotis criticizes the concept based on case law of an employment relationship that has been entered into 'willingly' and with the 'consent' of the employee, a concept that justifies, contrary to the author's own opinion, the placing of legal restrictions on their constitutional rights; Kondylis/Ktistaki/Tziraki, *Employee Code*. Interpretation by Article, passim.
341. Kondylis/Ktistaki/Tziraki, *Employee code: Interpretation by article*, passim; Lazarakos, 'The new code of civil, administration servants and legal entities' Employees (Law 3528/ 2007)', ToS 19 (2007) 709–733.

Chapter 4. Professional Secrecy

593. According to Article 371 PenCod, clergymen, lawyers, notaries public, doctors, midwives, nurses, pharmacists and others to whom confidential information is entrusted, usually on account of their occupation or professional capacity, as well as the assistants of these persons, face having to pay a fine or being imprisoned for up to one year if they disclose the confidential information which has been entrusted to them or which they have learnt as a result of their occupation or professional capacity (similar provisions are included in Articles 399–401 CCProc).[342] However, such an act is judged not to be unjust and remains unpunished if the perpetrator was seeking to carry out his/her duty or to protect an essential legal interest that he/she could not have protected in any other way (Article 371 § 4 PC).[343]

594. Furthermore, it is accepted that the protection of this confidential information is not restricted merely to what has been said within the framework of the sacrament of confession but extends to anything that has been confided to a cleric, on account of his capacity as a religious official. The exemption of clerics from examination as witnesses in court does not apply if the person to whom the confidential information relates permits such an examination (Article 400 § 1 CCProc).

595. The term 'clerics' in the above legal provisions does refer not only to those who belong to the Orthodox Church but also to those who belong to other creeds or religions, provided the sacrament of confession or something similar is recognized in these creeds or religions.

342. Papageorgiou, *Ecclesiastical law*, 203.

343. Kaiafa-Gbandi/Symeonidou-Kastanidou (eds), *The penal code and special penal laws*, 179; Margaritis/Paraskevopoulos (eds), *The penal code and special penal laws*, 273f; Kalfelis, *The penal code and special penal laws*, 126f.

Chapter 5. Medical Deontology

596. Within the framework of the application of L. 3418/2005, 'Code of Medical Deontology', doctors should respect the religious, philosophical, political and ethical views of their patients, without being influenced by them in the provision of their services (Article 8 § 4).

597. In the event of an urgent need for medical intervention in order to avert a threat to the life or health of a child, the public prosecutor of the Court of First Instance may himself, if the parents refuse, give the required permission immediately, following a request by the doctor in charge of the treatment or by the director of the clinic where the child is under treatment or by any other competent health authority (Article 1534 CC).[344]

344. For a more analytical interpretation *see* that by Pouliadis, in Georgiadis/Stathopoulos, *Civil Code*, vol. III: 'Family Law' [Arts 1505–1694]), 396–398; *Thessaloniki Court of Appeals 1433/2003*, Arm. 57 (2003) 1439–1443: termination of marital cohabitation and court settlement of the issue of parental care. The decision should aim to protect the interests of the child and should also be based on the constitutionally safeguarded principles of equality, legal equality of the sexes, free development of the personality and the freedom of religious conscience. Although the judge should not discriminate on the basis of the parents' religion, he/she should take into account the implications of each parent's religious convictions (e.g., if he/she is a Jehovah's Witness) in the exercise of parental care. Depending on the maturity of the child in question, the child's own opinion should be sought with regard to the issue of parental care or custody in the event of an urgent need for medical intervention. In order to avert a threat to the life or health of the child, the public prosecutor of the Court of First Instance may himself, if the parents refuse, give the required permission immediately. Reservations exist as to the full effectiveness of the provision in certain cases; *see Public Prosecutor of the Supreme Court (AP) 6/1992*, EllDni 33 (1992) 1528ff: the parents' refusal to consent to surgical intervention that is essential for the life of their minor child may be considered an abusive exercise of a right and not be taken into consideration. The doctor has a special legal obligation to proceed *lege artis* with the intervention, even if the parents refuse to consent or are not present. *See also* Manoledakis, *Childhood as an autonomous legal good in penal law*, 1107ff.

Chapter 6. Non-discrimination

598. In the landmark case of the European Court on Human Rights *Molla Sali v. Greece* (19.12.2018) was judged that the people belonging to the Muslim minority of the Greek Thrace may have the rights to live under the provisions of the Civil Code and not necessarily according to sharia. So, the application of the holy Islamic law (sharia) should not be obligatory for the Greek Muslims of Western Thrace. As for their family and inheritance cases, they can choose the application of civil law by the common courts, and not necessarily the sharia by the muftis. In this case, Greece was condemned for violation of the principle of non-discrimination (*see* more below: Part X: Matrimonial and Family Law).

599. State family law provides for the equality of spouses and joint decision-making in their exercise of parental care for their child. All relevant judicial decisions should respect the equality between the parents and make no discriminations on the basis of sex, race, language, religion, political or any other kind of convictions, nationality, ethnic or social origins or property (Articles 1510–1511 CC).[345]

600. Within the framework of the constitutional protection of the right to religious equality, which stems from the broader right to religious freedom, a host of relevant provisions have been enacted in more specific statutes. For example, Article 3 ('Equal Treatment of Detainees') of L. 2776/1999 ('Penitentiary Code') forbids any adverse discriminatory treatment of detainees, particularly that based on race, colour, ethnic or social origins, religion or ideological convictions.[346] Special treatment is reserved for detainees when it is justified by their religious or other convictions. According to Article 39 ('Exercise of Religious Duties') of the same law, religious education is optional and includes the right of the detainee to exercise his/her religious duties and communicate with a recognized representative of his/her religion or creed. All penitentiary institutions contain a place of worship or other suitable space in which acts of worship may be attended by any detainee who so desires. Detainees who are held in special detention areas or in treatment centres may be visited by priests in order to fulfil their religious duties. The priest or representative of another religion or creed is called upon by the Prison Committee to express his opinion on matters concerning his office.

345. Pouliadis, *supra.*, 268–275. *Single-Member Court of First Instance of Thessaloniki 1080/1995*, Arm. 49 (1995) 1160–1063: a request by a husband that his wife should be ordered to move out of the marital abode and that the parental care of his minor children should be entrusted to him on the grounds that his wife has changed religion is rejected. This fact, without the existence of other circumstances, does not in itself render marital cohabitation so intolerable as to justify the wife's change of abode. The court's settlement of the issue of parental care should be effected solely on the basis of the child's interest. The court should respect the equality of the spouses and make no discriminations on the basis of sex, race, language, religion, etc.

346. Stagkos, 'The fight against racism, xenophobia and discrimination in Greece today: The normative framework, public actions, and the European challenge', 159ff.

601. Under L. 3448/2006 (Article 35), for reasons of equal treatment, the cremation of the dead became possible, provided that the religious convictions of the deceased permitted it.[347]

347. *LCS 24/2004,* Law Social Security Review 46 (2004) 867–872: equal treatment for all those who choose to be buried or cremated; *Athens Court of Appeal 1702/1988*, EllDni 30 (1989) 366–367.

Chapter 7. Penal Law and Religion

602. The Greek Penal Law contains the following regulations with respect to the protection of religions in the Greek territory.

§1. Proselytism

I. Generally

603. Under the Greek Constitution, proselytism is prohibited (Article 13 § 2 section c' Const.), either for or against any religion.[348] According to the special penal legislation that is currently in effect (Article 4 § 2 L. 1363/1938, as it was replaced by Article 2 L. 1672/1939), proselytism is the direct or indirect attempt to penetrate into the religious conscience of another with the purpose of changing it, 'especially' when this is effected with the use of all forms of offers or promises, using deceptive means or by abusing the other's lack of experience or trust, or by exploiting the other's need and mental weakness.

604. The propagation of religious convictions by way of associations or assemblies, sermons or missionary work cannot be considered proselytism; neither can the sale, mailing or simple distribution of printed matter and advertising pamphlets, as long as these are not attempted using the unlawful means mentioned above.[349]

605. The offence of proselytism is punishable by a prison sentence and a monetary fine. For the substantiation of the crime of proselytism, it is not necessary that the intended purpose of the perpetrator was actually achieved or that the means which were used for the achievement of the criminal intent were expedient ('typical crime').

606. Because the prohibition of proselytism constitutes a precondition for freedom of worship, the administration is obliged, before granting a licence for the

348. About this so important issue, *see* in general: Androulakis, 'The punishability of proselytization and its constitutionality', NoV 34 (1986) 1031f; Christoforidis, 'Proselytization in favor of the prevailing religion, HellDni 22 (1981) 10ff; Ferrari, Globalization, postmodernism and proselytism, 13-27; Karakostas, Orthodox constitutional reasoning and the penal treatment of proselytization', EEN 54 (1987) 53–63; Krippas, 'The crime of proselytization, especially from the standpoint of instigation', PChr 30 (1980) 313–321; *ibid.*, 'Some remarks on proselytization from the standpoint of constitutional and criminal law', HellDni 22 (1981) 204–206; Ktistakis, Religious Freedom and the European Convention on Human Rights, 99ff, 297f, passim; Loverdos, 'Proselytization. On the unconstitutionality of the penal legislation relating to proselytization', 31ff, passim; Marinos, 'The concept of religious proselytization under the new Constitution', HellDni 25 (1984) 4–17; Lerner, Proselytism, change of religion and international human rights, 477ff; Mylonas, 'Translation: Comments on the case of Kokkinakis versus Greece', Y 4 (1994) 158–194; Philippou, 'The constitutional restrictions of religious freedom and the crime of proselytization (on the occasion of the judgment of Kokkinakis vs. Greece)', Chr. 1994, 6–38.

349. Manesis, 'The constitutional protection of the free circulation of printed material and its implementation in practice', ToS 3 (1977) 3ff; Papageorgiou, *Ecclesiastical Law*, 130f.

operation of a place of worship, to investigate whether the applicants for the licence practise proselytism, taking into consideration the overall activity of the members of the particular creed.

II. Case *Kokkinakis v. Greece* (25 May 1993)

A. *Facts, Legal Provisions, Court's Syllogisms and Decision*

607. Minos Kokkinakis was prosecuted by the Greek courts for having committed proselytism.[350] He appealed to the ECtHR, which reached an important decision on the matter. This was the first time the ECtHR declared a violation of Article 7 of the ECHR, yielding the principle *nullum crimen nulla poena sine lege certa et stricta.*

608. As judge L. Pettiti remarked, the case Minos Kokkinakis was the first one since the foundation of the Court, in which a judicial decision was made necessary on the topic of freedom of religion. It is not useless to observe that R. Ryssdal, the President of the ECtHR, mentioned this specific decision on the occasion of the annual beginning of the Court's works.

609. Mr Kokkinakis was born into an Orthodox family at Sitia (Crete) in 1919. After becoming a Jehovah's Witness in 1936, he was arrested about sixty times for proselytism, and imprisoned on several occasions. On 2 March 1986, Kokkinakis and his wife visited an Orthodox lady in the town of Sitia and started a discussion with her about religion. The lady's husband, a cantor at the local Orthodox Church, informed the police, who arrested Mr and Mrs Kokkinakis.

610. Both of them were prosecuted under Article 4 of L. 1363/1938 and were committed for trial at the Lasithi criminal court. The court convicted them, after overruling the objection that Article 4 of L. 1363/1938 was unconstitutional.[351]

611. Mr and Mrs Kokkinakis appealed against this judgment to the Cretan Court of Appeal, which quashed Mrs Kokkinakis' conviction and upheld her husband's,

---

350. On this very important case, *see*: Kyriazopoulos, 'Proselytization in Greece: criminal offence vs. religious persuasion and equality', 149–245; *ibid.*, 'Proselytization in Greece (*K*okkinakis judgment): criminal statute vs. "Nullum crimen nulla poena sine lege certa"', 357–395; Filou-Patsantara, 'The offense of proselytization in the European Court of Human Rights (Article 14 of obligatory law 1363/1938)', ToS 19 (1993) 821–842; Ktistakis, Religious Freedom and the European Convention on Human Rights, 297–310; Loverdos, 'On proselytization', in: Beis (ed.), Religious Freedom, 127–133; Mylonas, 'Translation-comments on the case of *K*okkinakis versus Greece', Y 4 (1994) 158–194; Papageorgiou, 'Freedom of religion: a case of discrepancy between the Greek and the European legal order, before the European Court of Human Rights', 215–222; Philippou, 'The constitutional restrictions of religious freedom and the crime of proselytization (on the occasion of the judgment of Kokkinakis vs. Greece)', Chr. 1994, 6–38; Stavrou, 'Proselytization and the right to religious freedom (on the occasion of the judgment of the European Court on the Appeal of Kokkinakis v. Greece', PChr 43 (1993) 964–977.
351. Troianos/Papageorgiou, *Religious legislation, 86-96.*

while at the same time reducing the duration of his imprisonment. Mr Kokkinakis appealed then to the Court of Cassation (Areios Pagos), where he claimed that the provisions of L. 1363/1938 contravened Article 13 of the Const., which safeguards the freedom of religion, particularly the right to profess publicly one's religious beliefs, and the right to act according to one's religious convictions. The Court of Cassation dismissed the appeal and stated, once more, that L. 1363/1938 in question was utterly compatible with Article 13 of the Greek Constitution.

612. Mr Kokkinakis had then (22 August 1988) recourse to the Commission of the European Court of Human Rights, once he had consumed all domestic means of judicial protection. Before the Commission, Kokkinakis claimed that his conviction for proselytism was infringing on his rights secured in Articles 7, 9 and 10 of the ECHR. Thus, the procedure focused on freedom of religion. In its report (3 December 1991), the Commission declared the application partly admissible and concluded that: (a) there had been no violation of Article 7 (by eleven votes to two), (b) there had been a violation of Article 9 (unanimously), (c) no separate issue arose under Article 10 (by twelve to one).

613. Article 7 of ECHR provides that:

(1) No one shall be held guilty of any criminal offence on account of any act or omission which did not constitute a criminal offence under national or international law, at the time when it was committed. Nor shall a heavier penalty be imposed than the one that was applicable at the time the criminal offence was committed.
(2) This article shall not prejudice the trial and punishment of any person for any act or omission which, at the time when it was committed, was criminal according to the general principles of law recognised by civilised nations.

614. Consequently, for a criminal provision to be in harmony with this article, it must be sufficiently precise and clear-cut. Kokkinakis, *inter alia,* augured that the Greek L. 1363/1938 on the prohibition of proselytism contained gravely indeterminate terms, rendering so imprecise the penal provision itself that this may be illimitably comprehended and applied.

615. The ECtHR, however, did not ascertain any breach of Article 7, maintaining that this article:

> (…) is not confined to prohibiting the retrospective application of the criminal law to an accused's disadvantage. It also embodies, more generally, the principle that only the law can define a crime and prescribe that the criminal law must not be extensively construed to an accused's detriment, for instance by analogy. This condition is satisfied where the individual can know from the

wording of the relevant provision and, if need be, with the assistance of the Court's interpretation of it, what acts and omissions will make him liable.[352]

616. Article 9 of ECHR provides:

(1) Everyone has the right to freedom of thought, conscience and religion; this right includes freedom to change his religion or belief and freedom, either alone or in community with others and in public or private, to manifest his religion or belief, in worship, teaching, practice and observance.
(2) Freedom to manifest one's religion or beliefs shall be subject only to such limitations as prescribed by law and necessary in a democratic society in the interests of public safety, for the protection of public order, health or morals, or for the protection of the rights and freedoms of others.

617. The guarantees of Article 9 ECHR appear in two aspects: they refer to the right of freedom of thought, conscience and religion, and they grant the manifestation of these freedoms. Thought, conscience, freedom of religion must be quite free. They are not susceptible to heteronomous restrictions or prohibitions; otherwise, the fundamental right of religious freedom is not fully protected.

618. Mr Kokkinakis professed that there is an insurmountable interpretative difficulty in tracing a demarcation line between proselytism and freedom to change another person's religion or beliefs. Everyone is free to preach his/her beliefs, to communicate the contents of a religion to other people, either alone or in community, both in public and in private.

619. In tune with the Commission, the Court reminded that Article 9 represented one of the foundations of a democratic society. It is:

> one of the most vital elements that go to make up the identity of believers and their conception of life, but it is also a precious asset for the atheists, agnostics, sceptics and the unconcerned (…). Furthermore, it includes in principle the right to try to convince one's neighbour, for example through 'teaching', failing which, moreover, 'freedom to change one's religion or belief', enshrined in article 9, would be likely to remain a dead letter (par. 31 of the Court's Decision).

620. According to the Court, the restrictions contained in paragraph 2 of Article 9 concern only the freedom of believers to manifest their religious beliefs, particularly in public worship. States may introduce limitations to this particular freedom,[353] for the sake of ensuring the coexistence of all religions and the specific set

---

352. Papageorgiou, 'Freedom of religion: a case of discrepancy between the Greek and the European legal order, before the European Court of Human Rights', 218.
353. On this subject, *see* in general Manfred Nowak/Tanjia Vospernik, *Permissible restrictions on freedom of religion or belief,* in: Lindholm/Durham/Tahzib-Lie (eds), *Facilitating freedom of religion or belief: A deskbook,* 147–172.

of goals referred to in paragraph 2 of Article 9. In the process of discovery of a reasonable solution, the Court set up consecutively three questions: (i) has there been any illicit state interference in the applicant's freedom of religion? (ii) was the interference permitted by law? (iii) was the interference necessary and so allowable in a democratic society?

621. It is most interesting that the Court held out that the applicable Greek law was not precise enough for a penal provision. The Court rightly avoided to take place on the issue of constitutionality of the law concerned, for the reason that this task belongs to the domestic courts. In the major premise of its syllogism, the Court suggested a distinction between 'permissible' and 'improper' proselytism. The decision alleged that there had been no proportionality between the applicant's activity and his conviction by Greek courts.[354]

622. No evidence was brought in as to whether Kokkinakis had truly attempted to persuade someone else by excessive means, that is through 'improper' proselytism. On the contrary, the 'victim' of Mr Kokkinakis' catechism testified before the penal Court of First Instance that the accused had simply talked to her about Christ, without having sought to proselytize her. Notwithstanding, the Greek Judge Valticos, member of the European Court, in explaining his dissenting opinion, asseverated that 'the term "teaching" in Article 9 refers to religious teaching in school curricula or in religious institutions, and not to personal door-to-door canvassing as in the present case' (page 30 of the Decision).

B. Critical Remarks

623. In the case *Kokkinakis*, the Greek penal legislation on proselytism was brought under scrutiny on two pivotal issues. Does the formulation of the Greek penal statute comply with the claim of precision, made in Article 7 of the Convention? Is the normative content of proselytism in Greek law in accordance with the freedom of religion in Article 9 of the ECHR? In both questions, one might raise some reasonable misgivings as to the rightness of the Court's resolution.[355]

624. The decision is quite correct in defending that, according to Article 7 of the Convention, only the law can define a crime and prescribe a penalty. But then, the

354. For example, *see* Drooghenbroeck, *La proportionnalite dans le droit de la convention europeenne des droits de l'homme. Prendre l'idee simple au serieux*, 433–435; Muzny, *La technique de proportionnalite et le juge de la Convention Europeenne des Droits de VHomme. Essai sur un instrument necessaire dans une societe democratique*, tom. I, 259.

355. Papastathis, *The application of religious laws in the hellenic republic,* 309f. As it is noted, various opinions have been put forth regarding the 'legal good' that is protected by the criminal statute of proselytism. The divergence of opinion on this matter is due not only to the legal-technical phrasing of the criminal statute on proselytization but also to the legal and political context of its enactment. A first opinion claims that the protected legal good is primarily the freedom of religious conscience and secondarily the protection of the prevailing religion and public safety. It is true that this ranking between legal goods can very well be overturned in practice and this has in fact already happened to a great extent. A second view supports that the legal good under protection is public

decision reduces the normative importance of this position, in accepting that the applicable Greek statute does not include some *intolerable* semantic elusiveness. Yet, the textual enunciation of the Greek statute apparently lacks in semantic clearness.

625. Furthermore, the decision makes a misstep, in arguing that it is permissible for a (defectively formulated) penal statute to become *interpretatively clearer* by jurisprudence, in the course of its application.

626. We may object that the principle *nullum crimen, nulla poena sine lege certa,* in the first place, must be served by the very linguistic formulation of any provision of penal law. If there is a prime deficiency of lucidity in the initial text of a criminal provision, this defect may never turn against the accused person's position: *in dubio pro libertate.* In this sense, the failure of precision and plainness in the legislative constitution of a crime may not be only later cured by jurisprudence. But even if we could accord such a discretionary authority to penal courts, the European Court may not selectively take into account the domestic jurisprudence, as it did in the case under dispute.

627. If the Court wanted to form a global view of the Greek jurisprudence on the issue of proselytism, it should reach the conclusion that the Greek jurisprudence is manifestly fluctuating in determining the normative content of proselytism. In cases like this, the jurisprudence of inferior criminal courts in Greece is rather keen to exculpate the defendant of all charges. This jurisprudential line justly construes restrictively the penal prohibition of proselytism. It accepts, for example, the free distribution or sale of leaflets with religious content.

628. Instead, the Greek Court of Cassation (Areios Pagos) seems to ignore the jurisprudence of inferior courts on the subject, by insisting on a wide and repressive conception of proselytism, which evidences a spirit of legal and political conservatism. In our opinion, this conception heavily offends the constitutional right of manifesting one's religious beliefs. Thus, the Courts of Cassation's Decision No 840/1986, in a way begging the question and without any further argumentation, stipulates that the gratuitous distribution of leaflets is punishable. The decision of the same Court 704/1988 has validated the conviction of a mother, simply because she had sent her children to the temple of the 'Free Apostolic Church of Pentecost', despite her ex-husband's objections!

629. As for Article 9 ECHR, the ECtHR considered the rights of thirds and so adopted a distinction between permissible and illicit proselytism. According to the minoritarian opinion expressed in the decision – which I find at this point better

---

security. The same view incorporates the protection of the prevailing religion among the most fundamental elements of public security. According to a third opinion, the criminal statute of proselytism protects the prevailing religion. On all these opinions, *see* more analytically: Kyriazopoulos, '*Proselytization in Greece (Kokkinakis judgment): criminal statute vs. "Nullum crimen nulla poena sine lege certa"*' 362f.

founded – proselytism is warranted as an expression of the freedom of religion, in the form of free teaching of religious dogmas, by virtue of Article 9 paragraph 1 ECHR. Even if one holds that certain limitations might be enacted in conformity with Article 9 paragraph 2, these restrictions may simply bear civil and certainly not criminal legal consequences.

630. It is to be hoped that L. 1363/1938 against proselytism will soon be abrogated, and that, in the meantime, the Greek jurisprudence, especially that of the Court of Cassation, aligns itself with the Court of Human Rights viewpoint. Behind the lines of the legal text, the true intention of the legislator in 1938, under circumstances of a military dictatorship, was to punish Jehovah's Witnesses for their refusal to join the military forces of the country. But this issue raises another controversial question, interrelated to that of freedom of conscience, within the Greek legal order, revolving around the problem of alternative forms or military service for reasons of conscientious objection.

§2. Criminal Offences Against Religious Peace

631. The criminal offences cited below are still included in the provisions of the Greek Penal Code, aiming to secure religious peace and the protection of the religious sentiment of the people.

632. The crime of 'obstruction or disturbance of religious assemblies' (Article 200 § 1 PC) aims at the unhindered exercise of a religious or worshipping activity, regardless of whether this takes place in a closed or open space. The crime is typical; consequently, it is not necessary that the intent of the perpetrator has been completed; attempt suffices since it is equivalent to a completed act. Moreover, as stated in paragraph 2 of the same article, any offensive or inappropriate act performed in places of worship of known religion is punishable. The property of a particular space as a place of worship shall be judged on the basis of the rules of the respective creed or doctrine. 'Acts which are offensively inappropriate' are those acts which, because of their cruelty, are deemed capable of offending the religious sentiment of others and which manifest disrespect for the sanctity of the place of worship.[356]

633. The removal of objects: (a) dedicated to holy worship, (b) from a place that is designated to holy worship, and (b) objects which are of artistic or archaeological or historical significance, with the purpose of illegally possessing them, constitutes a case of 'aggravated' theft (Article 374 Case a' PenCod, as it is modified by Article 5 of L. 4637/2019). For this crime, which is punishable by imprisonment of up to ten years, the law requires intent of simple theft (i.e., knowledge and volition to remove the item for the purpose of appropriating it) as well as intent of the perpetrator consisting in the knowledge, first that the object is dedicated to holy worship,

356. Troianos, *Lectures in Ecclesiastical Law, 103f;* Papageorgiou, *Ecclesiastical Law, 131f.*

second, that the place from which it was removed also has been designated for worship and, third, that the object is of artistic or archaeological or historical significance.

634. 'Usurpation of service of a religious minister' (Article 175 § 2 PC). By 'religious minister', the statute refers to the Minister of every religion that is known in Greece, as long as he has acquired this property in accordance with the rules of the respective creed. The usurpation is punished by imprisonment of up to one year or by a monetary penalty.

635. By L. 4285/2014 has been established as a criminal offence the public incitement of violence or hatred, as well as the public approval of crimes related to, among others, religious matters.[357]

636. According to Article 184 of PenCod, anyone who publicly in any way or through the internet causes or incites to a misdemeanour or to felony and thus endangers public order is punishable by up to one year in prison or a fine. That act shall be punishable by imprisonment for up to three years or a fine if it is an attempt to commit acts of violence against a group or a person determined on the basis of religion, race, colour, national or ethnic origin, genealogy, disability, sexual orientation, identity or gender characteristics.

637. After the issuing of L. 4619/2019, 'Ratification of the Penal Code (Criminal Code Codified)',[358] the following religious crimes are not any more punishable by the Greek Penal Code.

638. 'Malicious blasphemy' which – according to the abolished Article 198 § 1 PC – was the public and malevolent blasphemy of God.[359]

---

357. *AP 858/2020*: a condemnation of the abuse of an ecclesiastical office (Art. 196 of the previous Penal Code) and of the violation of Art. 1 of L. 927/1979, as amended by Art. 1 of L. 4285/2014 (public incitement to violence and hate speech).

358. GG A' *95/11.6.2019.*

359. The penalization of that behaviour had been covering every contemptuous or offensive manifestation of lack of respect towards God which could be considered blasphemy (therefore not civilized discussions, no matter how much doubt about the existence of God they may contain). 'Blasphemy' could be happened orally, in writing, with gestures, images and so on. The term 'God' was denoting the deity in accordance with the doctrines of every religion. 'Publicity' had been occurred when the act could fall under the perception of a vague number of persons, in addition to those towards whom the act is directed. From the aspect of its subjective substantiation, the crime was including intent (namely, the knowledge and the will to carry out the elements of the crime's objective substantiation) and malice (namely, that the act was committed with the purpose of showing contempt for God). About the previous law *see* indicatively Troianos, *Lectures in Ecclesiastical Law*, 102f; AP 1046/1991: whoever publicly and maliciously blasphemes God is punished by imprisonment. 'A public manifestation' occurs when the manifestation can be perceived by a vague number of persons, different from the ones towards which it is directed, regardless of whether this manifestation was witnessed by third parties, or whether it occurred in a public or private space. *See also*: Ravdas, *With a book opposite to God: Banned books for offending the religious sentiment*, 141ff; Tsakyrakis, *Religion versus Art*, passim.

639. 'Blasphemy concerning religions' (Article 199 PC) is the public and malicious statement against every religion known in Greece.[360]

640. 'Usurpation of a minister's sacerdotal vestments' (Article 176 PC). The crime was related to those who, lacking the right to do so, publicly were bearing the sacerdotal vestments or other insignia of a religious minister of any religion known in Greece. The prescribed sentence was imprisonment of up to six months or a monetary penalty. The special vestments or insignia of religious ministers are determined by the relevant provisions of every religion.

360. Troianos, *Lectures in Ecclesiastical Law,* 103; *AP 928/1984*: the commission of the crime of blasphemy concerning religions objectively presupposes the direct or indirect blasphemy against a religious teaching, which takes place with crude and vulgar expressions of the perpetrator, in writing or orally. The blasphemous behaviour may be directed against the doctrines, usages or symbols and utensils destined for holy worship.

Part VIII. Church Financing

§1. General Remarks

641. Already since the early Christian years the church realized that, in order to realistically pursue its spiritual work and the strong social presence and influence of the ecclesiastical organization, the utilization of real estate assets was among other things also required.[361]

642. The local ecclesiastical communities, by way not only of the voluntary contributions of their faithful people but also of their extra contributions, donations or inheritances, aimed to accumulate financial means and to form their own movable and immovable property, which over the next few centuries became immense. Factors that influenced this accumulation were, among others, not only the conservative nature of the church, which imposed an analogous spirit of management of its real estate property and other financial assets, but also the multifaceted direct and indirect financial support of the Byzantine state.[362]

643. Until the rule of Emperor Constantine the Great (AD 272-337), only natural persons (most habitually the bishops) were agents of ecclesiastical property, as it was stipulated in Holy Canon 26th of the Fourth Ecumenical Synod (AD 451; nowadays, the holy canons are protected mainly by Article 3 of the Greek Constitution). However, subsequently the Church and the ecclesiastical organizations (dioceses, churches, and monasteries) acquired property by lawful means and state recognition. This property was managed by the heads of these organizations, namely the bishops, vicars and Abbots.

644. The Fourth Ecumenical Synod was the first to enact canons on matters pertaining to ecclesiastical property, whereas later state provisions of the Justinian legislation systematize the administration and management of ecclesiastical property, regulating more specifically its acquisition, exploitation, taxation and disposition. A sizeable part of the revenues from the real estate property of the church was destined to cover the maintenance of its ministers, the practice of philanthropy and the provision of social welfare on the part of ecclesiastical foundations, such as orphanages, poorhouses, old age homes, and hospitals.

361. Indicatively *see* Papageorgiou, *Ecclesiastical Property*, passim; Liapis, *A brief introduction to ecclesiastical property,* 4ff.
362. Recently *see* the extended dissertation of Kollias, *The chrysobulls in Byzantine law*, 11ff.

645. The immovable monastic property was also quite extensive and it remained so throughout the duration of the Ottoman occupation, despite not only the cessation of state support, the imposition of polymorphous and extremely heavy 'contributions' to the conquerors but also the various damages that it was subjected to.

646. In Greece, today the ecclesiastical or religious legal entities (of public or of private law) are possessors and managers of their own (movable or immovable) property, for the realization of their objectives. The property of religions – that is protected by the Constitution, the ECHR[363] and several provisions of the Greek state of law – comes mainly from voluntary contributions, donations or bequests of the faithful, as well as purchases of property or financial investments.

647. Direct financial support on the part of the State is the payment of the salaries of Orthodox and Muslim clergy (muftis).[364] Except this, however, one cannot consider of minor importance the indirect financial assistance from the State, manifested in a series of tax exemptions in favour of almost all religions.

648. A significant part of the income, coming from the real estate of religious legal entities, is used for the upkeep of the clergy or monks, the practice of philanthropy and social welfare of institutions such as orphanages, nursing homes, hospitals and so on.

363. More lately: *ECtHR Liamberis v. Greece* (2020); *Kosmas v. Greece* (2017).
364. Papageorgiou, 'Ecclesiastical property and payroll of the orthodox clergy', TPDD 12/2018, 106ff.

Chapter 1. Direct Financing of Religious Communities

§1. Constitutional Protection of the Property of Religions

649. The movable and immovable property of various religious communities in the Greek territory is protected mainly by:

- the Article 13 Const. and 9 ECHR, in the wider context of conferring the right to religious freedom, in conjunction with Article 17 Const.,[365] which protects private property;
- the Article 18 § 8 Const., which refers to the big real estate of three monasteries as well as to that of the ancient patriarchates of the East;[366]
- the Article 105 § 2 Const., which protects the property of the monasteries of Mount Athos;[367]
- Article 1 of the First Protocol of the ECHR, concerning the peaceful enjoyment of property of legal persons.[368]

§2. The Legal Status of the Property of the Orthodox Church

650. The legal framework for the administration, management and protection of ecclesiastical movable and immovable property is not uniform on the entire Greek territory, primarily because of its division into the five ecclesiastical jurisdictions: (i) Autocephalous Church of Greece, (ii) Metropolises of the New Lands, (iii) Semi-Autonomous Church of Crete, (iv) Mount Athos and (v) ecclesiastical Eparchies of

---

365. Article 17 Const.: '(1). Property is under the protection of the State; rights deriving therefrom, however, may not be exercised contrary to the public interest. (2). No one shall be deprived of his property except for public benefit which must be duly proven, when and as specified by statute and always following full compensation corresponding to the value of the expropriated property at the time of the court hearing on the provisional determination of compensation. in cases in which a request for the final determination of compensation is made, the value at the time of the court hearing of the request shall be considered. […].' *See also*: Chrysogonos/Vlahopoulos, *Individual and social rights,* 399ff; Dagtoglou, *Constitutional law: Individual rights,* 851–957.

366. Article 18 § 8 Const.: 'Farmlands belonging to the Patriarchal Monasteries of Aghia Anastasia Pharmacolytria in Chalkidiki, of Vlatadhes in Thessaloniki and Ioannis the Evangelist Theologos in Patmos, with the exception of the dependencies thereof, cannot be subject to expropriation. Likewise the property in Greece of the Patriarchates of Alexandria, Antiocheia and Jerusalem and that of the Holy Monastery of Mount Sinai cannot be subject to expropriation.' On this issue, *see* Papastathis, *Nomocanonical studies,* 41–54; Venizelos, *The relations between state and church,* 97–99.

367. Article 105 § 2 Const.: '(2). Mount Athos shall be governed, according to its regime, by its twenty Holy Monasteries among which the entire Athos peninsula is divided; the territory of the peninsula shall be exempt from expropriation.' *See* Antonopoulos, *The constitutional protection of the regime in Mount Athos*, 275ff; Papageorgiou, *The legal institutions of Mount Athos*, 99–138.

368. Article 1 of First Protocol ECHR: 'Every natural or legal person is entitled to the peaceful enjoyment of his possessions. No one shall be deprived of his possessions except in the public interest and subject to the conditions provided for by law and by the general principles of international law.' *See* Sicilianos, *European Convention on Human Rights: Interpretation to articles,* 770ff.

the Dodecanese. The differences that exist in the ecclesiastical institutions of the aforementioned regions entail respective differentiations as to their current ecclesiastical property law.

651. The term 'ecclesiastical property' denotes here the movable or immovable property belonging to the totality of ecclesiastical legal entities (metropolises, churches, monasteries, various ecclesiastical organizations). By the term 'administration and management of ecclesiastical property', we refer to the legal framework which determines the competent organs and the procedure for the governance and utilization of this property.[369]

652. The property of metropolises. The provisions of Article 30 L. 590/1977, stipulating that the management of the metropolis' revenues is conducted by the respective metropolitan,[370] and Article 46 § 2 L. 590/1977, containing a legislative authorization for the promulgation of a relevant ecclesiastical regulation (which has not however been issued yet), refer to the administration and management of the property owned by metropolises.

653. The property of parish churches. The respective ecclesiastical council, which drafts the annual budget and the annual report (Ecclesiastical Reg. 8/1979),[371] is competent to administer the parish property. These acts, just like every other decision of the ecclesiastical council, are ratified by the metropolitan council (Ecclesiastical Regulation 263/2014).[372] The resources of parish churches are the revenues from the voluntary contributions of the faithful or from the sale of candles, revenues from box collections, donations, inheritances or bequests, the revenues from the movable and immovable property of the Church. The leases or sales of the parish property are effectuated by a bidding competition. The terms under which the competition is announced are drafted by the ecclesiastical council. In case of the

369. Articles 45–48 L. 590/1977 regulate more particular issues relating to the administration and management of ecclesiastical property and provide legislative authorizations for the issuance of regulatory decisions aiming to resolve such issues.

370. This provision is congruous with the respective definitions of holy canons, such as canons 38 and 41 of the Apostles (Canon 38: 'Let the bishop have the care of all the goods of the Church, and let him administer them as under the inspection of God. But he must not alienate any of them or give the things which belong to God to his own relations. If they be poor let him relieve them as poor; but let him not, under that pretence, sell the goods of the Church'; Canon 41: 'We ordain that the bishop have authority over the goods of the Church: for if he is to be intrusted with the precious souls of men, much more are temporal possessions to be intrusted to him. He is therefore to administer them all of his own authority, and supply those who need, through the presbyters and deacons, in the fear of God, and with all reverence. He may also, if need be, take what is required for his own necessary wants, and for the brethren to whom he has to show hospitality, so that he may not be in any want. For the law of God has ordained, that they who wait at the altar should be nourished of the altar. Neither does any soldier bear arms against an enemy at his own cost'). Today, the metropolitan is assisted in the exercise of his duties by the Metropolitan Council, applying the provisions of the Ecclesiastical Regulation 263/2014 regarding the organization, responsibilities and operation of the Metropolitan Councils.

371. For the whole text, *see* Troianos/Papageorgiou, *Religious legislation: Special legislation – bibliography – case law, 504-532.*

372. For the whole text, *see* Troianos/Papageorgiou, *supra*, 490–495.

sale of immovable property, an appraisal of its value on the part of the competent revenue service is carried out prior to the sale (15–16 Reg. 8/1979).

654. The property of monasteries. Until 1988, the administration and management of a large part of the real estate property owned by the monasteries of the Church of Greece belonged to the Organization for the Administration of Ecclesiastical Property (OAEP), which was established by L. 4684/1930 (codified by the P.D. of 14/22-9-1931).[373] Pursuant to Article 8 § 1 of L. 4684/1930, monastic property was distinguished into 'preservable' (which remained under the ownership and management of the monasteries) and 'disposable', whose liquidation was assigned to OAEP.[374]

655. However, OAEP was dissolved by way of Article 3 of L. 1811/1988, 'On the ratification of the Contract of Assignment to the State of the forest and agricultural property of the holy monasteries of the Church of Greece, which are signatory parties to this Contract'.[375] The legal entity of the Church of Greece was designated as the special successor of OAEP. However, its managerial authorities over the immovable ecclesiastical property are today exercised by the Ecclesiastical Central Financial Service (ECFS).[376]

656. L. 1700/1987 'On the regulation of matters of ecclesiastical property' (thirteen articles) constituted one more legislative attempt to detach a sizeable part of monastic property and dispose it for broader social purposes. L. 1700/1987 stipulated that upon its taking effect, OAEP would *ipso jure* handle the exclusive administration, management and representation of the entire real estate property of the monasteries. Presidential decrees would further determine all issues pertaining to the administration, management or assignment of monastic property.

657. The term 'immovable monastic property' was used to denote the agricultural property and any plots of land that were arable and permitted agricultural use, forests and forest lands more generally, pasturelands, grasslands, as well as quarries and mines.[377]

658. Subsequently, L. 1700/1987 stipulated that OAEP shall assign the use and exploitation of the generally non-urban monastic property to farmers, farmers' cooperatives and agents of the public sector. It also designated the manner in which OAEP would transfer this property to the Greek State, within six months of the law taking effect (Article 2 paragraphs 1–2 of L. 1700/1987).

---

373. *Ibid.*, 906ff.
374. *See* Ramiotis, *The Church within the Greek state,* 34ff, passim; Liapis, *A brief introduction to ecclesiastical property*, 82ff; *AP 1388/2010*.
375. The whole text, *see* in Troianos/Papageorgiou, *supra*, 1069–1089. *see also* Ramiotis, *The Church within the Greek State,* 21ff, passim; Liapis, *supra,* 113ff; Venizelos, *The relations between State and Church*, 95–103; CoS 5057/1987.
376. Liapis, *supra*, 119ff; Papageorgiou, 'Findings from the ecclesiastical case law of the council of state of the year 1987', 35ff.
377. Papastathis, *Nomocanonical studies*, 163ff.

659. It is underlined that for all the aforementioned plots of land, Article 3 § 1 A-B introduced a 'presumption of ownership' in favour of the Greek State, which was rebuttable only as long as the monastery's right of ownership derived from a deed of ownership.

660. Nevertheless, L. 1700/1987 remains inactive until this day because the presidential decrees that are required for the materialization of its stipulations have not to this day been promulgated. In any case, in 1988, the Holy Synod of the Church of Greece retreated from its initial negative stance, and the result, which came about on 11 April 1988, was the signing of a contract concerning the assignment to the Greek State of the property of those monasteries which agreed to sign this Contract.

661. Ultimately 149 monasteries participated in this Contract, as it is demonstrated in the Table that the Holy Synod attached to the Contract. In the end, the Contract of assignment of monastic property to the Greek State was ratified by the Greek Parliament by virtue of L. 1811/1988.

662. However, the enactment of L. 1700/1987 sparked a wave of harsh objections on the part of the Church. The harshest among them moved at a level of direct refusal to implement the law but also of public threats concerning the law's political cost.[378] But the most strident reactions pursued the judicial attack on the statutes of L. 1700/1987 and took two directions: on the one hand, the submission of a petition for judicial review (annulment) before the Greek Council of State and on the other the filing of an appeal before the European Court of Human Rights, whose seat is in Strasbourg (we will deal with the judicial development of both cases below).

663. Certain clergymen, laypersons, particular monasteries appealed to the Council of State, requesting the annulment of the ministerial decision which appointed members to the Central Board of Directors of OAEP. However, Council of State Decision No. 5057/1987, which was issued as a result, rejected the appeal of annulment.

664. As for the argument of the applicants that the provisions of L. 1700/1987 imposed an unacceptable confiscation of ecclesiastical property, since they deprived

---

378. The characteristic worth mentioning is that four of the seven members of the Board of OAEP were to be appointed directly by the Minister! As for Church of Crete, paras 3 and 4 of Art. 8 L. 1700/1987 stipulated that the above changes would be introduced in the Church after an 'opinion' would be submitted within one month by the Provincial Synod. It clearly stated that, if an idle period had elapsed, the application of L. 1700 would proceed without the conciliar opinion. The Provincial Synod of Crete, however, by a decision notified to the Prime Minister, directly and categorically refused any discussion on the subject, let alone come to an agreement with the State for the cession of monastic property. In consequence of the above, L. 1700/1987 has not yet been applied to the Church of Crete, neither has monastic property come to the hands of ODMP in Crete – although the relevant provision of L. 1700 which refers to this as well as to the dissolution of ODMP typically still applies, *see Court of Appeals 192/1991 of Crete*, HellDni 33 (1992) 1264ff; *First Instance Court Heraklion 367/1997* (not published in legal periodicals).

the holy monasteries of their estates and established restrictions of ownership that were contrary to Articles 17 and 7 § 3 section a of the Constitution, Council of State Decision No. 5057/1987[379] ruled that L. 1700 did not violate the constitutional protection of property rights, because property rights do not rule out the possibility 'that the legislative branch shall establish, on the basis of objective criteria and for the purpose of serving the public interest, limitations as to the extent and the content of property rights, under the precondition that through these limitations, property rights are not eliminated or rendered inactive with regard to their designated purpose'.

665. The second judicial challenge to L. 1700/1987 assumed the form of an appeal to the European Court of Human Rights on the part of certain monasteries and clergymen. The appeal held that the provisions of L. 1700 violated Articles 6, 9, 11 and 14 of the ECHR and Article 1 of its First Protocol.

666. The European Court of Human Rights, in its decision *Holy Monasteries v. Greece* (9.12.1994),[380] upheld that the provisions of Laws 1700/1987 and 1811/1988 violated Article 1 of the First Additional Protocol to the ECHR, which safeguards the right of the monasteries to the undisturbed enjoyment of their property.[381]

667. In an effort to comply, the Greek State proceeded with the enactment of Article 55 of L. 2413/1996, which restored to the prior status all those monasteries which did not sign the Contract ratified by L. 1811/1988 or which later acceded to it.[382]

668. After these events, monastic property is nowadays permeated by two systems of legal rules: that of the Contract ratified by L. 1811/1988, which relates to the Monasteries that were signatory parties to the Contract, and that of L. 1700/1987, which concerns all other Monasteries of the Church of Greece.[383]

669. Article 68 paragraph 1 of L. 4235/2014, which modified Article 47 paragraph 3 of SCCG, has introduced as a new notarian document for the ecclesiastical property the so-called register report (*ekthesi apografis*). The purpose of this new

379. Law & Politics 15 (1988) 233–248 (on pp. 249–260 and 261–292 are published the papers of Consultants N. Papadimitriou and A. Marinos). *See also* Papastathis, *Nomocanonical Studies*, 169f.
380. NoV 44 (1996) 287–305; HEED 15 (1995) 939–944. *See also* Sicilianos, *European Convention on Human Rights. Interpretation to Articles*, 776ff.
381. As it has been argued, a perception which is statist in nature and based on the premise that, since the Church of the prevailing religion is a legal entity under public law, it should accept intense legislative interventions concerning its ownership rights and its real estate property, is today contrary to the case law of the European Court of Human Rights, *see* Venizelos, *State and Church Relations*, 105ff.
382. For an application of Art. 55 L. 2413/1996 *see* at: *AP 411/1997*, NoV 46 (1998) 1435ff, HellDni 38 (1997) 1797ff; *First Instance Court Trikala 112/1999*, Arm. 54 (2000) 488ff; *First Instance Court Trikala 182/2001*, HellDni 42 (2001) 1432ff; *First Instance Court Piraeus 26/2002*, NoV 50 (2002) 721ff; LCS 333/2002.
383. Papastathis, *Nomocanonical Studies, 163-172*; Ramiotis, *The Church within the Greek State, 276ff.*

notarial document was, among other, to validate retroactively (ex tunc) the relative rights of ecclesiastical legal entities, that had weakened after a long time. It is noted that this is a common phenomenon in the cases of the old monasteries and temples, the establishment of which, as well as the consequent acquisition by them of their real estate, dates back to a much earlier time than the establishment of the modern Greek state.[384]

670. However, the very recent decisions of the Multi-Member Court of First Instance of Ioannina nos 27 and 28/2021 did not accept the retroactive application of the institution of the 'register report'.

§3. The Legal Status of Property of Religious Minorities

671. Muslims. For the Muslim wakfs of Western Thrace currently applies L. 3647/2008, 'On administration and management of the wakfs of the Muslim minority in Western Thrace and their property'.[385] Under Article 2 of this Law, the wakf is an endowment under the sacred Islamic law, including real estate and/or movable assets or annuity for a pious, charitable cause or for a philanthropic, religious, charitable institution, which either already exists or is established as a non-profit organization. The wakf property is this very wakf, and any other property, movable or immovable, dedicated to the proper functioning of the wakf.

672. The management of the wakf property falls under the law about charitable trusts and institutions. The members of the committees that manage the wakf property must respect the Muslim principles and traditions regarding its management. The wakfs are under the mufti's supervision.

673. The wakfs that existed when L. 3647/2008 came into force incorporate real estate and constitute separate legal entities of private law, operating as charitable institutions, serving the purpose which they were created for.

674. The wakfs that have been established after the above-mentioned law came into force incorporate movable and immovable property and are subject, as for their establishment and administration, to the provisions of the Civil Code regarding institutions, and as for their management to L. 3647/2008.

675. The wakf property per mosque or group of mosques in villages of Thrace outside the limits of the Municipality of Komotini, Xanthi and Didimoticho is managed by a Wakf Committee, which exercises its power on wakf property in

384. Papageorgiou, 'Ecclesiastical property: legislative and jurisprudential developments, property titles, the "register report" as a new notarial document', Arm. 73 (2019) 961ff.

385. For the whole text, *see* Troianos/Papageorgiou, *Religious Legislation. Special Legislation – Bibliography – Case Law, 1768-1776.*

accordance with the practices adopted at the establishment of wakf. Each Wakf Committee comprises three members, the President (Mouteveli), the treasurer and a member.

676. Furthermore, the management of the wakf estates of Dodecanese is under the responsibility of the 'Organization for the management of wakf property of Rhodes'. According to case law,[386] the above Organization is a legal entity 'with limited liability' with indirectly religious, and generally charitable or benevolent pursuits. This state is not affected by the investment on the part of the Organization of any funds available, since in this way its main purposes are in fact being served. Consistent with its charitable pursuits, the named Organization has so far made many donations to the Greek government, various municipalities, schools, Orthodox church organizations and Orthodox dioceses (metropolises) as well as to deprived citizens of the Dodecanese.

677. According to Administrative First Instance Court of Rhodes, Decision No. 50/2001, the Treaty of Lausanne (1923) does not apply to the Dodecanese since they were annexed to Greece by the Treaty of Peace signed on 10 February 1947 with Italy. Therefore, both the Organization for the Management of the Wakf Property of Rhodes and other philanthropic, charitable or religious institutions created by the Greek Muslims of the Dodecanese do not come under the category of minority legal entities, to which apply Articles 40 and 45 of the Treaty of Lausanne but constitute legal entities under the applicable provisions for all Greek legal entities.

678. 'Genuine Orthodox Christians' ('Old Calendarists'). Although the GOC adhere to the Orthodox doctrine, they must not be confused with the prevailing religion, as they have a special clerical hierarchy organization, with separate churches and monasteries.[387] Their religious communities are organized as private legal entities – usually in the form of the union – which manage their both movable and immovable property,[388] in the frame of rules laid down in respective statutes.[389]

679. Similar regulations apply respectively to various *Protestant Denominations* within the Greek territory, which, according to the prevailing law, have legal personality, but not in public law.[390]

---

386. CoS *4454/1984*, DFN 40 (1986) 360–361; *AP 1213/1991*, EEN 1993, 41–43; *Administrative First Instance Court of Rhodes 50/2001*, DiDiki 15 (2003) 1283–1286.
387. *Papageorgiou,* 'Statut constitutionnel des communautés religieuses des Anciens Calendaristes à l'ordre juridique de Grèce', 171ff.
388. Recognition of the property of the GOH according to L. 4301/2014 is contained in the decisions of the *Single Member Court of First Instance of Piraeus 2457/2015* ('Holy Metropolis of Piraeus and Salamis of the Church of the Original Orthodox Christians of Greece', Religious legal entity) and *Single Member Court of First Instance of Thivas 165/2015* (religious legal entity 'Holy Metropolis of Attica and Boeotia of the Original Orthodox Christians').
389. *Court of Appeal of Thessaloniki 546/2004*, HellDni 46 (2005) 913–915: the temples belonging to unions of GOC are not subject to any transaction [*see* AP 162/1996, HellDni 37 (1996) 1080–1082].
390. CoS 1558/1974.

680. The *Roman Catholic Church* in Greece as well as its organizational subdivisions are considered particular ecclesiastical legal entities according to the relevant canon law.[391] What is more, these ecclesiastical legal entities constitute independent entities concerning their obligations and rights, by the mere fact of belonging to the Roman Catholic Church.

681. However, with the decision of the *AP 360/1994*,[392] it was judged that the Catholic Church 'Panagia of Chania in Crete' as well as the local monastery of the Capuchins do not constitute legal entities, fact which deprived them of even the possibility to stand in court in order to defend their property rights. As this decision was particularly painful for the Greek Catholic minority, due to the fact that it essentially challenged its very existence, the Roman Catholic Church of Greece was forced to appeal before the European Court of Human Rights.

682. According to the decision *ECtHR Catholic Church of Crete v. Greece* (16-12-1997), the applicant has legal personality sui generis, like all the other Churches that existed in Greece before the introduction of the Civil Code.[393] Subsequently, the Greek government issued L. 2731/15.7.1991, which under Article 33 recognized the legal personality of the Catholic foundations that were established before the introduction of the Greek Civil Code (23 February 1946).

683. Finally, in Article 13 of L. 4301/2014 (Organization of the legal form of religious communities – Establishment of religious legal entities), the legal entities of the Roman Catholic Church were fully recognized by the Greek state as legal persons in private law.[394]

---

391. Asimakis, *Legislation and Jurisprudence for the Catholic Church in Greece*, 24ff and lately *Codex Juris Canonici*, passim.
392. D 26 (1995) 282–284: in the Third Protocol of the Protecting Powers, in London on 02/03/1830, it was not granted to the bishops of the Western Church any jurisdiction other than the purely intellectual and administrative, namely the one that is solely reduced to the internal order of this Church. In Greece, there have not been introduced any provisions of canon law of the Roman Catholic Church, which confers legal personality on monasteries established by acts of the bishop, as is the case with other religious institutions. Religious freedom, freedom of worship and religious equality are safeguarded for religious minorities. The right to establish religious associations and acquire legal personality is common for all the religious minorities, in accordance with the state laws. The different religious beliefs of minorities cannot constitute a legitimate reason for non-compliance with the above laws for the acquisition of legal personality, which is a prerequisite for acquiring the capacity to bring legal proceedings (Art. 62 a CCProc).
393. *ECtHR Catholic Church 'Panagia of Chania' v. Greece* (143/1996/762/963/16-12-1997), D 29 (1998) 567–578, with remarks of K. Beis; HEED 19 (1999) 205–210: the rejection of the appeals of the Catholic Church of Panagia of Chania by Greek courts, on the grounds that this Church did not have the requisite legal personality to bring legal proceedings, is a violation of Arts 9 and 14 ECHR, because it constitutes discrimination against the right of the specific Church for enjoyment of religious freedom and against the rights for access to court and respect for property. The religious communities, regardless of their legal personality, however, are subject to the rights guaranteed by the ECHR, which they may exercise in the name of their believers or members.
394. More analytically *see* Papageorgiou, 'Law 4301/2014 on the organization of the legal form of religious communities and the establishment of religious legal entities. A critical approach', Arm. 70 (2016) 570ff.

684. The Israelites. The local Israelite communities are recognized as self-governing legal entities of public law, with philanthropic, religious, charitable or educational purposes (Articles 1 and 4 of L. 2456/1920, 'On Jewish Communities'),[395] which run and manage the assets concerned, under their statutes.[396] For the promotion of the above objectives, the Israelite communities have hitherto established numerous charitable institutions, which engage in important social activity.[397]

§4. Revenues and Insurance of Clergy and Monks

685. The wages of the Orthodox bishops have been derived from the state budget since 1980 (Article 8 § 1 of L. 1041/1980).[398] The state budget is also burdened with the salaries of priests and deacons (L. 536/1945),[399] who have been integrated into the uniform salaries scale. However, their employment status does not equate them with civil servants.

686. Orthodox priests and deacons, in addition to their position in the parish church, may also at the same time occupy a position of teacher, receiving within certain limitations the wages of both positions.[400] Clergymen are entitled to also serve as ecclesiastical clerks in the offices of ecclesiastical legal entities, such as metropolises, receiving the salary of the highest paid position and two-thirds of the salary of the other.

687. Orthodox monks or nuns are sustained not only by their cenobitic monasteries but also through their own private property, in cases when this is permitted. If the monks or nuns engage in agrarian labour, they are insured by the Agricultural Insurance Organization (AIP) (Article 5 § 2 LD 1390/1973).

---

395. Troianos/Papageorgiou, *Religious legislation: Special legislation – bibliography – case law, 1737-1746.*
396. *Court of First Instance of Ioannina 8/1984*, DFN 38 (1984) 734–735: under Art. 9 of the Statute of the Jewish Community of Ioannina, approved by the RD of 03 Sep. 1937 (FEK A' 399), the Community's revenue is devoted to religious, educational, cultural and charitable institutions as well as to helping the needy in the Community. *See also*: *AP 440/1949*, EEN 17 (1950) 12; *Athens Court of Appeal 719/1949*, Them. 60, 366ff; CoS (Plenary Session) 236/1956, EEN 23 (1956) 678; CoS 485/1975, DiDni 13 (1975) 300–301.
397. As, for example, the charitable Israelite foundation 'Chaimoutso Kovo' in Thessaloniki. *See* relatively the opinions of Pelleni-Papageorgiou, 'Foundations of the Israelite Community of Thessaloniki', NoV 48 (2000) 618–620; Kerameus, 'Legal personality and state supervision of Israelite institutions in Greece', Arm. 30 (1976) 666–677, and, 'Israelite charitable institutions and the under the L. 2039/1939 supervision of the Minister of Finance', Arm. 30 (1976) 674–677; Fragkistas, 'Employee of the Israelite Community of Thessaloniki. Its legal character. Non application of provisions on contract labor', Arm. 5 (1951) 525–527.
398. Troianos/Papageorgiou, *Religious legislation: Special legislation – bibliography – case law,* 627f.
399. *Ibid.*, 616ff.
400. CoS 1030/1985.

688. The wages of the muftis are also covered by the state budget, as they also serve as religious functionaries of the Muslim minority of Western Thrace (Komotini, Xanthi, Didymoticho). The muftis are considered senior civil servants, with judicial powers. Their legal status is governed by the provisions of L. 1920/1991.[401]

§5. Real Estate as 'Non-market Goods': Meaning and Conditions

689. Things intended to serve religious purposes, and for as long this purpose remains the same, are considered 'non-market goods': i.e., either they cannot involve rights in rem – such as right of possession or ownership, they are non-confiscatable, inalienable and imprescriptible – or they can but under various restrictions (Articles 966, 971, 1054 CC).

690. As is acceptable though, the relevant provisions should be interpreted narrowly in order to include only those things that serve religious pursuits.[402] Consequently, all other ecclesiastical things may become subject to proprietary rights of natural or legal entities,[403] provided that such rights are not exercised in a manner contrary to the religious pursuits served by the holy things.

691. Finally, as for the privately owned churches, the law accepts that they are non-market goods, as long as they have been inaugurated and established in public worship.[404]

401. *See* relatively recent L. 4511/2018, 'Amendment of article 5 of the Act of Legislative Content "On Muslim Religious Officials" from 24.12.1990 (A 182), which was ratified with article only of L. 1920/1991 (GG A 11)'; CoS 466/2003; Tsitselikis, 'Le statut juridique de l'Islam en Grèce', 219ff.
402. Troianos, 'Privately owned churches and the Article 966 CC', ND 32 (1976) 95. This view was adopted by the current SCCG (L. 590/1977), defining (Art. 45 § 1) that the churches and the sacred vessels for the celebration of divine worship are 'non-market goods'.
403. *First Instant Court of Syros 88/2000*, ArchN 53 (2002) 494–497: the buildings around the monastery and its yard are not considered 'non-market goods', and are therefore subject to usucaption. In contrast, *First Instant Court of Volos 463/1996*, Arm. 51 (1997) 1012–1017: the monasteries and the buildings around them are thought to be as 'non-market goods', according to the relevant provisions of Greek Civil Code (Arts 966, 971), 'as the religious purpose pursued [by the monastery] cannot be realized only within the premises of the church'. Under *Athens Court of Appeal 7112/1982*, NoV 30 (1982) 1498, the building of the church as well as the property on which it is erected are not under usucaption (966 CC), as those two cannot de facto be separated.
404. *Athens Court of Appeal 4833/2006*, ChrIdD 7 (2007) 330–332; *AP 1178/2006*, NoV 54 (2006) 1482: the privately owned temples provide some individuals with the right to use them exclusively for their own and their families' religious needs. These temples, if they are inaugurated and established in divine worship, according to the sacred canons of the Eastern Orthodox Church of Christ, constitute 'non-market goods' (966 CC). Having the status of 'non-market goods', it is not incompatible to create legal relations of private law, if those do not impinge on serving the purpose of divine worship; similarly *AP 162/1996*, HellDni 37 (1996) 1080.

§6. Archaeological Legislation and Church Property

692. In accordance with the provisions of Articles 7 and 73 § 1 of L. 3028/2002, 'On the protection of antiquities and cultural heritage',[405] there should be preserved, regardless of their dating, the ownership rights of ecclesiastical entities in 'ancient'[406] movable or immovable monuments of religious nature (icons, sacred vessels, vestments, books, offerings, buildings, and so on),[407] already existing when this law came into force.

405. For the most important provisions of that law, *see* Troianos/Papageorgiou, *Religious legislation: Special legislation – bibliography – case law*, 104–143. *See also* the following studies: Karympali-Tsiptsiou, 'The possession of ancient movable monuments of its protection (under Law 3028/2002 "On the protection of antiquities and cultural heritage")', 1549ff; Troianos/Papadimitriou, 'The protection of religious monuments, according to L. 3028/2002', 584–591; Troianos, 'Ancient monuments in the Church of Greece', E. 83 (2006) 30–34.

406. Article 2 ('Meaning of terms') L. 3028/2002: 'For the application of the regulations of the present Law: a) … b) As monuments are perceived cultural objects which constitute material testimonies, belong to the cultural heritage of the country and deserve specific protection under the following divisions: aa) Ancient monuments or antiquities are all cultural objects dating back to the prehistoric, ancient, Byzantine and post-Byzantine times up to 1830, subject to the provisions of Article 20. Ancient monuments include caves and paleontological remains, for which there are indications that they are connected with human existence. bb) Newer monuments are the cultural objects after 1830, whose protection is necessitated by their historic, artistic or scientific significance, under the provisions of Articles 6 and 20. cc) Immovable monuments are the monuments that were connected to the ground and remain on it or in the seabed or at the bottom of lakes or rivers, and monuments located on the ground or the seabed or at the bottom of lakes or rivers and cannot be moved without damage to their value as evidence. Immovable monuments include installations, constructions and decorations and other items that form an integral part of them, as well as their immediate environment. dd) Movable monuments are the monuments that do not constitute property.'

407. *See also* Part XI: 'Religion and Culture'.

Chapter 2. Indirect Financing of Religious Communities

693. A series of favourable tax arrangements are provided for certain religious legal entities.[408] It should however be noted here that, because of the recent great economic crisis, there have been removed many tax exemptions that were in force previously. There is a general tendency to cut tax exemptions previously given in favour of ecclesiastical organizations, as evidenced by the decisions CoS 1731-1733/2018 on the exemption from income tax of Greek ecclesiastical legal entities, in relation with the European Community Court C-74/16/27.6.2017 *Congregación de Escuelas Pías Provincia Betania v. Ayuntamiento de Getafe*, as to the conditions of similar exemption enjoyed by the Roman Catholic Church in Spain.

§1. Inheritance and Donations Taxes

694. According to Articles 25 § 3 and 29 § 5 of L. 2961/2001 ('Code of Inheritance and Donations Tax'), the inheritances and the donations are subject to an autonomous taxation at a rate of 0.5%, if beneficiaries are the following:[409]

(a) Legal entities of public law, churches, monasteries, the 'Church of the Holy Sepulchre', the Monastery of Mount Sinai, the Ecumenical Patriarchate of Constantinople, the Patriarchate of Jerusalem, the Patriarchate of Alexandria, the Church of Cyprus, the Orthodox Church of Albania. It should be made clear here that the terms 'church' and 'monastery' refer to the churches, chapels and monasteries of every 'known' religion or belief – as required by the constitutional principle of fiscal and religious equality.
(b) Non-profit legal entities, which already exist or are lawfully established in Greece, as well as the corresponding foreign ones under the term of reciprocity.[410] A legal entity is considered to be non-profit when, in accordance with its statutes or founding act, and as is shown in practice through the activity which is actually performed, its pursuits are religious, charitable, philanthropic, educational, artistic or for the benefit of the nation. It should be clarified here that the legal entity retains its non-profit character even if from its activities derive revenue that is allocated to cover its expenses or if there is potential surplus (profit) that is allocated for further development of its activity and promotion of its pursuits.[411]

---

408. More details *see* in Papageorgiou, 'The special tax treatment of religions', Arm. 74 (2020) 953ff; *ibid., The tax regime of religions. Tax equality and religious freedom,* passim.
409. Papageorgiou, *The special tax treatment of religions*, 960f.
410. 'Foreign' is the legal entity that was established and functions on the conditions and terms of a specified foreign country, where lie its head offices. The foreign legal person should submit to the competent tax inspector, on the one hand the official data (documents) from its country of origin, regarding its lawful establishment, existence and objectives of the legal person, duly stamped by the Greek Consul in the country of origin, and on the other hand, the official translation of the foreign law, which provides the corresponding tax treatment of Greek legal persons.
411. CoS 1906-1910/1990, Accountant 37 (1990) 1152–1153.

695. More specifically, *religious* is the purpose, as prescribed in the statutes of the legal person and put into practice, which is designed to foster and disseminate the principles of a specific religion, 'known' in Greece.[412] For example, the Greek Evangelical Church of Katerini,[413] the Greek Evangelical Church of Alexandroupolis[414] and the Greek Evangelical Church of Thessaloniki[415] have been considered to be religious non-profit legal entities.

696. *Charitable* is considered the pursuit that is beneficial, wholly or partially, to the community. In addition, however, it is required that: (a) this pursuit should be the exclusive one of the legal person, (b) there should be proof of its realization and (c) the benefit of the pursuit should apply not only to the members of the legal entity but also to the general public.

697. The financial donations to temples, the monasteries of Mount Athos, the Patriarchates of Constantinople, Alexandria and Jerusalem, the Monastery of Sinai and the Orthodox Church of Albania are deducted from the income tax of the donator up to 10% of the total of his net income (Article 31 § 1gg of L. 2238/1994, as in force).

§2. Uniform Property Owners Tax

698. The United Property Owners Tax (UPOT) is imposed on properties located in Greece, which belong to natural or legal entities (Article 1 L. 223/2013, as in force after its amendment and by Law 4679/2018).[416]

699. However, according to Article 3 § 1 L. 4223/2013 (as in force), from the said tax are exempted among others: (a) the rights on real estate which belong to legal entities under public law and which are used exclusively for the fulfilment of the educational, religious, charitable, etc., purposes; (b) the legal entities of the known religions and dogmas according to § 2 of Article 13 of the Constitution, if they are used for the fulfilment of their worship, religious and public benefit work; and (c) the I. Monasteries of Mount Athos subject to the special constitutional regime, regardless of whether their properties are located inside or outside the Athos Peninsula.

412. CoS 385/1992, NoV 41 (1993) 874–875.
413. *AP 237/1968*, NoV 16 (1968) 738.
414. *Tax First Instance Court of Alexandroupolis 28/1972*, NoV 21 (1973) 554–557, comments by Panagopoulos.
415. *Tax First Instance Court of Thessaloniki 2174/1969*, Arm. 23 (1969) 876; CoS 1558/1974, DFN 29 (1975) 174–176.
416. Papageorgiou, *The special tax treatment of religions*, 961f.

§3. Real Property Transfer Tax

700. According to Article 6 Case c' L 1521/1950 (as amended by L. 1587/ 1950 and is in force today), fully exempt from the Real Property Transfer Tax, when they appear as buyers, are all public entities (and therefore all legal entities of public law of the Churches of Greece, Crete and Dodecanese, the Israelite communities and so on) as well as churches and monasteries.

701. As required by the constitutional principle of (religious and tax) equality, the above exemption from the Real Property Transfer Tax is extended to all the churches in general, of every known religion or denomination.[417] So, this tax exemption covers all the chapels or houses of worship, where people gather mainly to listen to the sermon or for common prayer and religious chants; to grant the above tax exemption the law does not demand for the chapels or houses of worship to constitute any kind of legal entity or engaging any charitable, artistic, educational or cultural activity.

702. The exemption from the Real Property Transfer Tax is not affected by the fact that the church or chapel belongs to a foreign legal person, denomination or faith, as the above-mentioned relevant provisions, since there is no provision limiting its application to Greek legal entities only, apply as well to foreign legal entities that operate in Greece in order to fulfil their religious pursuits.

§4. Value Added Tax

703. Article 2 § 2a L. 2859/2000 ('Code of Value Added Tax') exempted Mount Athos and a series of ecclesiastical or religious entities from levying this tax, depending on the nature of activities in which they engage. It should be noted here that even before Greek's accession into the European Economic Community (1979), especially Mount Athos had been exempted from the scope of VAT, under Article 3 (Title III: Territoriality) § 3, Case iv of the 6th Directive of the Council of European Community of 17 May 1977 (77/388/EEC).[418]

§5. Municipal Taxes

704. Temples of any religion are exempted from any municipal tax according to Article 82 § 1c of B.D. 20-10-1958 (as it is in force today).

---

417. *LCS 606/2000*; *Administrative Court of Appeal of Athens 4186/1987*, NoV 36 (1988) 989, with notes by Leontaritou; CoS 549/1991, NoV 40 (1992) 788–789 [= DiDiki 4 (1992) 747; Accountant 38 (1991) 1254–1255]: exempt from Real Property Transfer Tax is the purchase of property for housing a house of worship (Chapel) of the 'Church of Jesus Christ of Saints of the Last Days', which was founded in 1851; its head offices are in Frankfurt, Germany, and it has been recognized by the government of Hesse as a legal entity.

418. Papageorgiou, 'The special tax treatment of religions', Arm. 74 (2020) 967ff.

705. Full exemption of all religions and their legal persons is provided by the Real Estate Tax a kind of municipal tax introduced by Article 24 L. 2130/1993. The amount of Real Estate Tax is determined by a decision of the municipal or community council, and it is uniform throughout its administrative region, with a rate that ranges, depending on each local government authority provisions. However, Article 24 § 7 provides that Real Estate Tax is not imposed on all kinds of property belonging, *inter alia*, to

(a) the legal entities of public law;
(b) churches, monasteries, the 'Church of the Holy Sepulcher', the monastery of Mount Sinai, Mount Athos, the Apostolic Diakonia of the Church of Greece and religious institutions in general;
(c) the known religions or denominations, as to the properties used exclusively for public worship and services of religious nature;
(d) public charitable organizations;
(e) domestic non-profit legal persons, insofar as there is evidence that they pursue religious purposes or in a broader circle of philanthropic, educational, artistic, charitable or ecclesiastical scope. The exemption extends to foreign legal entities, as long as they pursue the same goals under the term of reciprocity.[419]

706. As stated by the decision of the Administrative First Instant Court of Thessaloniki no. 1064/1998, in accordance with the constitutional principles of religious and tax equality, the exemption from Real Estate Tax should be extended to any property of any 'known' religion, even if this is used not only for worship but also for educational purposes, since no such restriction holds for the prevailing religion either. A similar interpretation was also made by LCS 734/2001, stating that the exemption from every municipal or community tax, Real Estate Tax, duty or levy, concerns the churches of all known religions and not only those of the prevailing religion, as required by the Constitution itself, thus safeguarding equality among all known religions.

419. Papageorgiou, *supra*, *954ff*.

Part IX. Education

Chapter 1. Religious Education in Public and Private Schools

707. The fundamental basis of religious education in Greece is Article 16 § 2 Const., which stipulates that: 'Education constitutes a basic mission for the State and shall aim at the moral, intellectual, professional and physical training of Greeks, the development of national and religious consciousness and at their formation as free and responsible citizens.'[420]

708. At the same time, however, Article 2 of the First Protocol of the ECHR is also applied, which stipulates that everyone has a right to education and that states should respect the right of parents to ensure such education and teaching their children in conformity with their own religious and philosophical convictions.[421]

709. Consequently, one of the aims of school education is to develop the religious consciousness of pupils. In order to fulfil this State goal, religious education is taught as a compulsory subject in public and private elementary and secondary schools, where it largely reflects the principles of Orthodox Christian doctrine.[422]

---

420. Chrysogonos/Vlahopoulos, *Individual and social rights,* 316f, 371ff; Vlahopoulos (ed.), *Fundamental rights: Individual, social and political rights*, 319ff; Dagtoglou, *Constitutional law: Individual rights*, 683–694; Kyriazopoulos, 'Which model of the course of the religions is provided by the international human rights law and the constitution?', Proceedings of the Panhellenic Scientific Conference on the subject: *The course of religious, Reflections-Notes-Suggestions*, Laboratory of Pedagogy – Christian Pedagogy, Department of Pastoral and Social Theology, AUTh, Micheloudakis/Pepes (eds), Thessaloniki 2014, 277–297; Troianos, 'Religious education in the context of the individual right to religious freedom', 285f; Manesis, *Constitutional rights. Vol. A': Individual liberties-Lectures*, 252.
421. Sicilianos, *European Convention on Human Rights: Interpretation to articles*, 817ff; Troianos/Papageorgiou, *Religious legislation: Special legislation – bibliography – case law*, 5–10; Michailidis-Nouaros, 'The right to education under the European Convention of Human Rights (Art. 2 of the 1rst Protocol of the European Convention', 1ff.
422. Chrysogonos, 'Religious education and prevailing religion', 993ff; *Sotirelis,* 'Religion and education under the Constitution and the European Convention: from catechism to polyphony', passim; CoS 2176/1998, NoV 47 (1999) 139–143, with critical remarks by St. Tsakirakis. It should be stressed that the bulk of theoretical opinion is opposed to the catechetical and one-sided character that, according to the Ministry of Education, religious education should have in Greece. It is claimed, therefore, that there is a need for this subject to be based on a multicultural and religious studies approach: *see* Chrysogonos/Vlahopoulos, *supra;* Sotirelis, *Religion and education under the Constitution and the European Convention: from catechism to polyphony*, 330ff. It should also

710. According to the CoS (Plenary Session) 660/2018, the use of materials of a 'confessional' nature in religious education is compatible with the inviolable principle of religious freedom, provided it is exclusively directed at pupils who adhere to the Orthodox Christian faith, while pupils of other faiths and denominations and atheist pupils have the right to be completely exempted from religious education, without negative consequence. The State may include in the curriculum, as part of the content of other lessons, instruction in 'religious studies' presenting information and knowledge about other religions and denominations. The State may not, in regulating the content of religious education, deprive pupils adhering to a particular religion of the right to be taught exclusively about the doctrines of their own faith.

711. In a parallel interpretative way, the CoS 926/2018 (Plenary Session) judged that the teaching of the dogmas, moral values and traditions that make up the Orthodox Christian faith in the Lyceum in the context of religious education does not cause confusion with the teaching of other dogmas and religions. The religious education in Lyceum is compatible with religious freedom because it does not constitute a coercion in favour of the prevailing religion. It is addressed exclusively to students who adhere to the Orthodox Christian doctrine and not to the students of other Christian confessions, non-religious or atheist students who are entitled to complete exemption from the course. The State may include in the curriculum and education of a 'religious' nature information and knowledge about other religions and dogmas, but it may not, by regulating the content of the religious course, deprive students who embrace a particular religion of the right to be taught exclusively the doctrines of their faith.

712. Next year the Supreme Administrative Court judged that religious education in primary and lower secondary schools is directed exclusively at those pupils who adhere to the Orthodox Christian faith and not to pupils of other faiths or denominations or atheist pupils. The latter enjoy the right to religious freedom and may request their complete exemption from religious education, without any negative consequences. The State is obliged to make provision for the teaching of an equivalent religious education course of similar content or to include in the curriculum a 'religious studies' course presenting information and knowledge about other faiths and denominations other than the Orthodox faith (CoS, Plenary Session, 1749-1750/2019).[423]

713. The more recent and interesting ECtHR *Papageorgiou and others v. Greece* (31.10.2019) ruled that there had been a violation of Article 2 of the First Additional Protocol of the ECHR concerning compulsory religious education in

---

be noted that under CoS (Proceedings) 347/2002 (DA 2003, p. 623ff), it was accepted that the legislator should have the freedom to decide between a catechetical or religious studies teaching model for religious education in schools; moreover, it was added that the second of these two models was considered to be more in line with the constitutional protection of religious freedom (Arts § 1, 13 § 1, 16 § 2 Const.).

423. Venizelos, 'The ambiguity of recent jurisprudence around religious freedom and the subject of religion: Internal dialogue in the Council of State and deviations from the case law of the European Court of Human Rights', 19ff.

schools. The Court held that the procedure for exempting children from religious education, which consists in the parents' obligation to submit a solemn declaration in writing, ratified by the teacher, stating that their child is not of the Orthodox Christian faith, may risk exposing sensitive aspects of the parents' private life and is likely to deter them from submitting a request for their child's exemption, particularly if they live in a small and religiously compact society. When a Contracting State includes a religious education in its curriculum, it is obliged to offer at least one procedure enabling pupils to be exempted from that course, without requiring the parents to make known their religious or philosophical convictions, which constitute a matter of individual conscience. The Court held that there had therefore been a violation of the rights set out in the second sentence of Article 2 of Protocol No. 1, as interpreted in the light of Article 9 of the ECHR.

714. The subject is taught by regular elementary school teachers in elementary schools and by graduates of Theology Faculties in secondary schools. Both categories of teachers are regarded as civil servants and are paid by the State. However, neither the appointments of these teachers nor the religious education syllabus is controlled directly by the Church.

715. During religious education, it is not permissible to make offensive comments about other religions. For the same reason, relevant class material requires prior approval by the Ministry of Education and Religious Affairs.[424]

716. Pupils (or their parents) of other denominations or religions or of atheistic persuasion are entitled, by whatever means, to inform the headmaster of the school that, for reasons of religious consciousness, they do not wish to attend religious education lessons or to participate in other religious activities prescribed by the school curriculum.[425] In this case, the headmaster is officially obliged to immediately take all the necessary legal measures to ensure that these pupils do not participate in the above religious activities and do not attend religious education lessons.

717. A pupil's abstention from the above religious education and activities does not entail any form of school sanction (e.g., the recording of an absence in the attendance register, adverse comments in a pupil's record of conduct, disciplinary action). A pupil may even refuse to make a public recitation of prayer when they have other private reasons that justify, according to the rules of pedagogical science, this refusal (e.g., dysarthria, lack of confidence, psychological problems).[426]

718. As is apparent from L. 1566/1985, 'Structure and operation of primary and secondary education and other provisions', the aims of nursery schools do not

424. Ombudsman Act of 6-8-2002.
425. On this issue *see* Pouliadis, 'Parent and child relations: An interpretation of Arts 1521-1536 of the civil code', 253ff. However, *see* Argyropoulos, 'Freedom of religious conscience and the obligation to declare one's religious affiliation in public documents', 21ff.
426. CoS 3356/1995, NoV 43 (1995) 925–932, with a note by N. Frangakis.

include familiarizing pupils with ethical, religious, national, humanitarian or other values, nor, for that matter, does the children's age lend itself to such.[427]

719. In Greece, any religion or individual may, after obtaining permission from the State authority, establish a school that operates in accordance with the Constitution and laws of the country.[428] No one may be deprived of this right purely on the grounds that they belong to another denomination or religion. Such schools admit all pupils, regardless of their religious denomination.[429]

720. As Article 16 ('Appointments of teachers of other denominations and religions') of L. 1771/1988 stipulates, all nursery and elementary school teachers that are not Orthodox are appointed to and placed in multi-teacher State elementary schools or two-teacher State nursery schools. In these cases, these teachers only teach religious education to pupils of the same denomination or religion as themselves, provided that this subject is prescribed by the law.[430]

427. CoS 2702/1987, NoV 36 (1988) 821–822.
428. Troianos/Papageorgiou, *Religious legislation: Special legislation – bibliography – case law*, 80–85.
429. L. 4862/1931 'Concerning foreign schools'; L. 682/1977 'Concerning private schools of general education and school boarding houses'.
430. CoS 3390/2000.

Chapter 2. Religious Schools

721. Under L. 3432/2006, 'On structure and function of Ecclesiastical Education',[431] the structure for the provision of ecclesiastical education was reformed, with the particular aim of staffing the Orthodox Church with clerical and lay personnel of a high educational and moral standard.[432] The said structure consists of two tiers: a higher and a secondary-level one.

722. The first tier is composed of the 'Higher Ecclesiastical Academies' in Athens, Thessaloniki, Heraklion in Crete and the Vellas Academy near Ioannina.[433]

723. The second tier includes ten General Ecclesiastical Lykeia (upper secondary schools) with three years of studies and seven Ecclesiastical Gymnasia (lower secondary schools). Each of these schools is recognized as a public legal entity, which is governed and represented by its own school board. The provisions for the foundation, organization and operation of the ecclesiastical lower and upper secondary schools are the same as those applying to all other lower and secondary schools in the State secondary education sector.

724. All of the above ecclesiastical schools come under the supervision of the Ministry of Education and Religious Affairs. In addition, the Church of Greece always has the capacity to establish schools of further education for its clergy or lay personnel.

725. As for the religious education of the Muslims of Western Thrace, legal provision is made for the operation of a number of local religious schools which enjoy a special status and address the needs solely of the children of the Muslim minority. The legal framework for these Muslim schools is based on the Treaty of Lausanne (1923),[434] other international rules (such as those of the European Convention on

---

431. The last modifications of this law have been introduced with particular provisions of Laws 4386/2016, 4589/2019, 4610/2019 and 4653/2020.
432. CoS 1319/2019 (Plenary Session); CoS 775/2017. According to Art. 2 L. 3432/2006, 'the aim of the ecclesiastical education is to promote and train the clergy and secular officials of the Orthodox Church in Greece, so as to raise the level of their education and Christian ethos'. All the ecclesiastical schools are supervised by the Ministry of National Education and Religious Affairs (Art. 1 L. 3432/2006). Almost all ecclesiastical educational schools operate as boarding schools providing free of charge accommodation and meals to their students.
433. CoS 117-118/2007, TPDD 2/2008, 165f, with observations by C. Papageorgiou. The Higher Ecclesiastical Academies admit as students graduates from any Lyceum through the general university admission exams, provided that they are Orthodox Christians. Their graduates are exclusively appointed for the services of the Greek Orthodox Church and may not be appointed as teachers or professors in schools.
434. The Treaty of Lausanne equipped the Muslim minority with a unique legal status and particular rights that the government must protect, such as bilingual education, government salaries for muftis and other religious ministers, operation of mosques and the recognition of elements of Islamic Law (Shari'a) in family law matters.

Human Rights) and a complex set of internal provisions (laws, decrees, ministerial decisions) relating to primary and secondary education.[435]

726. A special category of Muslim schools consists of the 'Medrese' (seminaries) in Komotini and Echinos near Xanthi, which provide a basic education especially for Muslim teachers. Such seminaries have existed in Thrace since the Ottoman period and continued to operate after Thrace's annexation to the Greek State.[436]

---

435. *See*, in particular, L. 694/1977 ('Concerning minority schools of the Muslim Minority of Western Thrace'); L. 2341/1995 ('Regulation of matters concerning the educational staff of the minority schools in Thrace'); L. 3536/2007 ('Special regulations relating to immigration policy matters etc.'); P.D. 98/2007 ('Establishment of posts for Muslim State teachers in the minority State schools of Thrace'). *See also*: Antoniou, *Muslim immigrants in Greece: religious organization and local responses,* 155ff; Tsitselikis, *Muslims in Greece,* 79ff; Alivisatos, 'The constitutional treatment of religious minorities in Greece', in Dupay (ed.), *Melanges en l'honneur de Nicolas Valtikos,* Pedone, Paris 1998. Particularly useful is the material assembled by Baltsiotis/Tsitselikis, *Minority education in Thrace. Compilation of relevant legislation – commentary,* Athens 2001.

436. Under Article 36 of L. 3536/2007, as modified by Art. 53 of L. 4115/2013, 240 religion teachers for the teaching of Koran were appointed in Western Thrace. Religion teachers should be Greek citizens of the Muslim minority, holders of a certificate issued by a University Faculty of Theology in Greece or abroad, while in the latter case the certificate should be recognized by the National Academic Recognition Information Centre. For further details *see*: Kyriazopoulos, '*Restrictions on the freedom to teach minority religions*', 343ff; Askouni, *The education of the minority in Thrace*, Athens 2006.

Chapter 3. Theological Faculties and Religious Universities

727. When the first university of the modern Greek State was founded in 1837, the Theological Faculty of Athens was established together with the Faculties of Legal Sciences, Medicine and Philosophy.

728. Since 1932 the Theological Faculty, together with the Law and Philosophy Faculties, has formed part of the National and Kapodistrian University of Athens. Since then, the Theological Faculty has been producing graduates cultivated in all branches of theological science who go on to serve as either clergymen or teachers of religious education in State schools.

729. Today, there are two Theological Faculties in operation, one in Athens and the other in Thessaloniki. Both of these faculties contain two schools: the School of Theology and the School of Pastoral Theology. Originally, only graduates of the School of Theology were entitled to be appointed as State secondary school teachers; however, in 1983, under Law 151, graduates of both schools were granted the same entitlement. In 2016, a particular programme of Islamic studies has been created by the School of Theology of Thessaloniki (PD 45/2016).

730. Ecclesiastical education is also served within the jurisdiction of the Ecumenical Patriarchate by Ecclesiastical Schools or Seminaries, such as the Athonias School (in Mount Athos), the Patmian Ecclesiastical School, the Ecclesiastical School in Crete (*see* above) and certain others.[437]

437. Rodopoulos, *An overview of orthodox canon law*, p. 221, who also mentions of the Patriarchal Institute for Patristic Studies, which lies at the Holy Stavropegic Monastery of Vlatades in Thessaloniki. Important auxiliary tools and resources for theological studies are the libraries of the above Theological Faculties and Schools, of the Monasteries of Mount Athos and Patmos, of the Patriarchal Institute for Patristic Studies (Stavropegic Monastery of Vlatades), etc., as well as the periodicals published by the Church of Greece or by the Ecumenical Patriarchate.

Part X. Matrimonial and Family Law

Chapter 1. Legal Position of Religious Marriage

731. Article 1367 CC[438] established as equal in Greece the religious and the civil marriage. More specifically, according to the above article, marriage is celebrated either with the simultaneous and personal declaration of the intended spouses that they agree to it *(civil marriage)* or in a ecclesiastical ceremony of the Eastern Orthodox Church or by an official of another denomination or religion 'known' in Greece *(religious marriage).*[439]

732. The above declaration shall be made public in a festive manner before two witnesses, to the mayor or President of the community of the place where the marriage is celebrated, while those are required to prepare a relevant certificate immediately.

733. The conditions of the rite and every issue related to it are governed by the formal rules of the denomination or religion under which the rite takes place, provided they do not disturb the peace and proper order. The religious official is obliged to prepare the relevant certificate immediately. The contracting of civil marriage is not mutually exclusive with a church (ceremony) wedding under the religion and doctrine of both spouses.[440]

734. The contracting of civil or religious marriage requires authorization by the mayor of the place of residence of the intended spouses (Article 1368 CC). The Orthodox church wedding requires additionally the written permission of the local

438. Matrimonial and family law is contained in Book IV of the Greek Civil Code. The original provisions of this Book were quite conservative even for 1946, when they were adopted, modelled on the idea of patriarchal family. A wide revision of Greek family law was introduced by L. 1250/1982, which established civil marriage, and by L. 1329/1983, on the application of the constitutional principle of equality of men and women as well as about the partial modernization of family law. The mandatory character of most legal provisions about family law is an indication of its social interest; at the same time, the family law is liberal, marked by a considerable individualism. *See* more in Kotzambasi, *Handbook of family law*, passim; Chrysogonos/Vlahopoulos, *Individual and social rights*, 561ff, Athens [4]2017.

439. It is underlined that Art. 21 § 1 Const. declares that: 'The family, as well as marriage, motherhood and childhood years come under the protection of the State.' This constitutional reinforcement of the family as the most vital nucleus within society emphasizes the institutional nature of marriage, which is why provision is made to afford it the protection of the State; Kotzambasi, *supra*, 35ff.

440. Kotzambasi, *supra*, 58f.

bishop, a lack of which entails disciplinary and penal sanctions for the priest who will perform the mystery (Article 49 §§ 1–2 SCCG). The bishop himself is responsible for the spiritual dissolution or annulment of marriage as well, but only after he has received a copy of the irrevocable judgment for termination by divorce or annulment of marriage by the prosecutor (Article 50 § 2 SCCG).

735. The intended spouses must have reached 18 years of age. The court may, after hearing the intended spouses and those having custody of the minor, allow the marriage before reaching this age if its contracting is necessitated by an important reason.

736. When the marriage is celebrated with a declaration to the competent body of the local authorities, it is obvious that it constitutes a contract of civil law as well. However, marriage is considered as a kind of an agreement even when it is celebrated with a church ceremony, which is considered a type of marriage and not an essential condition for the existence of marriage.

737. The sham marriage (marriage of convenience) is not acceptable. Furthermore, in view of the contractual nature of marriage, those who do not have legal capacity may not contract marriage, while those who are partially able may do so but under the conditions laid down in Articles 1351–1352 CC.

738. Under Article 1354 CC, a second marriage may not be contracted before the irrevocable dissolution of the annulment of an existing one. However, spouses may repeat the celebration of marriage between them before their marriage is annulled.

739. In the case of religious marriage, the above-mentioned provisions of the Civil Code refer to the internal rules of each different religion. Each particular religious community enjoys the freedom to establish and modify its internal ceremonial and family law, as long as these religious provisions are not contrary to the general rules of Greek public order.[441]

740. According to the Orthodox canon law,[442] the sacrament of marriage is performed by a priest with the degree of bishop or presbyter. It is not necessary for him to belong to the clergy of the Church of Greece, as it is permissible for a marriage to be celebrated by an official from another autocephalous or autonomous Orthodox

441. *See*, for example, Papazissi, *Greek Jews and family law: From Judaic law to the civil law Code*, 385ff.

442. Orfanoudakis, *The holy canons and the constitution (a counter-comment or 'the other' interpretative approach)*, 82f; Rodopoulos, *An overview of Orthodox Canon Law*, 187, who underlines that the Christian Church proclaimed the institution of marriage to be a mystery, adding that 'from a legal point of view, in the first years of the Church and in later years, marriage was of civil importance, it was subject to civil jurisdiction and it had no direct connection to the Church'.

Church. Before the church ceremony wedding, the sequence of betrothal is also celebrated, but a separate celebration of the two constitutes an infringement rendering the offending cleric liable to disciplinary and penal sanctions (Article 49 § 3 SCCG).[443]

741. Major obstacles to the conclusion of the Orthodox religious – but not civil – marriage are the capacity of the priest or monk, the prior conclusion of three valid marriages and the difference in religion (not in dogma).[444]

742. A marriage is considered as non-existent, if there was neither declaration to the mayor nor church ceremony (Article 1372 CC). Null and void is considered the marriage that was celebrated in contravention of Articles 1350 CC (legal age), 1351 CC (legal impotence), 1352 CC (lack of consent of the judicial assistant), 1354 CC (impediment because of already existing marriage) and 1360 CC (impediment due to adoption).

743. The contracting of civil marriage does not constitute an impediment to a church wedding ceremony, which is celebrated according to the religion or doctrine of the spouses (Article 1367 CC). The religious official is required to prepare, immediately after the ceremony, the marriage certificate, as this constitutes evidence of the act. This is submitted to the registrar of the place where the ceremony took place (or, when abroad, to the Greek consular authorities), who in turn draw the registrar's marriage certificate in accordance with the certificate prepared by the religious official. If such a certificate was not issued or if it was destroyed, the interested parties may prove the actual fact of the celebration of marriage by any lawful means – as the law does not establish as exclusive evidence the registrar's certificates.

744. Under Article 1371 CC, when it comes to marriage between believers of different denominations or religions, the wedding ceremony is performed as required by the denomination or religion of each of the spouses, as long as it is recognized in Greece. In this case, the religious ceremony has to be performed twice, a complicated procedure that several times creates problems.[445]

745. The involvement of the Church in issues related to marriage and its dissolution (which once were entirely the responsibility of its institutions) also includes the spiritual dissolution or annulment of the marriage after an irrevocable judgment for dissolution of marriage by divorce or for its annulment (Article 50 SCCG and

443. About all these matters, *see*: Papageorgiou, *Ecclesiastical law*, 212ff; Rodopoulos, *An overview of orthodox canon law*, 185ff; Troianos, *Lectures in ecclesiastical law*, 352ff; Vavouskos, *Textbook of ecclesiastical law*, 272; Christophilopoulos, *Greek ecclesiastical law*, 238–245.

444. According to Encyclical 2320/19-5-1982 of the Holy Synod of the Church of Greece, a religious, though not a civil, marriage is not permitted for clergy of all ranks and monastics of the Orthodox Church. *See* Troianos/Papageorgiou, *Religious legislation: Special legislation – bibliography – case law*, 880–884.

445. 'There is an impediment against a religious marriage but not a civil one', Encyclical 2320/19-5 – 1982 of the Holy Synod of the Church of Greece.

Article 15 L. 1183/1981). When the judicial decision announcing the divorce is published, it is thereafter irrevocable; a copy has to be sent to the metropolitan of the residence of the man, who is responsible for declaring that the marriage is also dissolved spiritually (Article 22 § 4 L. 4509/2017, as it has been substituted with Article 97 of L. 4689/2020).

746. The spiritual dissolution or cancellation is necessary if one of the former spouses wishes to contract a new church wedding.[446] A marriage which is dissolved and then recontracted between the same persons is considered to be a new marriage, and therefore, for it to be regarded as valid, the same prerequisites are required.

747. According to AP 1428/2017,[447] the (civil) marriage between two persons of the same sex (homosexuals) is invalid. More specifically, the current national legal framework does not provide for the possibility of same-sex marriage since gender differences are considered a condition of the existence of marriage. This fact is considered to reflect the moral and social values and traditions of the Greek people, who do not accept the creation of marriage for same-sex couples. However, the possibility of free cohabitation of same-sex couples is provided by Law 4356/2015.

748. The 'cohabitation agreement' (simfono simviosis) consists of the agreement of two adults, regardless of gender (L. 4356/2015), by which they regulate their cohabitation, and which is signed by a notary.[448] The cohabitation agreement is not a marriage. However, the signing of this agreement has all the consequences of the marriage regarding the inheritance rights of the spouses, their claims from the marriage between them, the exercise of parental care as well as the presumption of paternity. So, a child may have two legal fathers. The agreement is legally terminated as a divorce after a unilateral declaration to a notary by one of the parties.[449]

749. The decisions CoS 2003-2004/2018 concern cohabitation agreements and the form taken by the certificate of registration of such agreements. According to the CoS, the relevant L. 4356/2015 safeguards the inviolability of the private life of the individual, at the core of which lies that individual's sexual orientation and sex life. Article 21 of the Constitution does not prevent the legislator from amending the provisions on the ways in which a family may be established or from recognizing other forms of cohabitation than marriage that can lead to the establishment of

---

446. It is remarked that although the Orthodox Church has always looked unfavourably on divorce and has stressed the moral obligation of the partners within it not to dissolve the marriage bond which has once been tied, it realized early that it was not possible to overlook human weakness and accepted in principle the possibility of the dissolution of the marriage of the spouses in this life and their remarriage, *see* Rodopoulos, *An overview of Orthodox Canon Law*, 200.

447. ChrIdD 18 (2018) 513ff.

448. Kotzambasi, *Handbook of family law*, 178ff.

449. Christodoulou, The New Cohabitation Agreement (after L. 4356/2015), Athens 2016; Papachristou/Koumoutzis/Tsouka, The Cohabitation Agreement. An interpretive guide to Arts 1–13 of L. 3719/2008, Athens 2009.

family bonds. The enactment and regulation of same-sex cohabitation agreements by L. 4356/2015 do not contravene the Constitution or any international treaties and do not prejudice the constitutionally safeguarded institution of marriage and the family. Neither does it challenge the Orthodox Christian religion, its constitutional position as the prevailing religion in Greece or the institutional role of the Church of Greece. Neither does it infringe on religious freedoms or the rights of Orthodox Christian Greek citizens, whether they be married, single, parents or without children.

Chapter 2. Legal Position of Religious Family Law

750. As it has already been noted, membership in the Orthodox Church is acquired through the celebration of the sacrament of baptism by the competent priest. The decision to celebrate baptism – that constitutes the entrance of a minor child into Church – is normally made by the parents, who exercise parental care and custody. The baptism is evidenced by a written confirmation of the priest, based on which the responsible registrar shall issue an appropriate entry in the registry books.[450]

751. However, the issue of selection and acquisition of the principal name is a separate one, which is established as an act of civil law, in the frame of the rights of custody of the minor and parental responsibility, although this act is not necessarily associated with the sacrament of baptism.[451] For this reason, if it is necessary to be changed the principal name of a child in the birth certificate (even if the name was given during the celebration of baptism), the mystery cannot be repeated, but a court judgment must be issued ordering such a change.[452]

752. Any dispute between the parents as to the choice of the name may be lifted by judicial decision (Article 1512 CC).[453] But in adulthood, the same applicant may seek a change of name if there are important reasons that necessitate this.[454]

753. Whereas previously the matrimonial and family matters of Greek Muslims of Western Thrace were obligatorily governed by the sacred Islamic law (sharia), this implementation has now become facultative (L. 4511/2018). After the case of the *European Court on Human Rights Molla Sali v. Greece* (19.12.2018), as for the

---

450. *ECtHR Stavropoulos v. Greece* (52484/18/25.6.2020): the birth certificate must not contain information from which the religious beliefs of the child or his/her parents can be deduced; *see also* Papageorgiou, *Ecclesiastical law*, 189ff; Rodopoulos, *An overview of orthodox canon law*, 35, 39, 117 and passim.
451. *AP 240/1975* (Plenary Session), NoV 23 (1975) 655f: the naming of minor children is not a component of the sacrament of baptism (which is celebrated only 'once'), but constitutes a legal act (legal transaction) that can be settled solely by the relevant provisions of the Civil Code; anyone who has custody of the person can, following the correction procedure of civil status documents (birth and other certificates), change the name given to the child, if the choice was not made by them. *See also* Troianos/Papageorgiou, *Religious legislation: Special legislation – bibliography – case law,* 875–880.
452. *First-Instance Court of Thessaloniki 38546/2009* (not published in legal magazines). The naming of a minor child is the right and duty of both parents, who have joint parental responsibility. The indicated on the birth certificate principal name of the child must be corrected according to the true intentions of the guardians, as this intention was expressed in the sacrament of baptism and attested by the statement of the priest who performed the baptism. In order to correct the birth certificate an irrevocable judgment should be issued, at the request of the guardians.
453. Pantelidou, *The name of the family,* EfAD 1/2012, 2ff; *Court of Appeals in Athens 558/1995*, HellDni 37 (1996) 358f: naming the minor child is part of parental responsibility; if the parents disagree on the name to be given, it is the court that makes the decision. *See also* Troianos/ Papageorgiou, *Religious legislation: Special legislation – bibliography – case law*, 875ff. Zervogianni, 'The religion of the child and the parental responsibility', 537ff.
454. *AP 573/1981*, NoV 30 (1982) 422–424, with Koumandos comments: vested interest, conditions and procedure for changing a person's name.

family and inheritance cases the Greek Muslims of Western Thrace may choose the application of civil law by the common courts, and not necessarily the sharia by the muftis.[455]

---

455. On these points, *see* Ktistakis, *The holy law of Islam and Muslim Greek Citizens*, 56ff and passim. *See also*: Council of Europe (2009), 'Issue reviewed: Human rights of minorities', Report by Thomas Hammarberg, Commissioner for Human Rights of the Council of Europe, following his visit to Greece on 8–10 Dec. 2008, CommDH (2009) 9, Strasbourg, 19 Feb. 2009, in: https:// wcd.coe-.int; Kotzambasi, 'The scope of implementation of the holy Muslim law in the family relations of Greek Muslims', HellDni 44 (2003) 57ff; Kotzambasi, *The family legal relations of Greek Muslim men and women*, 162ff; Kotzambasi, *Equality of the sexes and private autonomy in contemporary family relations (contractual freedom in divorce and limitations – artificial reproduction and biological differences – religious marriage and intercultural relationships)*, 45ff; Tsitselikis, 'The legal status of Islam in Greece', Die Welt des Islams 44 (2004) 402ff; Stavrou, 'The legal status of minorities in Greece today: The adequacy of their protection in the light of current human rights perceptions', 1ff. More generally, *see*: Nasir, *The Islamic law of personal status*, passim; Hodkinson Keith, *Muslim family law: a sourcebook*, 131ff, 219ff.

Part XI. Religion and Culture

Chapter 1. Religion and Art

§1. Religious Monuments

754. The Greek ecclesiastical and religious organizations are possessors of a huge number of cultural monuments. More specifically, currently applicable is L. 3028/2002, 'On the protection of antiquities and cultural heritage in general',[456] which in Article 1 states that its provisions apply to the (tangible or intangible) cultural heritage of the country, from the ancient times to the present, with a view to preserving the historical memory of generations and enhancing the cultural environment.

755. According to Article 7 of L. 3028/2002, the ancient immovable monuments dating back to 1453 belong to the State by ownership and possession; they are 'non-market goods'[457] and not susceptible of usucaption.[458]

756. Nevertheless, according to Article 73 of the same law, the already existing, when this Law came into force, ownership rights of the ecclesiastical legal entities

456. Court of Appeal in Thessaloniki 275/2018: ownership and criminal protection of ecclesiastical movable monuments, especially of great value; *Court of the First Instance Trikala 131/2017*: protection of the cultural and religious environment of the Sacred Area of Meteora. Any violation is an insult to the personality of the monks of the area; LCS 204/2017; CoS 1049/2017, on the protection of the monastic culture. For a detailed interpretation of L. 3028/2002 *see* the studies of: Tsivolas, *Law and religious cultural heritage in Europe, Springer Verlag 2014; ibid., The legal protection of religious cultural goods, Athens 2013;* Troianos/Papadimitriou, 'The protection of religious monuments, according to L. 3028/2002', ChrIdD 6 (2006) 584–591; Karympali-Tsiptsiou, Monuments and their possession (under L. 3028/2002, 'on the protection of antiquities and cultural heritage in general'), Athens 2004; *ibid.*, 'The possession of ancient mobile monuments and its protection (under L. 3028/2002, "on the protection of antiquities and cultural heritage in heritage"', Arm. 57 (2003) 1549–1559. Kyriazopoulos, 'The ecclesiastical cultural goods', in: *Cultural Heritage and Law*, Conference Proceedings, 3–4 Jun. 2003, Under the auspices of the Ministry of Culture, European Center for Public Law, Trova (ed.), Athens-Thessaloniki 2004, 497–507.

457. As it arises from the combination of Arts 966 and 971 CC, the objects which are dedicated to serve religious purposes and for the duration of this dedication comprise 'non-market goods'. This category encompasses in general churches, articles and vessels for worship, vestments and garments, liturgical books and icons. *See* more in Papageorgiou, *Ecclesiastical Property and National Cadastre*, 61ff.

458. On this issue *see also*: Karympali-Tsiptsiou, *Property and trust law in Hellas*, 231–238; Papageorgiou, *supra*, 67ff.

of the Church of Greece; the Church of Crete; the Dioceses (Metropolises) of the Dodecanese Ecumenical Patriarchate of Constantinople; the Patriarchates of Alexandria, Antioch and Jerusalem; the Monastery of Sinai; the Monasteries of Mount Athos; the Monasteries of St. Anastasia; the Pharmacolytria in Halkidiki, Vlattadon in Thessaloniki; and Evangelist John the Theologian in Patmos are still reserved, even if those rights are dating back to 1453. The same applies to the rights of all 'known' religions (Article 13 Const.)[459] or faiths (confessions) to ancient religious monuments.

757. Article 53 ('Monument theft') provides for imprisonment of up to ten years in case of theft (Articles 372, 374 PC)[460] if the stolen item was particularly valuable, or was removed from an immovable ancient monument or an excavated area, a museum, a storage area for ancient finds or any place where collections are kept.

758. The act of acceptance and disposal of proceeds of crime (Article 394 § 1 PC) is punishable by up to ten years in prison if the stolen item was particularly valuable and the perpetrator was aware that it was a product of a criminal offence.

759. Finally, anyone who destroys, damages, pollutes or alters in any way the form of a monument or cultural object will be punished with at least two years in prison. If the monument belongs to the offender, the imprisonment term is up to three years (Article 56 L. 3028/2002).[461]

§2. Religious Art

760. In Greece, there has been preserved a massive production of ecclesiastical art and religious culture (such as heirlooms, paintings, books, seals, priestly vestments), which are not protected by the provisions of L. 2121/1993, 'On intellectual property, related rights and cultural issues' because, due to the fact that they are very old, the protection of their intellectual property rights has expired a long time ago (*see Article 29*).[462]

---

459. About the meaning of this constitutional term, *see* Part I of the present monograph and Papageorgiou, *Ecclesiastical Law*, 125.

460. *See also* Art. 374, case a' ('aggravated' theft) of Penal Code, according to which the removal of objects dedicated to holy worship from a place that is designated for it with the purpose of illegally possessing them is punishable by imprisonment of up to ten years. For a theoretical analysis, *see* Manoledakis/Bitzilekis, *Crimes against property (Articles 372-384 Penal Code)*, 96–98. *Court of Appeal in Thessaloniki 275/2018*.

461. Karympali-Tsiptsiou, *Monuments and their possession (under L. 3028/2002, on the protection of antiquities and cultural heritage in general)*, 94ff, *ibid.*, 'The possession of ancient mobile monuments and its protection (under L. 3028/2002, "on the protection of antiquities and cultural heritage in general")', Arm. 57 (2003) 1549–1559.

462. *See also* more recently L. 4481/2017 on collective management of copyright and related rights, of which the main purpose is the adaptation of national legislation to Directive 2014/26/EU about the operation of collective management bodies or collective protection of copyright and related rights, the independent entities management, as well as the amendment of provisions of L. 2121/1993; Koumandos, Intellectual property, 281ff; Kallinikou, Intellectual property and related rights, 229ff.

Chapter 2. Religion and Media

761. In the context of the right to religious freedom, the religions in the Greek territory are entitled to providing and updating information not only for the faithful but also for every citizen concerned about their views on issues of public life. This can be done through television or radio broadcasts, through the internet as well as any other means of printed or electronic press.[463] It is worth noting here that the state media often broadcast – especially every Sunday – liturgies, ceremonies or rites of the Orthodox Church.

762. According to Article 14 § 3 Case a' Const., the seizure of newspapers and other publications, before or after their release into circulation, is prohibited. However, a seizure may be exceptionally ordered by the prosecutor, after the release of a publication whose content offends the Christian or any other 'known' religion. In such a case, the prosecutor, within twenty-four hours of the seizure, should submit the case to the Judicial Council. The latter, within the next twenty-four hours, should decide to retain or remove the order of seizure. Otherwise, the seizure is automatically revoked.[464]

763. The court, after at least three convictions within five years for committing crimes such as the above mentioned, orders a permanent or temporary cessation of publication of the paper. What is more, in 'severe cases', it may decide to prohibit the exercise of the journalistic profession by the person convicted.[465]

764. Moreover, in accordance with Article 15 Const., the protective provisions for the press in Article 14 Const. do not apply to films, radio, television or any other similar means of broadcasting speech or expression. The radio and television shall

---

463. Relevant is the Reg. of the Church of Greece 307/2018–2019 'Operation and organization of the Communication and Educational Service of the Church of Greece and its branches' (GG A 53/2019).
464. For constitutional approach of the whole issue, *see* Chrysogonos/Vlahopoulos, *Individual and social rights*, 330ff, 345ff; Dagtoglou, *Constitutional law: Individual rights*, 459–505; Manesis, 'The constitutional protection of the free circulation of printed material and its implementation in practice', 2ff. For substantial cases of censorship or judicial bans on books, on the grounds of offending the religious sentiments of citizens, which preoccupied the Greek society, *see* Ravdas, 'With a book opposite to God: Banned books for "offending the religious sentiment"', in the collective work: Loukides/Papadopoulou/Ravdas, *The trials of speech*, 141–265. On the same issue *see* Tsakyrakis, *Religious versus Art*, 191ff.
465. *First-Instance Court of Athens 5208/2000*, ToS 26 (2000) 572–582: the artefacts are not subject to the restrictions applicable to the press; there is no apparent malicious intent, on the part of the author of a literary book that is considered to revile the Christian religion, to offend the personality of Christians; *Court of Appeals of Athens 1013/1987*, Chr. 29 (1990) 31–39: the use of the name 'Jesus', as a distinctive feature of goods, poses a clear infringement of the personality of priests of the Christian religion; as this offence is clearly directed against their religious sentiments and the commercialization of the sacred name of the leader of their faith, the above priests may request, for this reason as well, the cessation of the infringement and its prohibition in the future (Arts 5, 13, 14 and 16 § 2 Const.); the special protection of the Church by the State is also evident in the Art. 14 § 3 Case a' Const., that exceptionally permits the seizure of newspapers and other publications for offending the Christian religion.

be under the direct control of the State. The control and imposition of administrative sanctions are under the exclusive competence of the National Broadcasting Council, which constitutes an independent authority. The direct control of the State aims at safeguarding the objectivity and equality in the transmission of information and news, as well as works of literature and art, the high-quality level of programmes as it is imposed by the social mission of radio and television and cultural development of the country as well as respect for human dignity and protection of children and youth.

Chapter 3. Religion, Civil Society and Public Debate

765. Over the recent decades, the ethnic and cultural diversity as well as an ever expanding revival of interest in the religious phenomenon are highlighted, among others, as the main features of European society.[466] More specifically, one may observe that religion 'returns' to Europe – although, as it is noted, it had never been 'gone', both in terms of social impact and awareness, and at the level of constitutional or normative regulation.[467]

766. The above data clearly relate to Greece as well – but perhaps on a smaller scale, compared to other European countries, as this country has not experienced secularization to such a high extent that was observed in Western Europe.[468] Nonetheless, one may find nowadays in Greece a broad mobilization of numerous religious organizations, whereas there are also frequent acute political conflicts between the Church and the State.[469] But there is here as well, an open dialogue on the constitutional and generally institutional position of various churches or religions, particularly those that afford a minority status.[470]

767. As it has already been noted, in contrast to most Western European countries – which over the last century in particular acquired the structure and morphological features of secularized societies – the degree of religiosity of modern Greeks has always remained high, and always in close connection of the vast majority of citizens with the 'prevailing' Orthodox Church (Article 3 § 1 Const.).[471] The fact of the highest religious homogeneity has always affected both the general ideological views of a very large part of Greek society and the public debate on issues related to the religious sphere.

768. The relevant dialogue is mainly directed around the national standards with respect to the traditional relations between Church and State, on the one hand, and

466. Deliyanni-Dimitrakou, *Comparative law and legal pluralism*, 93ff; *Kourtis, Signs of respect for cultural polymorphy in European Union law*, 96ff.
467. *See inter alia*: Zoumpoulakis, *God in town: Essays on religion and politics*, 11ff, passim, and, *Christians in the public space" Faith or cultural identity?* 145ff.
468. Diamantouros, *The origins of the modern state formation in Greece (1821-1828)*, 73–79; Close, *Greece (1945-2004): Policy-society-economy*, 159–162; Kitromilides, *New Greek enlightenment: The political and social ideas*, 377ff; Matalas, *Nation and orthodoxy: The adventures of a relationship*, 4ff.
469. Manitakis, *The relations of the Church with the nation-state under the shadow of the identity*, 74f, 174, passim; *Prinzipas, church and hellenism from 1821 till today: An historical overview*, 173–192; Papastathis, *Nomocanonical studies*, 163–172; Papadopoulou, *On the creed of identification cards*, 675ff;.
470. *See inter alia*: Alivisatos, *The constitutional treatment of religious minorities in Greece* 629ff; Papazissi, *The principle of equality and the woman of non-Christian religious minorities: the identity of the Jewish woman in Thessaloniki today*, 375–392; Clogg (ed.), *Minorities in Greece. Aspects of a plural society*, 24–47.
471. Papastathis, *The Hellenic republic and the prevailing religion*, 815ff.

the necessity of creating a more secular and tolerant society, on the other hand.[472] As main themes of the evergrowing and highly interesting dialogue may be considered the following:

- The concept of 'secularization' and the contemporary sources of modern Greek morality or religious conscience.[473]
- The social contribution of religious communities, especially among those sections of the population that face the most urgent need for charitable assistance.[474]
- The cultural role of religious traditions in the context of an increasingly growing multicultural modern Greek society.
- The interweaving of religious and political consciousness.[475]
- The influence of traditional religious values on secular conceptions pertaining to the organization of individual and social life.
- The law-comparative study of various religious traditions, especially of their regulatory/institutional side.[476]
- Increasing migration and the new forms of religiosity.
- The various changes in the traditional religious life of Greek society, after the massive influx of economic migrants, who represent a very different variegation of religious traditions and beliefs.
- Modern Greek civil society and Islam – the impact of religion on the political participation of Muslims.[477]
- The activity of various religious institutions and the civil society in Greece today.
- The religious communities as 'havens of consolation' from the cold logic of the market.
- The constitutional and in general institutional treatment of the so-called new religious movements.
- The fundamentalist aberration of religious beliefs and ways of avoiding the creation of social pockets of religious marginalization and fundamentalism.
- The religious belief, gender equality and equal rights to sexual minorities, accordingly, the position of women and gays.
- The new immigrant religious communities and school religious education.[478]

---

472. Stagkos, *The fight against racism, xenophobia and discrimination in Greece today. The normative framework, public actions, and the European challenge*, 160ff.
473. Manitakis, *The relations of the church with the nation-state under the shadow of the identity*, 23ff, 64ff, passim.
474. Papageorgiou, 'Legal and pastoral treatment of immigrants in Greece', in: Motilla Agustin (ed.), Immigration, National and Regional Laws and Freedom of Religion, 107–113.
475. Makrides, 'Orthodoxy in the service of anticommunism: the religious organization Zoe during the Greek civil war', 159ff; Mavrogordatos, *Orthodoxy and nationalism in the Greek case*, 117ff.
476. Deliyanni-Dimitrakou, *Comparative law and legal pluralism*, 93–201.
477. Kotzambasi, 'The scope of implementation of the holy Muslim law in the family relations of Greek Muslims', HellDni 44 (2003) 57ff, and, 'The family legal relations of Greek Muslim men and women', 29ff, passim; Menaidis, The religious freedom of Muslims in the Greek legal order, 40ff, passim; Antoniou, 'Muslim immigrants in Greece: religious organization and local responses', 155f; Tsitselikis, 'Muslims in Greece', in: Potz/Wieshaider (eds), Islam and the European Union, 79ff.
478. Chrysogonos, 'Religious education and prevailing religion', 993ff.

769. In the frame of the same public dialogue, the following questions constantly arise as well:

- Is there a need for redefining the hitherto legal restrictions on religious freedom? And, if so, to a broader or narrower direction?
- In general, is there a need for a redefinition of the content and implications of the right to religious freedom?
- What should be the position of the State towards religious ceremonies related to public order or public health, such as the ritual slaughter of animals by Jews and Muslims? Can and should the Jewish and Muslim communities improve the welfare of animals?[479]

770. Related questions arise in those cases that the State appears to have competitive claims towards religion. These problems can be solved only within the frame of a broad public dialogue held in good faith and in the context of an open society while considering all the parameters of the issues. It is certain that any state legislation should respect the fundamental right of self-government of religious communities, which constitutes one of the most important aspects of the right of individuals or organizations to religious freedom.

771. It is very often that the spheres of activity of religious communities and religious organizations overlap with areas of social welfare and education.[480] These are two areas in which the relations between religion and state should not be considered competitive but complementary and mutually assisting. In this way, the relationship between the activity within the state sphere with the respective religious one can only be constructive, showing goodwill to resolve conflicts, wherever (and whenever) those are incurred.

772. Towards the above direction can greatly contribute the decisions of the European Court of Human Rights (ECtHR), not only in those cases concerning Greece but also with their entire case law production. This is because the decisions of Strasbourg contribute to a more harmonious coexistence of various religious communities with the broader civil society.[481]

479. On religious slaughtery according to the Greek legal order, *see LCS 92/2017*.

480. *See*, for example, Maghioros, *Religion in public education*: *Rapport on Greece*, 195ff.

481. Chrysogonos, *The integration of the European Convention on Human Rights into the domestic legal order*. The Greek difficulties of adjustment to the European public order of human rights, 223ff; *ibid*., 'The significance of European Court on Human Rights case law for the Greek judge', 541ff.

Selected Bibliography

In Greek Language

Alivizatos N., *The constitution and its enemies in modern Greek history (1800-2010),* Athens 2011.

Androulakis N., *Fundamental concepts of the criminal trial*, Athens 52020.

Androulakis N., 'The punishability of proselytization and its constitutionality', NoV 34 (1986) 1031–1032.

Antonopoulos N., *The constitutional protection of the regime in Mount Athos*, Athens 21997.

Asimakis I., *The development of relations between Greece and the holy see (1820-1980). From French protection to the establishment of diplomatic relations*, Thessaloniki 2007.

Asimakis I. (ed.), *Legislation and jurisprudence for the catholic church in Greece*, Thessaloniki 2014.

Askitis Ar., 'The ombudsman and his limitations in the sphere of religious legal persons of public law', Arm 72 (2018) 33–45.

Askitis, 'Molla Sali (ECtHR): The "velvet condemnation" of Greece for the application of sharia in the inheritance disputes of Greek Muslims', in C. Papageorgiou (ed.), Law and Religions, Athens 2020, 23ff.

Avdikos Gr., *Constitutional problems and revision*, Athens 2020.

Beis C. (ed.), *Religious freedom*, Athens 1997.

Beis C., 'The revocation/termination of the patriarchal synodal act of September 4th 1928', D 35 (2004) 581–592.

Charalambakis Ar., *The new penal code*, Athens 2019.

Christophilopoulos An., *Greek ecclesiastical law*, Athens 21965 (reprinted ed. 2005).

Crysogonos C., 'Religious education and prevailing religion', ToS 25 (1999) 993–1024.

Chrysogonos C., 'The European Convention on Human Rights half a century later', ToS 27 (2001) 967–1007.

Chrysogonos C., *The integration of the European Convention on Human Rights into the domestic legal order. The Greek difficulties of adjustment to the European public order of human rights*, Athens-Komotini 2001.

Chrysogonos C., 'The protection of fundamental rights in Greece before and after the constitutional revision of 2001. A delineation of some introductory thoughts', DA 10 (2001) 529–541.

Selected Bibliography

Chrysogonos C., 'The significance of European Court on Human Rights case law for the Greek judge', DA 18 (2003) 541–551.

Chrysogonos C., *Constitutional law*, Athens-Thessaloniki 22014.

Chrysogonos C., 'The constitutional protection of the holy monasteries in private law (Hermitages/Hesyxastiria) and the L. 4559/2018', NoV 68 (2020 1773–1790.

Chrysogonos C./Vlahopoulos Sp., *Individual and social rights*, Athens ^{4}2017.

Close D., *Greece (1945-2004): Policy – society – economy*, Athens 2005.

Codex Juris Canonici, Athens 2020.

Dagtoglou Pr., *General administrative law*, Athens-Komotini ^{4}2012.

Dagtoglou Pr., *Constitutional law. Individual rights*, Athens-Komotini ^{4}2012.

Deliyanni-Dimitrakou Chr., *Comparative law and legal pluralism*, Athens-Thessaloniki 2008.

Dervitsiotis A., *The establishment of a church as a component of religious freedom*, Athens 2010.

Deliyanni-Dimitrakou Chr. (ed.), *Religious freedom. Contemporary legal issues*, Athens-Thessaloniki 2019.

Diamantouros N., *The origins of the modern state formation in Greece (1821-1828)*, Athens 2006.

Dimopoulou A.-K., 'Religious freedom in the context of the case law of the EctHR', in: Deliyanni-Dimitrakou Chr. (ed.), *Religious freedom. Contemporary legal issues*, Athens-Thessaloniki 2019, 45–60.

Feidas Vl., 'The function of the distinct roles of church and state and the responsibility of the polity', E 78 (2001) 232–247.

Feidas Vl., 'The constitutional entrenchment of the patriarchal act of 1928', D 35 (2004) 903–915.

Filou-Patsantara A., 'The offense of proselytization in the European Court of Human Rights (article 14 of obligatory law 1363/1938)', ToS 19 (1993) 821–842.

Frazee Ch., *Orthodox church and Greek independency (1821-1852)*, Athens 1987.

Glykatzi-Arhweiller E., *The political ideology of the Byzantine empire*, Athens 1988.

Goulas D., *The discriminations due to religious symbols in the workplace*, Athens-Thessaloniki 2019.

Holy Community of Mount Athos, *The regime of Mount Athos*, Thessaloniki 1996.

Kalfelis Gr., *The penal code and special penal laws*, Athens 2005.

Kallinikou D., *Intellectual property and related rights*, Athens-Komotini 22005.

Kambourides C., *Modern Greece through Ottoman archival sources. Economy, institutions and society in the 17th century Thessaly*, Thessaloniki 2009.

Karympali-Tsiptsiou G., *Monuments and their possession (under L. 3028/2002, 'On the protection of antiquities and cultural heritage in general')*, Athens 2004.

Karympali-Tsiptsiou G., *Legal regime of monuments (collectors: antiquities dealers – traders of more recent monuments)*, Athens-Thessaloniki 2009.

Kitromilides P., *New Greek enlightenment. The political and social ideas*, Athens 32000.

Kollias B.-Al., *The chrysobulls in Byzantine law*, Athens 2020.

Konidaris I., *Legal theory and practice concerning 'Jehovah's Witnesses'*, Athens-Komotini ^{4}2005.

Konidaris I., *Lessons of ecclesiastical law*, Athens-Komotini 2020.

Kontidis Th. (ed.), *Catholicism*, Athens 2000.
Kotzambasi Ath., 'The scope of implementation of the holy Muslim law in the family relations of Greeks Muslims', HellDni 44 (2003) 57–72.
Kotzambasi Ath., *The family legal relations of Greeks Muslim men and women*, Thessaloniki 2003.
Kotzambasi Ath., *Equality of the sexes and private autonomy in contemporary family relations (contractual freedom in divorce and limitations: artificial reproduction and biological differences – religious marriage and intercultural relationships)*, Athens-Thessaloniki 2011.
Kotzambasi Ath., 'Religious freedom in family law', in: Deliyanni-Dimitrakou Chr. (ed.), *Religious freedom. Contemporary legal issues*, Athens-Thessaloniki 2019, 33–44.
Kotzambasi Ath., *Handbook of family law*, Athens-Thessaloniki 2021.
Koumandos G., *Intellectual property*, Athens-Komotini [8]2002.
Kourtis V., 'Signs of respect for cultural polymorphy in European Union law', in: A. Manitakis/V. Kourtis (eds.), *Commemorative volume for giota kravaritou*, Athens-Thessaloniki 2011, 97–126.
Krembenios D., *The jurisprudence of the council of state on ecclesiastical matters according to the current constitution*, Athens-Thessaloniki 2018.
Ktenidis I., 'Religious freedom and equal treatment under the light of the recent case law of the Court of Justice of the European Union', in: Deliyanni-Dimitrakou Chr. (ed.), *Religious freedom. Contemporary legal issues*, Athens-Thessaloniki 2019, 11–32.
Ktistakis G., *Religious freedom and the European Convention on Human Rights*, Athens-Komotini 2004.
Ktistakis G., *The holy law of Islam and Muslim Greeks citizens*, Athens-Thessaloniki 2006.
Kyriazopoulos K., *Limitations to the freedom of teaching of the minority denominations*, Thessaloniki 1999.
Kyriazopoulos K., 'Church and state in modern Europe', *Encyclopedia of religious freedom*, Catharine Cookson (ed.), Routledge, Great Britain, 2003, 56–60.
Kyriazopoulos K., 'The orthodox cultural area from Athens to Moscow and minimal guarantees of religious freedom', *Materialien Der 5. Internationalen Tagung zum Thema – Kulturelle Identitat Der Europaischen Union Und Religioser Pluralismus*, Trier 18.-19. September 2006, Herausgegeben von Jozef Krukowski, Josef Isensee, Miroslaw Sitarz, Kultura I Prawo, Kultur Und Recht, Wissenschaftliche Gesellschaft der KUL, Katholischen Universitat Lublin Johannes Paul II, Lublin, 283–330.
Lentzis D., 'The European Union law against discrimination on grounds of religion in employment', in C. Papageorgiou (ed.), *Law and religions. Greece-Europe*, Athens 2020, 79–112.
Liapis I., *A brief introduction to ecclesiastical property*, Athens 2020.
Liapis I., *Church property and salaries of the clergy*, Athens 2012.
Makridis V., 'The orthodox church in the 20th century: a historico-sociological survey', *Commemorative volume for Penelope Agallopoulou*, Vol. II, 860ff.
Manesis Ar., 'The constitutional protection of the free circulation of printed material and its implementation in practice', ToS 3 (1977) 1–36.

Selected Bibliography

Manesis Ar., *Constitutional rights,* Vol. A': *Individual liberties-lectures*, Thessaloniki ^{4}1982.

Manitakis Ant., *The relations of the church with the Nation-State under the shadow of the identity*, Athens 2000.

Marinos An., *Relations between church and State under the constitution of 1975 and the new statutory charter of the church of Greece*, Athens 1984.

Marinos A., *Church and law. Theory and case law*, Athens 2000.

Matalas P., *Nation and Orthodoxy. The adventures of a relationship*, Crete 2003.

Mavrias C., *Constitutional Law*, Athens ^{5}2016.

Mavrias C./Pantelis A., *Constitutional Texts*, Col. A., Athens-Komotini ^{4}2007.

Menaidis S., *The religious freedom of Muslims in the Greek legal order*, Athens 1990.

Menevisoglou P., An historical introduction to the holy canons of the Orthodox Church, Stockholm 1990.

Michailidis-Nouaros G., 'The right to education under the European Convention of Human Rights (article 2 of the 1rst Protocol of the European Convention', *Anthology in Honor of Phaedon Vegleris*, Vol. I: *The crisis of state institutions*, Athens 1988, 1–34.

Orfanoudakis S., 'The separation of State and Church. Necessity or palillogy?', *Association of Jurists of Northern Greece: State and Church Relations in view of the revision of the Constitution*, Athens-Thessaloniki 2008, 1–27.

Orfanoudakis S., 'The holy canons and the Constitution (a counter-comment or "the other" interpretative approach)', Arm 35 (1981) 82–83.

Orfanoudakis S., *The principle of proportionality in the Greek legal order. From its implementation in case law to its constitutional entrenchment,* Athens-Thessaloniki 2003.

Panagiotakos P., *System of Ecclesiastical Law during its enforcement in Greece*, Vol. C: *The Penal Law of the Church*, Thessaloniki 21999.

Papachrysanthou D., *Athonite monasticism. Principles and organization*, Athens 1992.

Papachrysanthou D., *The administration of Mount Athos (1600-1927). A brief historical overview*, Athens 1999.

Papadopoulou L., 'On the creed of identification cards', ToS 26 (2000) 675–723.

Papadopoulou L., 'Religion and Constitution in Greece and Europe today: ten brief comments on current issues', in: Deliyanni-Dimitrakou Chr. (ed.), *Religious freedom. Contemporary legal issues*, Athens-Thessaloniki 2019, 63–87.

Papageorgiou C., 'Findings from the ecclesiastical case law of the Council of State of the year 1987', Arm Scientific Yearbook 17 (1996) 31–47.

Papageorgiou C., *The Orthodox Church of Crete: Institutions and Administrative Organization under its Statutory Charter (L. 4149/1961)*, Chania 2001.

Papageorgiou C., *The tax regime of religions. Tax equality and religious freedom*, Athens-Thessaloniki 2005.

Papageorgiou C., *The legal institutions of Mount Athos*, Thessaloniki 2009.

Papageorgiou C., 'The Community Law on public works and ecclesiastical self-administration. The integration of Regulation 55/1974 relating to ecclesiastical works with Directive 2004/18/EC', Arm 65 (2011) 361–382.

Papageorgiou C., *The limits of ecclesiastical self-administration*. I: *Regulatory jurisdiction*, Thessaloniki 2012.

Papageorgiou C, 'L. 4301/2014 on the organization of the legal form of religious communities and the establishment of religious legal entities', Arm. 70 (2016) 573–584

Papageorgiou C., *Ecclesiastical Property and National Cadastre*, Athens-Thessaloniki 2017.

Papageorgiou C., *Ecclesiastical Law*, Athens 2019.

Papageorgiou C., 'Ecclesiastical property: legislative and jurisprudential developments, property titles, the "register report" as a new notarial document', Arm. 73 (2019) 961–976.

Papageorgiou C., 'The constitutional review and the question of religious neutrality', in Dimopoulou A.-K., Religious freedom. Contemporary legal issues, Athens-Thessaloniki 2019, 3–10.

Papageorgiou C., 'The constitutional revision and the issue of religious neutrality', in: Deliyanni-Dimitrakou Chr. (ed.), *Religious freedom. Contemporary legal issues*, Athens-Thessaloniki 2019, 3–10.

Papageorgiou C., 'The special tax treatment of religions', Arm. 74 (2020) 953–969.

Papageorgiou C., *Ecclesiastical Property: Studies – Opinions – Comments on Jurisprudence*, Athens 2020.

Papageorgiou Niki, *The Religion in Greek Political Changeover. Limits and Ambiguities*, Thessaloniki 2018.

Papakonstantinou K., 'The general clause of good morals. An historic-legal approach', Yearbook of the Research Center for the History of Greek Law 40 (2007) 307–328.

Papastathis Ch., *Nomocanonical Studies*, Trikala-Athens 2009.

Papazissi Th., 'The principle of equality and the woman of non-Christian religious minorities: the identity of the Jewish woman in Thessaloniki today', *'We' and 'Others'. A reference to tendencies and symbols*, National Centre for Social Research, Athens 1999, 375–392.

Pavlopoulos P., 'The legal nature of the administrative bodies of Mount Athos and the collection of the fines that it imposes according to the Code for the Collection of Public Revenues', D 28 (1997) 547–558.

Philippou D., 'Religious equality and the principle of the interpretation of laws in accordance with the Constitution. A comment on decision 1064/1998 of the Single-Member Administrative First-Instance Court of Thessaloniki', DA 7 (2000) 689–696.

Philippou D., 'The protection of the cultural environment and the protection of freedom of worship', *State-Law-Administration, Volume of scientific studies in honor of Epameinondas P. Spiliotopoulos*, Athens-Komotini 2000, 701–722.

Philippou D., 'The freedom of religious conscience and the obligation to give an oath. Comments on decision 2601/1998 of the Council of State', DA 2 (1999) 409–423.

Pouliadis Th., 'Parent and child relations: An interpretation of articles 1521-1536 of the Civil Code', in Georgiadis A./ Stathopoulos M., *The Civil Code, Vol. VIII: Family Law (articles 1505-1694)*, Athens 2007, 253–303.

Selected Bibliography

Prinzipas G./Karagiannis G., *Church and Hellenism from 1821 till today. An historical overview*, Athens 2005.

Rallis C., *The penal law of the Orthodox Eastern Church*, reproduction: Athens 1985.

Ravdas P., 'With a book opposite to God. Banned books for "offending the religious sentiment"', in the collective work: Loukides Mirto/Papadopoulou Vasiliki/ Ravdas Pantelis, *The trials of speech*, Athens 2002, 141–265.

Salachas D., 'Administration and organization of the Catholic Church. Church and State relations according to the Catholic Church, with a special reference to Greece', in the collective work: Th. Kontidis (ed.), *Catholicism*, Athens 2000, 265–319.

Sicilianos L.-Al. (ed), *European Convention on Human Rights. Interpretation to Articles*, Athens 22017.

Sotirelis G., *Religion and education under the Constitution and the European Convention: from catechism to polyphony*, Athens 1993.

Sotirelis G./Xiros Th., *The fourth revision of the Constitution of 1975 (2014-2019). Introduction, History, Proposals, Amendments, Reports, Ballots, Resolution, Sources, Scientific Articles, Press Publications*, Athens 2020.

Stagkos P., The fight against racism, xenophobia and discrimination in Greece today. The normative framework, public actions, and the European challenge, *in:* Papadimitriou D./Cavounidis J. (eds.), *Managing migration: The Greek, EU, and international contexts, Greek* Migration Policy Institute (IMEPO), Athens 2006, 159–175.

Symeonidou-Kastanidou El., *Abuse of power and human rights*, Athens-Thessaloniki 2013.

Svoronos N., *The Greek nation. Origin and formation of the new Hellenism*, Athens 22004.

Troianos S., *Lectures in Ecclesiastical Law*, Athens-Komotini 21984.

Troianos S./Papageorgiou C., *Religious Legislation. Special Legislation – Bibliography – Case Law*, Athens 2009.

Troianos S./Papadimitriou M., 'The protection of religious monuments, according to L. 3028/2002', ChrIdD 6 (2006) 584–591.

Tsakyrakis St., *Religion versus* Art, Athens 2005.

Tsironis Th., *Church in Politics (1913-1941)*, Thessaloniki 2010.

Tsivolas Th., *The legal protection of religious cultural goods*, Athens-Thessaloniki 2013.

Vavouskos C., *Textbook of Ecclesiastical Law*, Thessaloniki 51989.

Venizelos Ev., *The relations between State and Church*, Thessaloniki 2000.

Venizelos Ev., 'The European Constitution and the religious phenomenon', in the volume by the same author: *The challenge of the European Constitution*, Thessaloniki 2003, 119–146.

Venizelos Ev., *Lessons of Constitutional Law* (revised edition) Athens 2015.

Venizelos Ev., 'The ambiguity of recent jurisprudence around religious freedom and the subject of religion. Internal dialogue in the Council of State and deviations from the case law of the European Court of Human Rights', NC 1/2020, 19–31.

Vlahopoulos Sp., *Fundamental Rights. I*ndividual, social and political rights, Athens 2017.

Zervogianni L., 'The religion of the child and the parental responsibility', ToS 2020, 537–558.
Zoumpoulakis St., *God in town. Essays on religion and politics*, Athens 2002.
Zoumpoulakis St., *Christians in the public space. Faith or cultural identity?*, Athens 2010.

In Foreign Languages

Ahdar R./Leigh I. (eds), *Religious freedom in the liberal State*, Oxford 2005.
Antoniou D., 'Muslim immigrants in Greece: religious organization and local responses', *Immigrants & Minorities* 22 (2003) 155–174.
Antonopoulos N., 'La juridiction civile des autorités athonites', RHDI 19 (1963) 236–245.
Basdevant-Gaudemet Br./Berlingò S. (ed.), *The Financing of Religious Communities in the European Union – Le financement des religions dans les pays de l'Union européenne*, European Consortium for Church and State Research, Proceedings of the Meeting in Messina, 16–19 November 2006, Peeters, Leuven-Paris-Dudley, MA 2009.
Beck Hans-Georg, *A History of the Orthodox Church in the Byzantine empire*, vols. I-II (trans. L. Anagnostou), Athens 2004.
Cranmer F., 'National' Churches, territoriality and mission, *Law and Justice. The Christian Law Review* 149/2002, 155–177.
Doe N., 'The notion of a national Church: a juridical framework', in: *Law and Justice. The Christian Law Review* 149/2002, 77–91.
Doe N. (ed.), *The portrayal of religion in Europe: the media and the arts – Le portrait de religion en Europe: les médias et les arts*, European Consortium for Church and State Research, Proceedings of the Conference, Cardiff, 21–24 November 2002, Peeters, Leuven-Paris-Dudley, MA 2004.
Doe N./Sandberg R. (ed.), *Law and Religion: New Horizons*, European Consortium for Church and State Research: Law and Religion Studies 7, Peeters, Leuven-Paris-Walpole, MA 2010.
Economidès C., 'Le Mont Athos et le Droit International', in: Tachiaos A.-E. (ed.), *Mount Athos and the European Community*, Institute for Balkan Studies 241, Thessaloniki 1993, 47–53.
Emilianidis Ac. (ed.), *Religious Freedom in the European Union*, in: European Consortium for Church and State Research, Proceedings of the Meeting, Nicosia (Cyprus) 15–18 November 2007, Peeters, Leuven-Paris-Walpole, MA 2011.
Evrigenis D., 'Réflexions théoriques sur la Déclaration Commune relative au Mont Athos', in: Tachiaos A.-E. (ed.), *Mount Athos and the European Community*, Institute for Balkan Studies 241, Thessaloniki 1993, 13–17.
Ferrari S./Cristofori R. (ed.), *Law and Religion in the 21st Century. Relations between States and Religious Communities*, International Consortium for Law and Religion Studies, Cultural Diversity and Law, Ashgate, England-USA 2010.
Flauss J.-F. (ed), *La protection international de la liberté religieuse*, Bruxelles 2002.
Frazee Ch., 'Catholics', in: Clogg R. (ed.), *Minorities in Greece. Aspects of a plural society*, London 2002, 24–47.

Selected Bibliography

Friedner L. (ed.), *Churches and other Religious Organisations as Legal Persons*, European Consortium for Church and State Research, Proceedings of the 17th Meeting, Höör (Sweden), 17–20 November 2005, Peeters, Leuven-Paris-Dudley, MA 2007.

Garcia-Pardo D., 'L'enseignement et l'étude du droit ecclésiastique de l'État dans les Universités de Grèce, Espagne, France, Italie et Portugal', in: González del Valle J.-M./Hollerbach Al. (ed.), *The Teaching of Church-State Relations in European Universities*, European Consortium for Church and State Research, Peeters, Leuven-Paris-Dudley, MA 2005, 171–195.

González del Valle José María/Hollerbach Alexander (ed.), The Teaching of Church-State Relations in European Universities, European Consortium for Church and State Research, Peeters, Leuven-Paris-Dudley, MA 2005.

Gouttenoire A./Marguénaud J.-P./Andriantsimbazovina J./Levinet M./Sudre F., *Les grands arrêts de la Cour européenne des Droits de l'Homme*, Paris 2007.

Harris D./O' Oboyle M./Warbrick C./Bates E., *Law of the European Convention on Human Rights*, Oxford 2009.

Hill M. (ed.), *Religion and discrimination law in the European Union – La discrimination en matière religieuse dans l'Union européenne*, European Consortium for State and Church Research, Proceedings of the 23rd Congress, St Stephen's House, University of Oxford, Institute for European Constitutional Law, University of Trier (Germany) 2012.

Karympali-Tsiptsiou G., *Property and Trust Law in Hellas*, Kluwer Law International 2013.

Kyriazopoulos K., 'Proselytization in Greece: criminal offence vs. religious persuasion and equality', The Journal of Law and Religion 20 (2004–2005) 149–245.

Kyriazopoulos K., 'Proselytization in Greece (Kokkinakis judgment): criminal statute vs. "Nullum crimen nulla poena sine lege certa"', Anuario De Derecho Eclesiástico Del Estado xxii (2006) 357–395.

Kyriazopoulos K., 'New Religious Movements in Greece: The Recognition of Religious Organizations in Greece', in: *The State, the Orthodox Church and Religions in Greece*, Ch. Papastathis/Gr. Papathomas (eds.), Katerini 2008, 323 – 337.

Kyriazopoulos K., 'The ecclesiastical cultural goods', in: *Cultural Heritage and Law*, Conference Proceedings, 3–4 June 2003, Under the auspices of the Ministry of Culture, European Center for Public Law, E. Trova (ed.), Athens-Thessaloniki 2004, 497–507.

Kyriazopoulos K., 'Which model of the course of the religions is provided by the International Human Rights Law and the Constitution?', Proceedings of the Panhellenic Scientific Conference on the subject: *The course of religious, Reflections-Notes-Suggestions*, Laboratory of Pedagogy – Christian Pedagogy, Department of Pastoral and Social Theology, AUTh, S. Micheloudakis – E. Pepes (ed.), Thessaloniki 2014, 277–297.

Lindholm T./Durham C. W./Tahzib-Lie B. G. (eds), *Facilitating Freedom of Religion or Belief: A Deskbook*, The Netherlands 2004.

Madeley J.T. S. (ed.), *Religion and politics, The International Library of Politics and Comparative Government*, England-USA 2003.

Maghioros N., 'State and Church in Greece: "To reform or not to reform"?', Droit et Religion 2 (2006–2007) 497–502.

Maghioros N., 'Religion in Public Education – Rapport on Greece, in: Robbers Gerhard (ed.), *Religion in Public Education – La religion dans l'éducation publique*, European Consortium for State and Church Research, Proceedings of the Conference in Trier, 11–14 November – Actes du colloque, Trèves, 11–14 November 2010, Institute for European Constitutional Law, University of Trier (Germany) 2012, 195–216.

Makrides V., 'Orthodoxy in the service of anticommunism: the religious organization Zoë during the Greek Civil War', in: Philip C./Thanassis S. (eds), *The Greek Civil War*, London 2004, 159–174.

Marinos A., 'La liberté réligieuse dans la nouvelle constitution grecque', *Église et Droit (Théorie et Jurisprudence)*, Athénes 2000, 192–197.

Mavrogordatos G., 'Orthodoxy and nationalism in the Greek case', in: Madeley J./Enyedi Z. (eds), *Church and State in contemporary Europe*, Ambington 2003, 117–136.

Nasir J., The Islamic law of personal status, The Hague-London-New York, 2002.

Papadopoulou L., 'State and Church in Greece', in: Robbers G. (ed.), *State and Church in the European Union*, Germany 32019, 171ff.

Papageorgiou C., 'Freedom of religion: a case of discrepancy between the Greek and the European legal order, before the European Court of Human Rights', in: *Jurisdiction in Europe. Towards a common legal method, Erasmus Intensive Seminar On Legal Theory*, Münster 1997, 215–222.

Papageorgiou C., 'Statut constitutionnel des communautés religieuses des Anciens Calendaristes à l'ordre juridique de Grèce', in: *Les Cultes et l'État en Grèce. Les identités religieuses dans la République hellénique*. Quatrième colloque sur la notion d' 'Églises nationales', L' Année Canonique 45 (2003) 171–176.

Papageorgiou C., 'Le cadre nomocanonique des relations du Patriarcat Oecumenique avec l'Église semi-autonome de Créte', L' Année Canonique 46 (2004) 159–168 [= Contacts, Revue Francaise de l' Orthodoxie, No 210, Paris, Avril-Juin 2005, 133–148].

Papageorgiou C./Papastathis Ch., 'Formes de collaboration conventionelle ou non-conventionelle entre l'État et les communautés religieuses en Grèce', in: Puza R./Doe N. (ed.), *Religion and law in dialogue: covenantal and non-covenantal cooperation between state and religion in Europe*, [European Consortium for Church and State Research, Proceedings of the Conference, Tübingen, 18–21 November 2004], Peeters, Leuven-Paris-Dudley, MA 2006, 65–77.

Papageorgiou C., 'The application of the freedom of religion principles of the European Convention on Human Rights in Greece', in: Ac. Emilianides (ed.), *Religious Freedom in the European Union*, Proceedings of the 19th Meeting of the European Consortium for Church and State Research, Nicosia (Cyprus), 15–18 November 2007, Peeters, Leuven-Paris-Walpole, MA 2011, 187–198.

Papageorgiou C., 'Die Verpflichtung, anlässlich der Eidesleistung seine religiöse Überzeugung vor Gericht zu erklären, verletzt die Gewissens-und Religionsfreiheit. EGMR 21. 2. 2008, 19.516/06 (Alexandridis /. Griechenland)', ÖARR 58 (2011) 372–379.

Selected Bibliography

Papageorgiou C., 'Legal and pastoral treatment of immigrants in Greece', in: Motilla A. (ed.), *Immigration, national and regional laws and freedom of religion*, European Consortium for Church and State Research, Proceedings of the Conference – Actes du colloque, Madrid (12–15 November 2009), Peeters, Leuven 2012, 107–113.

Papageorgiou C., The right to religious equality under the Greek Law, in: M. Hill QC (ed.), *Religion and discrimination law in the European Union – La discrimination en matière religieuse dans l'Union Européenne*, European Consortium for Church and State Research, Trier 2012, 165–168.

Papageorgiou C., *An Introduction to Hellenic Ecclesiastical Law*, Thessaloniki 2012.

Papageorgiou C., 'The special treatment of religions in the context of Greek Penal Law', in: N. Doe/M. Kotiranta (ed.), *Religion and criminal law – Religion et droit pénal*, European Consortium for Church and State Research, Proceedings of the Conference – Actes du colloque, Järvenpää, Finland (2–5 October 2008), Peeters, Leuven 2013.

Papastathis Ch., 'The Nationality of the Mount Athos Monks of non-Greek Origin', Balkan Studies 8 (1967) 75–86.

Papastathis Ch., 'The Statute of the Athonic Russian Cells' Brotherhood according to the constitutional laws of Mount Athos', *Actes du Premier Congrès International des Études Balkaniques et Sud-Est Européennes* 4 (Histoire XVIII-XIX ss.), Sofia 1969, 523–528.

Papastathis Ch., 'The application of religious laws in the Hellenic Republic', in: Caparros E./Christians L.-L. (eds), *La religion en droit comparé à l'aube du 21 siècle – Religion in comparative law at the dawn of the 21th century* [XVe Congrès International de Droit Comparé – XVe International Congress of Comparative Law], Bruxelles 2000, 307–321.

Papastathis Ch., 'Religious self-administration in the Hellenic Republic', in: Robbers G. (ed.), *Church Autonomy. A Comparative Survey*, Peter Lang, Frankfurt am Main 2001, 425–450.

Papazissi Th., 'Greek Jews and Family Law: From Judaic Law to the Civil Law Code', *The Jewish Communities of Southeastern Europe, from the fifteenth century to the end of world war II*, Institute for Balkan Studies no 259, Thessaloniki 1997, 385–396.

Puza R./Doe N. (ed.), *Religion and law in dialogue: covenantal and non-covenantal cooperation between state and religion in Europe – Religion et droit en dialogue: collaboration conventionelle et non-conventionelle entre état et religion en Europe*, European Consortium for Church and State Research, Proceedings of the Conference, Tübingen, 18–21 November 2004 – Actes du colloque, Tübingen, 18–21 November 2004, Peeters, Leuven-Paris-Dudley, MA 2006.

Renucci J.-F., *Article 9 of the European Convention on Human Rights: Freedom of thought, conscience and religion*, Human Rights Files no 20, Council of Europe Publishing, Strasburg 2005.

Robbers G. (ed.), *Church autonomy. A comparative survey*, Peter Lang, Frankfurt am Main 2001.

Robbers G. (ed.), *State and church in the European Union*, Germany 32019.

Robbers G. (ed.), *Religion and public education – La religion dans l'éducation publique*, European Consortium for State and Church Research, Proceedings of the Conference in Trier, 11–14 November - Actes du colloque, Trèves, 11–14 November 2010, Institute for European Constitutional Law, University of Trier (Germany) 2012.

Rodopoulos P., *An overview of orthodox canon law*, USA 2007.

Scandamis N., 'La Communauté Européenne et le Mont Athos', in: Tachiaos A.-E. (ed.), *Mount Athos and the European Community*, Institute for Balkan Studies 241, Thessaloniki 1993, 119–123.

Shadid A.R. W./Koningsveld P. S. (eds,), *Intercultural relations and religious authorities: Muslims in the European Union*, Leuven-Paris-Dudley, MA 2002.

Tachiaos A.-E. (ed.), *Mount Athos and the European Community, Institute for Balkan Studies* 241, Thessaloniki 1993.

Tsitselikis C., 'Muslims in Greece', in: Potz R./Wieshaider W. (eds), *Islam and the European Union*, European Consortium for Church and State Research, Leuven-Paris-Dudley, MA 2004, 79–107.

Tsitselikis C., 'Le statut juridique de l'Islam en Grèce', *Les Cultes et l'État en Grèce. Les identités religieuses dans la République hellénique. Quatrième colloque sur la notion d 'Églises nationales'*, L' Année Canonique XLV (2003) 219–242.

Tsitselikis C., 'The legal status of Islam in Greece', Die Welt des Islams 44 (2004) 402–431.

Tsitselikis C., *Old and new Islam in Greece. From historical minorities to immigrant newcomers*, Brill – Nijhoff 2012.

Uitz R., *Freedom of religion in European constitutional and international case law*, Strasbourg 2007.

Yataganas X., 'Declaration commune relative au Mont Athos (intervention)', in: Tachiaos A.-E. (ed.), *Mount Athos and the European Community*, 'Institute for Balkan Studies no 241', Thessaloniki 1993, 83–84.

Selected Bibliography

Index

The numbers here refer to paragraph numbers.

Index

Index

www.ingramcontent.com/pod-product-compliance
Lightning Source LLC
Chambersburg PA
CBHW071435230926
51846CB00001B/244